Working on Cruise Ships

Working on Cruise Ships

Sandra Bow

Revised by
Deborah Penrith
and Victoria Pybus

Distributed in the USA by
The Globe Pequot Press, Guilford, Connecticut

Published by Vacation Work, 9 Park End Street, Oxford
www.vacationwork.co.uk

WORKING ON CRUISE SHIPS
By Sandra Bow

First edition 1996
Second edition 1999
Third edition 2002
Fourth edition 2005

Copyright © Vacation-Work 2005

ISBN 1-85458-338-7

Cover design by mccdesign ltd

Illustrations by John Taylor

Typeset by Brendan Cole

Printed and bound in Italy by Legoprint SpA, Trento

Contents

INTRODUCTION

DECK DEPARTMENT

HOTEL DEPARTMENT

CONCESSIONAIRES

TECHNICAL & ENGINEERING

MEDICAL DEPARTMENT

CHOOSING A SHIP: WHICH LINE?

WHICH SHIP?

OTHER OPTIONS

CRUISING ITINERARIES

ADDRESSES OF CRUISE LINES & OTHER COMPANIES

APPENDICES

Preface

No other industry has grown quite so fast in the past seven years as the cruise industry except, possibly, the IT sector. Millions of Americans, an estimated 10.6 million in 2004, and hundreds of thousands of Britons take cruises each year. At any one time there are dozens of new cruise ships under construction preparing for launch one, two or three years hence and each new ship means an average of more than 2,000 new jobs.

Many modern cruise ships are simply mobile leisure resorts with casinos, cinemas, swimming pools, fitness centres, lecture halls and even golf courses, so the range of jobs is enormous – anything from the usual hotel staff to fortune tellers, florists, gentlemen hosts and priests. Wages are generally similar to those on land but the gratuities can be good and because most jobs come with full board and lodging, the opportunities for saving money are excellent.

The ships themselves are getting larger thanks to the rivalry between industry giants Carnival, ultimate owner of Cunard's *Queen Mary II* launched in 2004 (2,600 berths), and Royal Caribbean, owner of the *Freedom of the Seas* (due to enter service in 2006), and which will carry 3,600 passengers and 1,360 crew, not to mention an as yet unnamed Costa ship that will house 3,800 passengers and is to be launched in 2007. There have also been attempts to target younger cruise passengers by the likes of P&O with their Ocean Village concept, and in 2005 the pared down cruise arrived, courtesy of easyCruise. At the other end of the scale from super cruise ships are small 'intimate' versions carrying 120-150 passengers such as Australia's Captain Cook Cruises. The variety and growth of cruise ships means an ever-increasing number and diversity of jobs for people with vastly different skills and experience to work at sea. In this fourth edition of *Working on Cruise Ships* we explain the types of work available and who is eligible to do it.

In addition, there are the well-documented opportunities for travel to all corners of the globe, from Alaska to Spitzbergen or Bermuda to Hawaii, and for romance under the glorious sunsets of the Caribbean and Mediterranean. Not so well documented are the long hours and hard work, but in the end it is all worthwhile. Good luck and *bon voyage*.

Sandra Bow
July 2005

Introduction

WHY CRUISE LINES NEED PEOPLE LIKE YOU

Now that holidays are accessible to more and more people, tourists are continually searching for new ways of spending their time and money. Cruising – once the preserve of the wealthy – offers a different kind of travel experience, which is attracting a wider range of holidaymakers than ever before. As companies compete for the biggest slice of this expanding market, cruising has become a huge growth industry with smaller lines buying more ships, major lines building bigger ships, and all these vessels needing crew members to work on them. America is the biggest supplier of customers: in 2004, 10.6 million Americans took cruise holidays compared with 922,000 Britons. At the last count there were more than 155,000 cruise ship workers (compared with 15,000, thirty years ago).

Think of a cruise ship as a floating town and you will realise that many of the jobs and skills required on land are also needed at sea. Engineers, doctors, cashiers, secretaries, hairdressers, musicians, electricians, croupiers, cleaners, nurses, lecturers, personal trainers, photographers, waiters, carpenters, shop assistants... virtually all occupations from auctioneering to zither playing, have at one time or another been carried out at sea. The list is huge. And so are the opportunities because, unlike on shore, vacancies occur very frequently.

A large cruise ship may employ over a thousand crew, many of whom are only at sea for short periods. People move on, settle down, get promoted, fall sick or simply go on leave. Some crew members may use savings earned on ships to set up businesses back home. Others may get married or decide to spend more time with their families. But whatever the reasons, the turnover of employees is enormous.

This, combined with the overall expansion of the industry, means that there are thousands of exciting job opportunities, all waiting to be filled by the right people.

FACING THE FACTS

So let's start at the beginning. Why do you want to work on cruise ships in the first place? Is it for the travel? The money? Or just to get out of the rat race and enjoy life?

You will already have some conceptions of what ship life is like. It is possible that some of these are misconceptions. Here then are some of the more common reasons for going to sea – and the reality behind the myths.

'I want to see the world'

Working on ships is still one of the best ways to see the world. Cruising is a huge industry and most of the major companies have vessels sailing, literally, all over the globe. It should be pointed out, however, that the amount of time you can expect to spend on shore in exotic ports of call will depend greatly on your working schedule. Not all crew are able to get off at every stop. But even the most overworked seafarer can expect to catch a good glimpse of life in foreign lands and will certainly see more of the world than working nine to five in Boringtown.

Of course, if the travel aspect is your main incentive for working at sea, do try and explore as far from the ship's berth as time permits. The dock areas of many, otherwise beautiful, cities can often give a rather sordid first impression, so never judge a port by its port. Also, if you really intend seeing as much as possible of your destination, make a point of venturing ashore with like-minded individuals. Too many 'Jolly Jack Tars' never make it beyond the nearest sleazy bar.

While ashore, be warned that ship's crew are often seen as easy prey for dealers of drugs and other contraband. However much you may stand to gain, bear in mind that cruise lines are universally stringent in their rules on illegal drugs and that some countries even equip their ports with armed militia and sniffer dogs. If you are caught smuggling illegal substances or goods, not only will your job be on the line, but you may find yourself at the mercy of a foreign (and possibly corrupt) legal system, and in a country where the penalty could be a death sentence.

Employees in the staff sector (e.g. gift shops, casino, health and beauty, photography, shore excursions, entertainment/social staff) often have the most free time in port, as in the case of Jim Withers, a 26 year old sports instructor from Merseyside, who admits:

Until I started working on cruise ships, I had to save like crazy for every holiday abroad, which was usually nothing more than a ten-day bash with some mates in Benidorm. But in the four years I've been at sea, I've scuba-dived in the Caribbean; waterskied in the Greek Islands; jet-skied in Mexico; parasailed in the Seychelles, and I've actually been paid to do it! Plus, when you consider all the numerous countries I've been lucky enough to visit around the globe, there's no way I could have possibly saved enough by working on land to go to them all. Why earn money to see the world, when you can see the world and earn money at the same time?

Exactly. Which brings us to...

'I want to earn good money'

This is a real possibility although, as with all sectors of employment, salaries vary considerably depending on the type of work you do. Some jobs at sea pay well, often far higher than comparable positions onshore. But you must remember that shipboard earnings cannot be calculated at an hourly rate. Most seamen, irrespective of rank or duties, work long and unsociable hours.

Other jobs may appear to be poorly paid. But don't be put off by a seemingly low basic wage. In general, cruise passengers tip well, and it is not uncommon for an employee's gratuities to exceed the earnings of someone else on a good 'basic'.

The real financial advantage, however, of working at sea is not how much it is possible to earn but how much it is possible to save. There is considerable potential for saving money on cruise ships, largely because the sort of everyday expenses one incurs on land are substantially reduced. Food, accommodation and of course transportation are provided, thus eliminating all those shopping, household and car bills. Your laundry is done free (or at a reduced rate) and a drink in the crew bar will almost certainly cost less than in your local.

Some cruise ship stalwarts have become very wealthy, even millionaires, by investing their (often tax-free) earnings wisely. Whilst many employees work at sea for only a few years, before using their savings to facilitate a mortgage, business venture or other financial goal on shore.

'I want to work in a cosmopolitan environment'

Cruise ships must be among the most cosmopolitan workplaces imaginable. For economic as well as geographic reasons, cruise lines tend to employ many different nationalities – possibly as many as fifty or sixty – per ship. And on some cruises the passenger list represents just as much variety.

Note that to overcome stringent registry regulations and, it has to be said, to enable companies to hire 'cheap labour', many ships are registered under 'flags of convenience', such as Panama, Liberia and the Bahamas. For example a ship might be registered in Panama though owned by an American company, based in Europe, with mostly Norwegian officers, British staff and Filipino crew.

You may become the favourite of an aristocratic widow

'I want to rub shoulders with millionaires'

Cruise ship passengers come from all walks of life and it is fair to assume that, especially on longer and more expensive cruises, you may encounter some very wealthy individuals. Whether you actually rub shoulders (or, indeed, anything else) with them, depends largely on your job on the ship. Social staff have more direct dealings with the passengers than most, but it is not unknown for a barman to become the favourite, or even the husband, of some lonely aristocratic widow. There seem to be more opportunities for male employees than female in this regard, mainly due to the large numbers of unattached ladies on most passenger lists. If a liaison with an ageing millionairess (the average age of cruise passengers is 54), appeals to you, fine. But don't make it your main objective in choosing a career at sea or you may be disappointed.

'I want fun, sun and romance'

As in other walks of life, being at sea is largely what you make of it. You will probably encounter both fun times and sunny days during your time on the ship, but don't forget that you are planning a working trip and not a vacation. If, after applying for a job as a busboy, you picture yourself sipping champagne in the spa like the models in the glossy brochures, you will definitely be in for a shock. As for romance, the following accounts might provide some insight:

Yes, there's something about cruising that is romantic. It's a holiday atmosphere, and it's easy to get caught up in what are basically holiday romances. People come and go so frequently on ships that lasting relationships are rare. My cabin-mate was heartbroken when her boyfriend disembarked, but within a week she was seeing someone else.

Annie Davies (Casino Cashier)

As a cocktail waiter working in the passenger bars, I suppose you could say I see it all. It seems to me that a lot of young (and also not-so-young) female passengers come onboard obviously looking for romance. Of course they all go for the stripes (officers) first and if they can't get lucky with them they flirt their way down the ranks. I've never understood the attraction of men in uniform but it certainly works. I once knew a DJ who wore his tuxedo even off duty because it was such a hit with the women.

Pedro Parrondo-Sanchez (Cocktail Waiter)

As a female working at sea, especially in the medical department, I am very aware of the level of promiscuity onboard. Some employees can be seen with a different passenger every cruise and a lot of the crew risk sexual disease, including HIV, by frequenting red light areas in foreign ports. I know by the number of cases of VD I treated after our last visit to Thailand!

Vanessa Miller (Nurse)

Having watched The Love Boat, I was actually disappointed when I first came onboard. I didn't see one dashing officer and half the crew were gay. I ended up seeing guys I would never have dated on land, mainly as company to go ashore. A case of 'Hobson's Choice', really.

Sylvia Blake (Masseuse)

I wasn't even looking for romance when I joined the ship since I still had a girlfriend back home. But I used to go off onshore with a crowd of the entertainers and, with the best will in the world, it's hard to stay faithful in such exotic locations. I've been seeing Karen (one of the dancers) for over a year now and we intend getting married in June, so I hope this particular shipboard romance will last.

Andrew Savage (Shore Excursions Assistant)

They go for the officers first

'I want to escape the pressures of work/home/family etc.'
Running away to sea has always been seen as an easy solution to problems at home and in the short-term it can be. Certainly there is a freedom of lifestyle attached to working in a perennially holiday atmosphere. But don't forget that any difficulties, whether personal, marital or financial, will still be waiting for you when you return, and may even have grown more insoluble during your absence. On this note, many crew members find that they end up losing touch with former friends and colleagues while they are away or discover they no longer share the interests of old friends when they

return home. Loneliness on shore is an occupational hazard.

Terry Donahue, a gift shop assistant from West Yorkshire, describes his return home on leave:

When I first got offered a job in sales at sea, my colleagues in the department store were really pleased for me. A few of them even said they wished they could have got a job on ships too. I sent them the odd postcard and we kept in touch. But the first night that I went down the pub after working nine months in the Caribbean, I found it difficult to keep the conversation going. I'd been away so long I was out of touch with local events – I didn't even know the season's football results – and if I mentioned all the things I did overseas, it appeared as if I was showing off. Although most of my old friends still made me welcome, they didn't want to hear about my travels, and I felt a few people actually resented me for it. In turn, I guess I found their same old life-style boring. It's a shame really, but we seem to have lost that common link.

'I want a job that's right for me'

Deciding what type of work is exactly right for you is, of course, a very subjective issue. One person's idea of a challenge may be nothing short of a trauma to someone else. An easy workload to some people means pure humdrum to others. But presuming you are prepared to be flexible and have the stamina to endure the frequently long working hours – not to mention the equally long social hours – there is in all likelihood a job at sea that's right for you. While considering the opportunities open to you, concentrate, at least in the first instance, on areas of employment in which you may have some experience.

And a word of advice. If the type of position you'd prefer isn't on offer or seems out of reach at the present time, don't be deterred from accepting a job that you may consider beneath your ability. There are always promotion possibilities on ships, far more than in comparable situations on land. Opportunities often arise unexpectedly, so that capable (and occasionally even incapable) people may suddenly find themselves thrust into a totally different role or department. But much rests on being in the right place at the right time. And the right place is on the ship.

So don't miss the boat.

APPLYING FOR A JOB

There is a lot of competition for jobs on cruise ships and you may wonder where to start. After considering the kinds of job for which you might be suited and weighing up the pros and cons of the various cruise lines based on the information in this book and the cruise lines own websites, it is time to get down to the business of landing a job at sea (if that isn't a contradiction in terms). As with any form of job hunting, the more possible employers you contact, the better the odds of being accepted. So apply to as many cruise lines, agencies, etc., as possible. Then, should you receive more than one offer of employment, you are in a stronger position to negotiate and/or choose the best terms and conditions. This does not mean, however, that you should not be selective. Do your homework and target companies that you feel are most likely to require your particular skills.

You can use a placement agency such as the ones listed in this book. This is not essential as it is just as easy to apply direct to the cruise lines by post or through their websites and by applying direct you will avoid paying an agency placement fee. The decision is yours. Large cruise ships hire the bulk of their staff, particularly entertainers through specialist agencies. Such staff remain employees of the agency that places them, usually on one ship after another for several years (see *Concessionaires*).

Another factor to consider is the minimum age. Most cruise ships are reluctant to hire anyone under 21, though some 18, 19 and 20 year olds have found suitable employment. For work in areas such as bars or casinos you will certainly have to be over 21.

Confirming the Contact Details

The first step in launching your assault on cruise ship companies is to ascertain the correct address of the department which is relevant to the work you are seeking. It is essential to address your application to the appropriate department (preferably using the name of the relevant person) because it is most unlikely that a speculative application will be forwarded to the correct person or even the correct department. Remember too that major cruise lines may have offices around the globe and it is no use applying to their UK division for jobs in a particular department if all the recruitment for that line of work is handled in Miami.

When clarifying details, ask for the name and job title of the person to whom you should directly apply and use that name in all correspondence.

Your letter will have much more impact than one addressed to an anonymous 'Dear Sir/Madam' or 'Dear Personnel Officer'. (Specific names have not been included in this book since personnel changes in the industry are frequent and such information would soon be out of date). Note that unsolicited faxes and e-mails are generally considered 'junk mail' and almost invariably hinder rather than help.

Cruise line offices are notoriously busy so it is not surprising that unsolicited telephone calls are not encouraged. Unfortunately, phoning may be the only viable means of obtaining the name and department you need. If you ring at an off-peak time (late afternoon, perhaps) the person answering your call may be more approachable, but be prepared for them simply not to give you the information you require. If this is the case (or you end up talking to an answering machine) then a 'To whom it may concern' via their head office may have to suffice. But whatever reaction you receive from the voice on the line, remember that they are unlikely to have any bearing on your employment prospects and your priority is to get your details to the person who does.

When phoning, don't forget global time differences, e.g. Miami and New York are five hours behind London. To give your prospective employer an alarm call is not a good idea.

With the increasing popularity of the internet, many cruise lines now have worldwide websites and these can be a valuable source of information for job-seekers. Some cruise lines advertise job vacancies on the internet and the e-mail address provided means the application goes to the right person.

The Application Procedure

Having ascertained the name and business address of your target, present your details as professionally as possible. Type or print all communications and always include a covering letter. Set out your CV (résumé) clearly and enclose photocopies of references or other relevant information. Enclose a photograph, preferably one that shows some personality. For jobs in the social/entertainment department a large publicity shot is a good bet. Some companies will send you an official form to fill in (or you can download one from their internet site). If so, don't be afraid to enclose additional information, as long as it is relevant to your application. The more skills and/or qualifications you can offer, the more likely it is that you will be offered a job.

Sometimes you may be offered employment solely on the strength of your application; at other times you may be required to attend an interview. Yet again, you may not even receive a reply. A follow-up telephone call may be beneficial in the latter instance, on the lines of 'I just wanted to make sure you've received my details'. Remind them that you're still alive and waiting. Occasionally it works.

Don't become too disillusioned if you hear nothing. Your details could lie for months in a filing cabinet, only to be dug out and a job offered, requiring you to join a ship in Acapulco in two days time.

Company files are, however, regularly renewed. So if you haven't been contacted within six months and you still wish to be considered for employment, it is advisable to send a fresh application. It is also worth noting that cruise line employers almost always telephone applicants to offer them an interview (or a job) rather than using other forms of communication. If your mobile phone is frequently switched off; a message facility is vital so that you don't miss your chance.

A final point of which all applicants should be aware is the increasing trend for cruise ship employers to reply to those whom they do not wish to interview by postcard rather than letter. Such open reply cards are very impersonal and comprise a series of sentences along the following lines, one of which will be ticked:

a) At this time we do not have anything available for your area of expertise, but we will keep your information on file for possible future engagement.
b) Before we can fully consider your application we need to receive the following further information ....
c) We are sorry but you do not meet the requirements or area of experience we require but we thank you for your interest in our company.

The lack of confidentiality attached to this method of reply may be disconcerting for those who do not wish their private correspondence to be read by their postman, neighbours, current employers, other family members and anyone else who has access to their mail. Unfortunately, there is not a lot that can be done about it, as this is the reply system adopted by many of the major lines.

On-the-Spot Applications

The old-fashioned approach of asking at the gangway for an impromptu interview might work if you happen to live in a port town and are prepared to spend your time loitering around the docks. Ships that frequent ports as part of a regular itinerary may be especially interested in taking on local crew members, particularly if they are inadvertently caught short-staffed, as it may be cheaper and more convenient than recruiting elsewhere. Note, however, that security is often tight and you would probably be lucky to get in the port gates, let alone on the ship. Also, many lines insist that recruitment is authorised by their office-based staff. Personal contacts or recommendations will obviously help your case, but be prepared for rejections and referrals.

Making a Favourable Impression

Considering that major cruise lines receive hundreds of job applications per week, it is important to make a good first impression. One busy personnel manager offers some 'dos and don'ts' on preparing to make an application or attend an interview:

> *Too many applicants have obviously not bothered to learn anything about our company or the type of product we are marketing. I get people wanting to work as youth counsellors on vessels that never have children onboard or deal blackjack on ships without a casino. All they had to do was pick up a copy of our brochure and they would have realised that they were wasting their time and ours.*

So what other application 'blunders' does he encounter?

> *Vagueness is very common. It's no use sending in a general 'give us a job' style of letter without any reference to the sector in which you are hoping to find work. Recruitment for each division of a ship, whether housekeeping, entertainment, catering, etc., is handled by a different onshore office or department. If an application arrives without specifying the type of job for which it is intended, the only filing system it's likely to see is the nearest trash can.*
>
> *Neither are we interested in people who are clearly only looking for a good time with no responsibility or commitment. You would be amazed at the number of applicants who think working on ships is going to be one long holiday and a means of visiting lots of exotic ports, as though the work is incidental. Of course, the travel opportunity is an incentive, and there's nothing wrong with that. But I would be wary of hiring anyone who stressed that*

angle above, say, their commitment to providing a good service. I've even asked applicants why they wish to work on cruise ships and received unsuitable answers like, 'Well, I've got a few months off and I want to have some fun' or 'I want to be like Julie on the Loveboat' or 'Because I need to get out of the country for a while.' Needless to say, they didn't get the job.

What we're looking for is professionalism and commitment. If someone is not smartly dressed at an interview, why should I presume they'll be smartly dressed at work? If someone can't be bothered to show an interest in our company and understand the differences that set us apart from our rivals, why should I think they're going to show any commitment? If someone appears to me as rude or miserable or lacking in confidence, why should I imagine they'll be seen any differently by the passengers? We're really not asking a lot. But you've got to show us that you're the one that we want.

Klaus Kappeler, a bartender from Germany, has recently managed to do just that, by changing his approach:

When I first started trying to get work on ships I was just too honest. I've done a lot of different jobs and I stupidly listed them all in my application, thinking the varied experience would go in my favour. Actually it went against me, because companies thought I was unreliable and wouldn't stick with them for long. So, once I realised this, I adjusted my CV and took out all the jobs that weren't really relevant to the work I was seeking. I've known students looking for vacational work who have also chosen not to tell the whole truth as, understandably, companies are reluctant to employ people who they think are not going to last. It's a case of making your face fit, telling them what they want to hear. Within six weeks of sending off my revised details I had a phone call from Miami offering me a job in the Caribbean.

Interviews

If you are asked to attend an interview, stick to the same kind of rules that you would for any other type of job, that is:

- ◌ Be punctual.
- ◌ Dress smartly and conservatively (definitely no jeans). Over-

the-top/sexy fashion statements and outrageous hairstyles may get you noticed in a nightclub but they won't get you work on a luxury cruise ship.

○ Ask probing questions about the company, about the job, the hours, salary, length of contract, promotion prospects, etc.

○ Be prepared to give answers to standard questions, such as 'Why do you want this particular job?'/'Why do you think you are suited to this type of work?'/'Why did you apply to this particular company?'

○ Establish your personal strengths for the job, i.e. any relevant skills, qualifications or experience, together with factors such as personality, availability and aptitude.

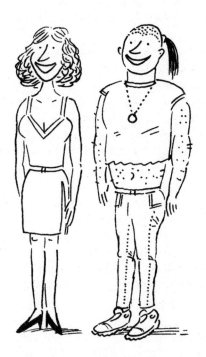

Sexy fashion statements and outrageous hairstyles won't help you get work

Contracts

All cruise lines and reputable agents or employers should issue you with a contract before you start work and this is generally renewed each time you return from leave. As with any contract, read the small print and raise any queries before signing (though this is tricky in the cases when you don't see the contract until you board the ship). Contracts are for between four and twelve months of work. Before signing on the dotted line, you will want to clarify the following points:

○ **Transport**. Will you be expected to travel to the ship at your own expense or will your prospective employer foot the bill? And are you responsible for booking your own flights etc. or will they make the necessary arrangements and reservations for you?

○ **Uniforms**. Are you expected to pay for your own uniforms (if required) or are they provided free of charge? Also, do you need to take uniform items with you or do you pick them up onboard?

○ **Insurance**. Will you be covered by your employer's insurance or will you need to take out a personal policy? If you are covered, what are you covered for? If it is only for health you may want to insure separately against loss or damage to personal effects.

○ **Tax**. Will your earnings be subject to tax (or other) deductions, or will you be liable for your own tax declarations?

○ **Payment**. When will you receive your first payment and what form will it take? (cash on the ship, direct credit to a bank account, company cheque, etc.)

○ **Special requirements**. Will you be expected to provide any special items or clothing for your new job? (chef's knives, photographer's cameras, carpenter's tools, evening dress, particular style/ colour of shoes, etc.)

○ **Contract conditions**. What are the terms of the contract? How long is it for? Is the full duration of the contract subject to the successful completion of a trial work period?

○ **Commission**. Are you liable to pay commission on your earnings and, if so, for how long? Note that some agencies include contractual clauses, demanding commission on extended or follow- up contracts or additional offers of work, even if they have absolutely nothing to do with setting up the ensuing contract and you have procured it independently.

○ **Any other expenses**. Will there be any hidden expenses that you have not been told about (e.g. a deduction for food and accommodation)?

Since the demise of unions in the merchant fleet, it should be stressed that many ships' contracts are barely worth the paper they are written on. There is little, if any, job security at sea. But this works both ways: while it is relatively easy for companies to break their side of the bargain, neither are they likely to rush straight to the law courts if you should happen to break yours.

If you are told that your contract won't be available until you board the ship, be sure to obtain a letter or document (even a fax copy) from your future employer, stating the date you are to commence work and the vessel you will be joining. Carry this with you when passing through foreign immigration as proof of your reason for entering the country where you are to pick up the ship. This particularly applies if you are a non-US citizen entering the United States.

Taking the Job

This brings us to the vital subject of availability. Cruising, more than any other, is an industry where 'he who hesitates is definitely lost'. So if a job is offered at short notice (and presuming you are reasonably happy with the terms and conditions), take it. Even if it means dropping everything and flying to Honolulu, take it. And even if you are not quite sure what you are letting yourself in for, take it. Because if you don't take it, such an opportunity may never be offered to you again. *Carpe Diem* ('Seize the Day').

WHAT TO EXPECT

If you are in the financial position to take a holiday abroad, why not plan a cruise as your next vacation? It is often possible to book a cruise for a comparable price to other types of package holiday, and it would at least give you an insight as to what to expect. During the course of your vacation, you would have the opportunity to talk first-hand to those already working onboard, and you might even make some useful contacts for future employment.

Those who are heading for their first contract at sea will no doubt be anxious about what life will be like. This section provides answers to some of the most commonly asked questions about working and living conditions.

Q: How long will I work at a time?
A: This really depends on your job on the ship and the particular cruise line. If you are having to pay your own transport costs you will naturally want to work for as long a stretch as possible instead of flitting home every other month. If, on the other hand, the company is paying your costs, you may want to take frequent leave. The minimum stretch of work for regular employees (as opposed to visiting entertainers, etc.) is usually about three months, although some crew members may choose to work for up to a year without a break. With occasional exceptions, most members of a ship's company are officially self-employed and are therefore not paid when on leave.

Q: Will I get a day off?
A: Very unlikely. Irrespective of your position on the ship (with the possible exception of certain members of the entertainment department) you will be required to work every day. Of course, you will have time off, maybe whole mornings, afternoons or evenings, as the case may be. But most crew members work long and often anti-social hours, seven days a week.

Q: What if I have an accident or fall ill?
A: The cruise line will usually cover any medical costs for accidents, injuries or general illnesses of ship's personnel, whether incurred on or off-duty, at sea or on land, as long as the crew member is in the ship's service at the time (i.e. has 'signed on' as all crew members must do on joining or re-joining a ship). When an employee leaves a ship (even to go on leave with the intention of returning), he or she signs off and is no longer covered by the company's insurance.

While in service, crew members are entitled to the ship's medical services free of charge and may even be admitted to the ship's hospital for a short recuperation period. Nevertheless if you require medication for an ongoing condition, take a supply with you rather than assume that the ship's medical centre will have what you need in stock. Dental problems are usually treated by shoreside dentists and the costs are incurred either by the crew member or the cruise line, depending on the nature of the complaint.

If an employee becomes so ill or is so seriously injured that he/she is unable to fulfil his/her contract and has to return home or be admitted to a shoreside hospital, the company is unlikely to pay treatment charges and (in most cases) is not liable for sickness pay. It must be stressed, however, that this is an area of great discrepancy and it is well worth checking on a company's medical policies before accepting a contract. Better still, take out a personal insurance policy that will also give you travel cover. In the United Kingdom, Marcus Hearn & Co. Ltd., (Marcus Hearn House, 65-66 Shoreditch High Street, London E1 6JL; ☎020-7739 3444; fax 020-7739 3444; www.marcushearn.co.uk; mail@marcushearn.co.uk) offers a policy which covers people who intend working overseas, as opposed to simply taking a vacation.

Q: What if I miss the ship?
A: If you miss the ship at any time during your sea-going career, the local ship's agent can help you to pick it up again, even though you will almost invariably be responsible for flights, accommodation and any other costs incurred. Missing the ship can be an expensive mistake; it may even cost you your job. Always check the 'All Aboard' time before going ashore (all crew members should usually be aboard one hour before sailing).

Q: Will I receive special safety training?
A: Obvious risks such as fire, stormy weather, collisions and flooding are ever-present when working at sea. Specialist training to enable crew members to cope with the eventuality of life-threatening situations is a priority of all reputable cruise lines.

Generally, all new crew members will be requested to attend a safety course within a short time of joining the vessel. This course should cover emergency procedures, lifeboat/raft instruction and basic fire fighting. In addition, all crew members will be expected to attend regular crew safety drills and some will also be requested to assist with the passenger safety drills. It should be pointed out that in the course of these (particularly crew) drills you may be expected to assist in physical, grimy and even potentially dangerous activities which you may consider irrelevant to the job for which you were hired. Manicurists and ballroom dancers be warned.

Ships sailing out of American ports also have to pass both stringent US coastguard inspections (which affect all crew members) and United States Public Health (USPH) inspections concerning hygiene and sanitation (which involve a great number of the crew).

It is advisable to familiarise yourself with the emergency routes from your cabin and workplace as soon as possible after joining a ship. Make sure you know the location and understand the operation of watertight and fire doors, and also how to use the fire extinguishers and launch the lifeboats/rafts. This is not just to satisfy the US coastguards but for your own peace of mind, so that you will know how to bail yourself out if those designated to help you are nowhere to be found.

Q: Are there many rules and regulations?
A: Naturally, there will be certain rules and regulations. Some ships are much harder to work on than others in this respect. It is fair to assume that whatever your rank you will be bound by rules concerning appearance, time-keeping and conduct. Some companies may even operate a penalty system, whereby employees are financially penalised or refused shore leave for misdemeanours.

Certain areas of the ship may be out of bounds, depending on your job and rank, and permission to socialise in passenger areas may be subject to not occupying bar stools or sitting in large groups of staff members. Perhaps the least popular rule to be enforced on some ships is the curfew system, whereby all off-duty employees other than senior officers must vacate the passenger areas by a specified time at night.

Any crew member amassing several verbal or written warnings for offences is liable to be dismissed, as is anyone unfortunate enough to miss the ship without a very good excuse. Drunkenness, swearing and fighting, particularly in passenger areas, will nearly always result in dismissal (especially if your opponent was higher ranking than you!).

If getting fired seems to be something of an occupational hazard, getting re-hired, possibly by another cruise line within the same week, may come just as easily. Your claim of 'unfair dismissal' will almost certainly fall on deaf ears, but your new employer may not ask too many questions either.

Suffice to say, most of the regulations appear worse on paper than they do in practice, and in the unlikely event that you do face disciplinary action, take consolation in the knowledge that, unlike your predecessors, you won't be flogged or keelhauled.

Q: What should I wear?
A: All officers, staff and crew members wear the uniform allocated to their job when on duty, with the exception of entertainers and social staff members who wear their own clothes for occasions like cocktail parties. In the evenings, ship's personnel not in uniform should adhere to the pas-

senger dress code, which may range from very formal to casual, depending on the nature of events. Note, however, that even 'casual' does not include T-shirts or jeans (unless of course it happens to be Wild West Night).

Typical evening dress codes for the passengers and non-uniformed employees are:

○ *Formal* – Evening/cocktail dress for women, tuxedo/dinner jacket (black tie) for men
○ *Informal* – Dress/suit for women, business suit/jacket and tie for men
○ *Casual* – Dress/trousers for women, collared shirt (no jacket/tie required) for men
○ *Theme* – Dress appropriate to the theme, e.g. 50s/60s, Black & White, Tropical, Country & Western, etc.

Uniformed officers will also be expected to follow the evening dress codes, wearing dress uniform on formal nights. Your company will advise you of their requirements.

Most officers and many crew members are expected to buy the uniforms required for their job. However, policies on uniforms vary considerably from company to company and some lines will provide good quality uniforms free of charge. Do check on this before accepting a job offer, as uniform costs may eat into your profits, particularly if you are not looking for a long-term career. Footwear is not normally provided and there may be certain stipulations, such as shoe colour or heel height. In the main, however, common sense prevails, especially bearing in mind that many crew members spend long hours on their feet.

Additional regulations may concern hairstyles (particularly for those handling food) and general appearance (no earrings for male employees, for instance).

Naturally, during your free time and on trips ashore you may wear whatever you like, although it should be noted that most cruise lines are averse to personnel wearing jeans or cut-away shorts in passenger areas even in their free time.

LIVING CONDITIONS

Q: What will my accommodation be like?
A: Your accommodation will depend on the status given to your par-

ticular job and the ship on which you are working. Officers and other senior employees will generally have single accommodation with en-suite shower/toilet facilities. Accommodation for staff (and this includes casino, health & beauty and shop concessionaires) is variable and may be single or shared, depending on your job and the cabin allocation for your department. Managerial and 'one-off' staff positions generally warrant good standard single accommodation with en-suite facilities, while other staff positions may involve sharing with one or (rarely) two other employees (usually of the same department). Some staff members and entertainers may be allocated passenger accommodation, and often these are cabins that for reasons of location, noise, etc., would be difficult to sell but are nevertheless quite acceptable.

Cabins allocated to crew – i.e. non-managerial restaurant and bar staff, cabin stewards and 'ratings' – are often shared by two to four people (usually of the same department), subject to space availability. Crew accommodation on newer ships tends to be superior to that on older ones.

Possibly the best crew accommodation currently afloat can be found on the *Europa* (Hapag-Lloyd) and the *Crystal Harmony* (to be renamed *Asuka II* in 2006) and *Crystal Symphony* (belonging to Crystal Cruises). Other ships with good crew quarters include the *Asuka* (NYK) and the ships of Seabourn Cruise Line.

Q: What about the food?
A: Again, your dining place will be subject to your rank or job status. Officers usually eat in the Officers' Mess with waiter service while crew members dine in the self-service Crew Mess. Staff members, entertainers and concessionaires have the most variable allocations, depending on the ship. Larger ships may have a Staff Mess with waiter-service or self-service while smaller ships may reserve a section of a passenger restaurant for staff. Officers and staff members are usually permitted to eat at passenger buffets as long as they give priority to the guests. Certain senior officers and members of the social/entertainment sector may also be expected to host a passenger table for dinner on specified evenings.

While passenger food is of a reasonable to excellent standard, crew food can be variable even on the best of ships. So if you get a good deal (and crew food can be good) eat well, as tomorrow you may prefer to diet.

Q: What if I get seasick?
A: If you are generally prone to travel sickness, it may be a good idea to

take some form of remedy until you find your sea legs. Medication is usually freely available on board, but if you still find yourself suffering:

O Try to get fresh air. Go out on the deck if you can and look out at the horizon, not down at the waves. Alternatively, keep to the middle of the ship and on as low (and therefore stable) a deck as possible.

O Eat dry salted crackers and non-greasy foods. Ginger (including ginger ale) is a favourite remedy. Generally, avoid alcohol, although it must be said that an occasional 'stabilizer' (combination of port and brandy) has helped many a sea dog regain his swagger.

O Concentrate on some activity or busy yourself to take your mind off the nausea. Try and work through it; you may have no choice.

Above all, don't let the prospect of seasickness put you off working on ships. Many of the most popular routes tend to be in calmer waters and it is not a myth that even so-called bad sailors get better over a period of time.

Q: What leisure facilities are there for the crew?
A: Generally, the bigger the ship, the better the facilities for crew members. Larger ships may have a crew gymnasium, sunbathing area, library and even specialist facilities such as a computer centre. Most ships will have a Crew Bar and/or Recreation Room, although bar opening hours may be subject to restrictions.

Crew facilities are important on a ship, since crew members (and this includes waiters and bar staff) are not usually allowed in passenger areas except to work. The ship's officers may have a Ward Room (Officers' Bar) and officers generally have access to all (certainly, most) public rooms, including (discretional) use of the passenger pool, sauna, gymnasium, etc. Staff, entertainers and certain concessionaires also have public rooms privileges (these vary from ship to ship) and on larger vessels they may also have their own Bar or Recreation Room.

Q: Do I have to do my own cleaning?
A: Officers and certain staff members and entertainers will be allocated a cabin steward(ess) to attend to the general cleaning (but not tidying!) and servicing of their cabins. Although the steward's wages are paid by the

company, good service should be rewarded with a tip.

Lower ranking crew members are generally responsible for the cleaning and servicing of their own cabins, although a small fee may well secure the assistance of one of the cabin stewards. (In fact, ship-wise employees soon learn that an odd backhander or service bartered can considerably improve the quality of life in all areas of work and accommodation). Towels and bed linen are supplied and laundered free of charge by the ship.

The cabins of all personnel, even senior officers, may be subject to frequent inspections. The main purpose of these is not to snoop into your personal belongings but to ensure against risks caused by vermin, structural damage and fire hazards.

Q: What about my personal laundry?
A: Most ships will have self-service laundry facilities especially for the ship's personnel. (It must be said, however, that the condition of some of the washing machines and dryers may leave a lot to be desired). Crew members' uniforms and overalls are usually cleaned free of charge by the ship's laundry service and there are generally special rates for personal items sent to the onboard laundry.

Q: Will I be able to adapt to my new surroundings?
A: This is something you will never know until you step aboard your first ship. Everyone finds things hard for those first few days, even seasoned crew members joining a new vessel. But whether or not you take to the lifestyle and enjoy it or are tempted to disembark at the next port really depends on you.

Joining a ship for the first time can be hard, especially if you've never really been away from home or travelled that much before. What makes it especially difficult is the fact it's not just a new job, it's a whole new lifestyle.

You may find your working hours a lot longer and less social than before. Then at the end of a hard day you might have to share a cabin with someone you don't know and possibly don't even like. You can't get away from your colleagues like you can on land. You can't just go home at five o'clock, put the kettle on and forget about work. You may not be able to get off the ship for days at a time. There might be more petty rules and regulations than you've been

used to, the food may be lousy, you feel institutionalised and you're
missing your family or partner back home. These are all things that
newcomers find difficult to handle.

Plus, it's easy to become burnt out, not only by the work but also
because experiences and emotions are heightened by being per-
manently in transit. There's far less stability at sea than onshore.
People come and go. You make friends and live with them for 24
hours a day for several months, then they get off and you never
see them again. The same with relationships. Tearful farewells are
more commonplace at sea than on land. What could be more dra-
matic or poignant than sailing out of port, while your disembarked
lover stands, suitcase in hand, on the pierside?

Even ordinary activities like going to a bar or hiring a jeep are
much more exciting in a strange and foreign country. You become
more streetwise, more self-sufficient. But so much depends on the
individual. Ship life tends to suit people who are independent and
a bit adventurous, but I would say to anyone with doubts, 'Try it'.
Whether it will be the best time or the worst time of your life – and it
will probably be both – the main thing is having the guts to walk up
the gangway.

Jonathon Globerman (Crew Purser)

Q: How can I maintain contact with home?
A: Receiving news from home is a highlight for most employees on
cruise ships. Your family or friends can write to you via your company
head office where crew mail is then forwarded to the ship through worldwide port agents. Alternatively, mail may be sent directly to the port
agents (addresses are usually available from the Crew Purser). It must be
stressed, however, that some port agents are better than others at passing
on crew mail. Be sure to tell contacts to mark all correspondence very
clearly with your name, rank/position and the name of your ship, and
advise them not to send you valuable items unless absolutely necessary.
You will generally be able to send mail from the ship's onboard post box
(to be posted ashore by agents shortly after sailing). You can send and
receive e-mails, faxes and telephone calls round-the-clock via the ship's
satellite. But this is an expensive option for routine conversations and
most crew members phone home via mobile phones or from shoreside
telephones and calling stations.

You may also want to consider taking members of your family
onboard. A temporary visitors' pass is usually all that is required to allow

family members and friends on to visit. If you wish to have relatives staying onboard, then special cruising rates normally apply. Some cruise companies offer very good deals for family members and, subject to your rank and length of service, your next-of-kin might even travel free for a specified time. It is generally not possible, however, for family members, spouses or children to remain onboard for more than a vacation (unless, of course, they are also employees). The Crew Purser on your ship should be able to give you the company's policies on travel for family members.

Q: What will the passengers be like?
A: Of course, there is one factor common to every single cruise ship and every single cruise line, and that is the passengers. Cruise ship passengers come in a variety of shapes and sizes but, in spite of recent successes in attracting a wider family market, most cruisers still fall into the 'Fair, Fat and Forty (Plus)' category. Pity then the poor steward who, when asked to assist a gentleman trying to find his wife, was told to look for a lady who was 'short with grey hair and glasses,' a description that could easily have fitted the majority of females on the guest list.

Many passengers may also be spending their retirement nest egg, which is possibly one of the reasons why cruising is one of the few industries not to have been badly affected by recent economic recessions.

Vincent Ardito, a 68-year-old regular cruiser from Philadelphia explains why he keeps coming back:

The way I see it, my wife and I have worked hard all our lives and we deserve to enjoy our retirement. When we were younger we couldn't afford to travel. We were too busy bringing up a family and paying the bills. Now the kids have families of their own and we've got a lot of catching up to do.

But why take a cruise as opposed to any other type of vacation? Doris Campbell, from Essex, England, would never consider anything else:

I first took a cruise with my sister the year after my husband died, and I've travelled on 16 cruises since. What I like most is the convenience. You visit umpteen different countries and yet you only unpack once. And because your transport is also your hotel, you can leave all your valuables safely onboard when you go ashore. On the ship, everything is so handy. Whether you attend a lecture, swim in the pool or browse in the shops, it's all just a deck or two away. And there's so much to do that I'm never bored.

But the main pleasure for me is the evening's entertainment. I love watching the shows and listening to the classical concerts. I also enjoy ballroom dancing, but all the dance halls back home are gone now, so it's wonderful to be able to dance onboard to a proper big band. I tend to choose ships that have gentlemen hosts as they always make good partners, with no strings attached. As an older single woman, I wouldn't feel comfortable going out alone at night on land. But at sea, I can dance the night away, go in any of the bars, watch a film or show on my own, and not have to worry about getting back to my hotel. I feel safe on the ship. It's a sort of home from home.

Considering factors such as rough weather, steep gangways and the use of tender boats, it is somewhat surprising that cruising proves so attractive to many physically-challenged passengers, with an increasing number of ships offering facilities such as wheelchair-accessible cabins. Less surprisingly, it is also the dream vacation for romantics, would-be romantics, honeymooners and those celebrating anniversaries or other special occasions.

But while lovers may stroll the decks under the same old moon, for those who remember the age of the great liners, cruising just 'ain't what it used to be'.

Tony Andrews, a Chief Steward of some 20 years experience, reflects:

Oh yes, cruising has changed. It used to be an elegant experience, attracting the cream of society. Now, everyone and anyone takes a cruise. Standards have dropped enormously, but it's inevitable because what used to be reserved for the élite is now a mass market tourist industry, a change for which the cruise lines themselves are responsible. They keep building bigger and bigger ships that hold so many passengers, it's impossible to maintain the kind of personal service that we used to give.

In addition, they offer really cheap deals in order to fill all those empty cabins, hoping that the passengers will spend, spend, spend once onboard. Some of them do, but a lot are just cheapskates. And it's always the ones who have paid the least who complain the most. We get couples paying next-to-nothing for a ten-day holiday, which includes round-the-clock service, food and entertainment, and they do nothing but moan about the fact that they don't get caviar or fresh lobster every meal. You feel like telling them that if they were at home they'd be lucky to get bed & breakfast for the price.

Unfortunately, I feel the tendency for customers to demand more for less is something that affects not only cruising, but the whole tourism industry. They all like to think that they are sophisticated travellers, but fewer people dress appropriately for dinner any more, and the ones who do will often change into 'something more comfortable' straight afterwards, which means you frequently see passengers wandering around in T-shirts on formal nights.

Yes, it's definitely the end of an era, but we all have to come to terms with the changes in the industry. When I'm faced with a particularly tricky customer, I don't let it get to me. Instead, I remind myself that, in spite of everything, I'm still earning a very good living at their expense.

FINANCIAL MATTERS

One of the most important issues to consider is whether or not you have to pay your own travel expenses to join the ship. Officers, entertainment staff and senior personnel will generally have their flights and travelling expenses paid for and arranged by the company. Concessionaires may have their expenses paid and arranged by the companies that employ them. But the majority of the crew will have to pay, at least in the first instance, for their own transport to and from the ship. Some cruise companies have a policy of paying a percentage of flight costs or reimbursing travelling expenses after a fixed period, but it really does vary from line to line, which is another good reason to shop around if you are in a position to do so. Whatever, the situation should be specified in your contract. Cruise lines tend to start off the way they mean to go on, so that those which cover transport and uniform costs tend to be more generous employers in other respects.

Many people wonder whether they will have to contribute towards food and accommodation. Sometimes, staff members who are employed by an independent concessionaire do have some deductions made for living expenses. But the vast majority of employees receive free food and accommodation, while senior officers and social staff members may even receive an additional drinks allowance.

On this subject: 'Health Warning: Working at sea can seriously damage your liver.' Alcohol on passenger ships is cheap (or even 'on the house') and very available and it is no coincidence that a high ratio of employees become heavy social drinkers.

With the exception of certain senior officers, most ship's personnel are paid in cash (usually twice a month and often in American dollars) by the Crew Purser on the ship. Many ships also offer crew banking facilities to transfer payment or to arrange for a portion of the salary to be automatically sent to a home account. Members of the ship's company who are employed by an organisation or agent other than the cruise line may be paid independently (by cheque or direct credit) by their employer.

Seafarers' Benefits Advice Line 0845 7413318

We are a Citizens Advice Bureau telephone helpline offering free advice to merchant seafarers and their immediate families.

You can call us from abroad on (44) 20 8269 0730 or ring from the UK on our local rate number 0845 7413 318.
E-mail sbal@btinternet.com   Web www.seabal.co.uk

We are open Monday to Friday from 10am until 12.30pm.
Outside of these times messages can be left, all calls are returned.

A service funded entirely by the
Seamen's Hospital Society

The tax situation for people working at sea is generally very favourable. Since most ships are registered in tax haven countries and also because many crew members are classified as self-employed, tax is seldom withdrawn at source. Rather, you will be personally responsible for declaring your earnings to the tax office (or not, as the case may be). Rulings in this matter are not always clear and regulations vary from country to country. In the UK, the Citizen's Advice Bureau provides a

Seafarers' Benefits Advice Line (☎0845-7413-318 (local rate); +44 20-8269-0730 (from abroad). The Seafarers' Benefits Advice Line also has a very useful website at www.seabal.co.uk which has a number of links to other sites that will be of use to prospective seafarers. Local tax offices currently issue Help Sheet IR205(S). Many seafarers are legally exempt from tax duties, but much depends on how many months per year they are employed at sea. There are plenty of tax exiles currently working on cruise ships, but don't presume a three-month contract in the Baltic will save you from the Bogey Man.

PRACTICAL PREPARATIONS

Visas and Documents

Obviously you will need a full passport and, subject to the route your particular ship is taking, you may need visas to visit certain countries. Generally, this is not a problem, and any necessary visas will be arranged for the crew by the Crew Purser in conjunction with local officials in each port.

If you are sailing to or from American ports and you are not a US citizen you will definitely need a Crew Members' Visa (C-1/D). This is available from US Embassies, is valid for five years from the date of issue and costs £60 from the London US Embassy. To obtain your C-1/D, you will need to supply written proof (such as a contract) of an offer of employment at sea. If in doubt, check with your prospective employer.

Don't forget to check if you will be stopping at any ports in countries which require a vaccination certificate, such as those in which yellow fever is prevalent. Also, most cruise lines will request proof of a recent successful medical examination and some may also require you to submit results of an HIV test. If there is insufficient time to undergo a medical examination before you join the ship, you will probably be required to have one on board. Be aware that a history of epilepsy, mental disorder, heart disease or other major illness could seriously impair your chances of employment at sea.

Joining the Ship

Crew change-overs usually take place on the same day as passenger change-overs (with predictably chaotic results), with most employees joining their ship at its base port. An exception to this would be when a 'handover' period is required, usually in the case of senior personnel where the new employee is to learn the ropes from the outgoing employee or to ensure continuity. If this is the case, employees may be asked to embark days or even weeks before assuming their positions of responsibility. Most lower ranks, however, simply learn the ins and outs of their jobs while actually doing them.

On this note, don't expect a 'settling in' period or a chance to recuperate from jet lag. Whatever your rank, you will probably have to start work as soon as you arrive, sometimes even before you unpack, and this can come as a shock after a long, gruelling journey. Cruise ship employees frequently cover almost as many miles by air as they do by sea and unless you are fortunate enough to be embarking in a local port, you will probably have to fly half way around the world to join your ship.

If your cruise line arranges your travel, do not expect a convenient journey. In order to get the cheapest deal, you may be put on flights with different airlines and badly timed connections, perhaps necessitating a stopover in some obscure hotel miles from the airport. Companies rarely seem to take into consideration that after paying for the cost of your overnight accommodation and the taxi fare trying to find it, they could have probably flown you directly to your ship for less. But that is cruise lines for you.

On arrival at your destination you should be met by a ship's representative, such as a local shipping agent, who will escort you to the vessel. Sometimes, because of flight arrangements, you may arrive the day before the ship is due, in which case the agent will arrange overnight accommodation and transport you to the ship in the morning. It should be stressed that despite assurances to the contrary things do not always run according to plan. The most common problems, together with their suggested solutions, are as follows:

a) There is no-one to meet you at your destination.
Phone the ship's agent to collect you from the airport. If you arrive in the middle of the night, check into a convenient hotel (it is not unknown for abandoned employees travelling on company expenses to 'inadvertently' select the most expensive) and then contact the cruise line or ship's agent in the morning. If you have to make your own way to the ship, take a taxi and keep receipts of any expenses for reimbursement.

b) Your luggage goes missing.
Make sure you give the airport officials all details, including contact numbers of your cruise line and their local shipping agent and the name of

your intended ship. Inform your cruise line and/or the ship's agent of the situation, as they can help to follow things up on your behalf. With luck your luggage will be forwarded to the vessel at the next convenient port of call (see also below *What to Take*).

c) You miss your sailing.

If you are delayed by Customs or Immigration officials through no fault of your own, try to get a message to your cruise line or their shipping agent, as sometimes they can help resolve immigration problems. If you miss the ship because of such delays, the agent should make the necessary arrangements for you to join the vessel at the next convenient port.

The main thing to remember about joining a ship abroad is to BE PREPARED. If possible, always take the following with you:

○ At least one major credit card to cover hotel and/or emergency expenses. (Note that Visa is the world's most widely accepted card.)

○ Enough cash (preferably in the currency of your destination) to cover incidental expenses, and a supply of travellers' cheques (preferably in US dollars, the world's most widely accepted currency) to tide you over until you receive your first wages (which will be at least two weeks).

○ Copies of any appropriate insurance policies (see also the question, 'What if I have an accident or fall ill?').

○ A copy of your contract and/or a letter/fax of offer of employment to show upon request to overseas immigration officials. This particularly applies if you are a non-US citizen entering the United States.

○ The name/address/telephone number of your cruise line and, if different, your direct employer. And *don't forget the name of your ship*. This is not as silly as it sounds. Your company may have several vessels, possibly with similar names, in the same dock at the same time, and embarrassing mistakes such as going up the wrong gangway do happen.

○ The name/address/telephone number of the shipping agent used by your cruise line at your port of embarkation, including an 'outside office hours' number. Get this information from your cruise line's head office prior to departure.

○ Your passport and any necessary visas or medical certificates (as mentioned above).

What to Take

The answer to the question of what to pack is a resounding 'as little as possible'. In the same way that tourists usually take too much with them on holiday, so new employees tend to take far too much on their first ship. Just because you're at sea doesn't mean you're on a desert island. You will still have access to pharmacies, supermarkets, boutiques, stationers and department stores in many ports of call and in some cases on the ship itself. So do you really need those six bottles of lotion, twenty-five CDs, mega-size shampoo and conditioner, eleven or twelve T-shirts (you're bound to buy more), umpteen pairs of shoes, outfits you wouldn't even wear at home and your entire library including *War and Peace*?

Your cabin is unlikely to offer even a fraction of the space of your

Do you really need to pack your entire library?

bedroom at home, especially if you have to share it. You will probably spend most of your working time in uniform anyway, and your hours on shore may necessitate little more than a pair of shorts, so be ruthless. Remember too, that crew members usually accumulate additional items on their travels and these may include anything from duty free sound systems to life-size carvings of African giraffes! If your luggage is bursting on the way out, how on earth will you carry it on the way back?

You will, of course, need to choose what to leave in as well as out, and this will depend on:

O *Your itinerary.* Whether you include sweaters or swimwear will be subject to the general climate of your intended route. If your itinerary is variable, so will your wardrobe need to be varied, but do keep the quantity of each variation to a minimum.

O *Your job.* Entertainers may need to include costumes; social staff should bring cocktail/formal wear; and most employees will require uniforms.

O *Your ship.* Different vessels have different dress codes but as a rule of thumb the longer and more expensive the cruise, the glitzier the evening wear and smarter the day wear for social and other non-uniformed staff (see the answer to the question 'What should I wear?' in the section *What to Expect* above).

Also, several easy-to-pack items that few first-time crew members consider, but which you may find useful are:

O *Small hand torch* – in case your cabin or indeed the whole ship is plunged into darkness during a power failure or emergency situation.

O *Sewing kit* – for speedy repair of hanging hems, lost buttons, etc.

O *Handful of clothes pegs* – to hang hand-washed items to dry.

O *Travel alarm clock*

O *Small padlock* – to secure travel bags and onboard personal effects.

O *Tube of shoe whitener* (if applicable)

O *Swiss-style army knife* – or at least a corkscrew/bottle-opener.

When packing, take into account that your luggage could go missing *en route* to the vessel. Always label your baggage clearly with the name of your ship, your cruise line and the shipping agent in your destination port. If you have more than one item of luggage, split the contents so that you don't have all uniform/formal wear in one case, for example, and all casual/sports wear in the other. The same applies to jewellery, pairs of shoes, underwear, etc. This way, even if one case goes missing, you should have enough in the other(s) to tide you over until its eventual arrival.

If you intend making a career out of working at sea, it is worth investing in hard, durable cases (such as those by Delsey or Samsonite) which should survive the attentions of even the most frenzied baggage-handler.

THE HIERARCHY

On the majority of ships there are three categories of employee and this hierarchy creates a marked class system: officer, staff and crew.

Officers (those wearing stripes) are free to make use of most ship facilities and enjoy superior living quarters. Note, however, that shore leave for senior officers may be restricted by responsibilities and that junior officers might earn less than many staff and crew members.

The 'Staff' sector consists of shop staff, hairdressers, beauticians, entertainers and cruise staff, casino staff, photographers and others working for concessionaires (explained later). Their status is the most variable, differing from job to job and ship to ship but, in general, staff members enjoy access to passenger areas (they are always the last to leave the disco!) and do well for time off in port.

The largest number of employees are classed as 'crew'. This includes non-managerial bar and restaurant personnel, cabin stewards and cleaning staff, galley and laundry personnel, and deck and engine 'ratings'. Crew leisure activities are more circumscribed (socialising may be confined to the 'crew bar') and living quarters may be quite cramped and spartan. This particularly applies on older ships, where it is not uncommon to find crew members sharing four to a small cabin in the least desirable part of the vessel. The redeeming feature of this system is that there is usually scope for promotion. Note, however, that crew-ranked jobs such as waiters and cabin stewards often have greater earning potential than some officers. Hardly surprising then that crew members have been known to turn down promotion if it means losing out on tips.

Who Wears What?

Maritime officers wear stripes on their epaulets or the base of their jacket sleeves to denote their rank. The colour (if any) between the stripes and optional accompanying symbol signifies their department of work, according to the following traditional guidelines:

Deck:	No colour – Diamond
Hotel:	White – Clover leaf
Technical & Engineering:	Purple – Propeller
Electrical:	Purple – Electric Current
Medical:	Red – Caduceus (i.e. staff of Hermes)
Communications:	Green – Radio signal
Security:	Brown/no colour – 'S'

While it must be stressed that different cruise lines do not always allocate the same status to jobs of the same title, this listing may serve as a general guide:

Four Stripes:
Captain
Chief Engineer
Hotel Manager
Staff Captain
Staff Chief Engineer

Three Stripes:
Assistant Hotel Manager
Chief Electrician
Chief Officer
Chief Radio (Communications) Officer
Cruise Director
Executive Chef
Food & Beverage Manager
Medical Officer (Doctor)
Purser

Two and a Half Stripes:
Assistant Food & Beverage Manager
Assistant (Hotel/Crew) Purser

Bars Manager
Chief Security Officer
Chief Steward
First Officer (Deck, Engineering, etc.)
Housekeeper

Two Stripes:
Nurse
Second Officer (Deck, Engineering, etc.)
Second Purser

One and a Half Stripes:
Senior Secretary
Third Officer (Deck, Engineering, etc.)
Third Purser

One Stripe:
Cadet
Fourth Officer (Deck, Engineering, etc.)
Fourth Purser
Petty Officer

Note that high-ranking managers, chefs, maître d's and senior social staff members may have officer status and privileges, even though they don't actually wear stripes.

It may be easier to appreciate the different degrees of status attached to particular areas of work by considering the employment structure of the ship as a whole. Turn to *Appendix 2* at the end of the book for a typical cruise ship's 'Family Tree of Jobs'.

ABC OF JOBS AT SEA

Let's go back to basics and identify the types of work opportunities that exist on cruise ships. In later chapters, we will be looking at the jobs themselves, their requirements, their availability and how to apply for them. But first, check out the range of possibilities. There are about 200 of them listed below, and the list is far from exhaustive.

Most jobs at sea fall into one of four categories: Deck, Hotel (including Catering, Concessionaires and Entertainment), Technical & Engineering (including Electrical and Communications) and Medical. Each of these departments offers a great many different job opportunities, all of which are discussed later in the book.

You may have already considered some of the options. Others you may not have even thought of. But all of these jobs can be found at sea. As you go down the list, it is to be hoped that you will discover at least one or two titles that appeal. Bear them in mind for future reference. It will make selecting your potential job as easy as ABC.

The following jobs are available to both men and women, at least in theory. Titles such as manager, actor, director, masseur, etc. do not assume a gender preference.

Accommodation Services Manager
Accountant
Actor
Aerobics Instructor
Art Auctioneer
Assistant Bar Manager
Assistant Cruise Director
Assistant Food & Beverage/Catering Manager
Assistant Hotel Manager
Assistant Housekeeper
Assistant Maître d'
Assistant Manager *(Shop, Spa, etc.)*
Assistant Purser
Assistant Steward

Baggage Master
Baker
Ballroom Dancer
Banker
Bar Steward
Bar Waiter
Bars Manager
Beautician
Beauty Salon Manager
Bellman
Berthing Officer
Bookkeeper

Bosun
Buffet Chef
Busboy
Butcher
Butler

Cabin Steward
Captain
Carpenter
Cashier
Casino Manager
Casino Technician
Catering Assistant
Catering Manager
Chef de Cuisine
Chef Entremetier
Chef de Partie
Chef de Rang
Chef Saucier
Chief Electrician
Chief Engineer
Chief Officer
Chief Photographer
Chief Radio Officer
Chief Security Officer
Chief Steward
Children's Counsellor
Chiropodist

Choreographer
Classical Musician
Cleaner
Cocktail Pianist
Cocktail Waiter
Commis Chef
Communications Engineer
Computer Technician
Concierge
Crew Purser
Croupier
Cruise Director
Cruise Sales Manager
Cruise Staff Member

Dancer
Deck Carpenter
Deck Officer
Deckhand
Dentist
Desktop Publisher
Disc Jockey
Dishwasher
Doctor

Electrical Assistant
Electrician
Engineer
Engineering Assistant
Entertainer
Executive Chef

First Officer *(Deck, Radio, Purser, Engineering, etc.)*
Fitness Instructor
Florist
Food & Beverage/Catering Manager
Fourth Officer *(Deck, Radio, Purser, Engineering, etc.)*

Galley Assistant
Garbage Handler
Gardener
Gentleman Host
Group Escort
Guest Lecturer/Expert *(e.g. Archaeologist, Arts & Crafts, Astrologer, Astronomer, Bridge, Cartoonist, Celebrity Speaker, Finance, Gardening, Golf, Hand-writing Analyst, Palmist, Self-improvement, Tarot Card Reader, and so on)*
Gymnasium Supervisor

Hairdresser
Head Chef
Head Waiter
Head Wine Steward
Host/ess
Hotel Engineer
Hotel Manager
Hotel Purser
Housekeeper

Inspector *(Casino)*
International Host/ess

Joiner
Journalist
Junior Officer *(Deck, Radio, Purser, Engineering, etc.)*

Kennel Hand

Laundry Assistant
Laundry Master
Librarian

Maître d'

Manicurist
Manifest Officer
Masseur
Medical Dispenser
Medical Orderly
Motorman
Musical Director
Musician

Navigator
Nurse
Nursery Assistant

Office Clerk
Officer Cadet *(Deck, Engineering, etc.)*
Opera Singer
Ordinary Seaman (OS)

P.A. *(Personal Assistant)*
Pantry Steward
Pastry Chef
Photographer
Physiotherapist
Pit Boss *(Casino)*
Plumber
Port Lecturer
Porter
Priest
Principal Medical Officer
Printer
Programme Co-ordinator
Public Rooms Manager
Purser

Quartermaster

Rabbi
Radio Officer
Radio Room Assistant

Rating *(Non-officer: Catering, Deck, Hotel, etc.)*
Receptionist *(Purser's)*
Restaurants Manager

Safety Officer
Sales Assistant
Secretary
Security Officer
Second Officer *(Deck, Radio, Purser, Engineering, etc.)*
Senior Nurse
Ship's Service Manager
Shop Manager
Shore Excursions Assistant
Shore Excursions Manager
Social Director
Sound/Lighting Engineer
Sous Chef
Spa Assistant
Spa Manager
Sports Director
Staff Captain
Staff (Deputy) Chief Engineer
Stage Manager
Stage Technician
Stores Assistant
Stores Manager

Tailor
Technical Engineer
Television Station Manager
Third Officer *(Deck, Radio, Purser, Engineering, etc.)*

Unskilled Assistant *(Catering, Office, etc.)*
Upholsterer

Vegetable Chef

Waiter   Yeoman
Water Sports Instructor   Youth Counsellor
Wine Steward

Is there anything listed that might be suitable for you? If so, you will need to know more about the type of work for which you are aiming. To find out more about the specific departments and their requirements, we'll take each one step by step, deck by deck.

THE UNOFFICIAL CHARTS

Just for fun, with all listings in no particular order:

Top Ten Best Bets for General Employment Opportunities

1. Carnival Cruise Lines
2. Princess Cruises
3. Royal Caribbean International
4. Holland America Line
5. Costa Cruises
6. P & O Cruises
7. Norwegian Cruise Line
8. Celebrity Cruises
9. Cunard Line
10. Star Cruise

Top Ten Jobs for Time Off in Port

1. Featured Entertainer
2. Casino Staff Member
3. Gift Shop Assistant
4. Musician
5. Disc Jockey
6. Sports/Fitness Instructor
7. Photographer
8. Cruise Staff Member
9. Cruise Sales Manager
10. Port Lecturer

Top Ten Potential Money Earners

1. Captain
2. Cruise Director
3. Headlining Entertainer
4. Hotel Manager
5. Maître d'
6. Food & Beverage Manager
7. Chief Engineer
8. Doctor
9. Purser
10. Casino Manager

Top Ten Jobs for Perks

1. Captain
2. Cruise Director
3. Hotel Manager
4. Maître d'
5. Shore Excursions Manager
6. Food & Beverage Manager
7. Port Lecturer
8. Bars Manager
9. Doctor
10. Purser

Top Ten Most Glamorous Jobs

1. Captain
2. Doctor
3. Headlining Entertainer
4. Social Hostess
5. Dancer
6. Deck Officer
7. Fitness/Water Sports Instructor
8. Dance Band Singer
9. Disc Jockey
10. Any Officer with three or more stripes

Top Ten Best Bets for Native English-speaking Job-hunters

1. Gift Shops/Retail
2. Hairdressing/Beauty
3. Photography
4. Casino
5. Cruise Staff/Entertainment
6. Shore Excursions
7. Sports/Fitness
8. Hotel Management/Pursers Office
9. Medical
10. Technical/Engineering

Top Ten Silly Questions from Passengers

1. Does the crew sleep on board?
2. Do these stairs go up as well as down?
3. Is it seawater in the swimming pool, because it moves around so much?
4. Can we walk ashore when we anchor off?
5. How far are we above sea level?
6. What time is the Midnight Buffet?
7. *(To the waiter)* Is the fish caught each day by the crew?
8. *(To the captain, at his reception party)* Who's driving?
9. *(To the featured entertainer)* Do you hope to go into Show Business one day?
10. *(To anyone who works onboard)* So, when are you going to get a real job?

Ten Things You Should Know Before Going to Sea

1. You start on ships for the travel, you stay on ships for the money, you end up on ships for ever.
2. The ship's laundry master will insist it is the salt air that has shrunk your best formal wear.
3. The obligatory crew lifeboat drill is always scheduled for your morning off.
4. Attractive females don't need security passes.
5. If travel broadens the mind, working on ships stretches the imagi-

nation.
6. Nobody has ever said that ship life was fair.
7. Local taxi drivers will always rip you off.
8. Never tell passengers about your favourite hideaway bar, beach or restaurant.
9. If you were sexually unsure at the beginning, you will be totally confused by the end.
10. Cabin walls have ears.

And just for the Ladies...

Ten Things Your Mother Never Told You

1. All male crew members are single – even the married ones.
2. The ship's photographer cannot make you a movie star.
3. Neither does the DJ have recording 'contacts'.
4. You can't teach an old sea-dog new tricks.
5. An officer is not always a gentleman.
6. The crew drag queen will never return your lipstick.
7. Gangways weren't made for stilettos.
8. Buoys will be buoys.
9. Never lend your cabin key to the guy who says he's lost his.
10. Beware of Greek officers bearing gifts.

And everything else your mother told you still applies.

Deck Department

Your image of the deck department may include swarthy mariners scaling the rigging or their latter-day counterparts stacking up sun loungers. However, the real workings of the Deck Department are rather different. One could say that the members of the deck department are ultimately responsible for getting the ship safely from A to B. They include the deck officers navigating on the bridge, the quartermasters at the wheel, the deck 'ratings' (non-officers) chipping and painting the hull, and the ABs (Able Seamen) manning the launches to shore.

Opportunities for Deck Officers

The head of the deck department is also the master of the entire vessel, the *Captain* (salary range $6,000-$10,000 per month). He has absolute rights of control over the ship and all those (passengers as well as crew) who sail in her. In other words, what the Captain says goes. As well as overseeing navigation, a Captain's daily routine is largely taken up with paperwork, inspection tours, attending social events and meeting with the various heads of department. Also, international maritime law dictates that only the Captain is allowed to sign verification of the daily entries in the ship's log book, such entries providing an important record of nautical and navigational data, together with reports concerning passengers and crew.

The Captain's assistant is the *Staff Captain* (salary range $5,000-$7,000) and it is he (rarely she) who is second in command of the vessel. The joke is frequently told that the Staff Captain does all the work and the Captain takes all the glory, and certainly much of the day-to-day running of the ship, together with disciplinary and crew matters, will fall onto the Staff Captain's desk. The Staff Captain will also be a certified Master in his own right and able to take over command at any time, if necessary.

Third in Command is the *Chief Officer*, whose responsibilities include overseeing the maintenance of the body of the ship, i.e. the exterior paintwork, the decks and the hull. He may also arrange for supplies of fresh water and fuel and the disposal of sewerage and garbage, vital services to which most passengers remain oblivious.

The *First Officer* (there may be several of these) will spend most of his working hours on the bridge doing watch duty. The bridge is always manned, even in port, and the navigation and safety of the vessel are the responsibility of the officer on duty.

Watch duties on ships always follow the sea-going tradition of four-hourly cycles, i.e. 8am-noon, noon-4pm, 4-8pm, 8pm-midnight, midnight-4am, and 4-8am. This way, an officer on the 4 to 8 watch, for example, must be on duty from 4am to 8am and again from 4pm to 8pm, so that his watch hours total eight in every 24.

The job of *Safety Officer* is either held by one of the senior officers alongside their other duties or, on larger ships, is a full-time position in its own right. The Safety Officer is responsible for the training and implementing of all safety procedures at sea, including the prevention and combat of fire, possibly the worst hazard on any ship. Note that the master controls for the fire-detection system (including deck plans with indicator lights to locate the problem area) and the watertight doors, which can divide the lower part of the vessel into compartments, are generally located on the bridge.

Training for Deck Cadets

The previously-mentioned posts are all high-ranking positions which bring with them a salary of upwards of £17,000-£45,000 a year depending on rank. These are attained only after years of study and practical apprenticeship. For newcomers, the first step to becoming a Deck Officer is to apply directly to shipping companies to be taken on as an *Officer Cadet*. Once accepted, the company will pay your salary (starting pay is approximately $250/£125 per week /£5,000-£8,000 a year) and sponsor you throughout your training.

Acceptance as an officer cadet usually requires the following from UK applicants: that they:

- Be aged between 16 and 22 years
- Possess at least four GCSEs, including English, Maths and a Science subject, or (for a shortened cadetship) two A-levels
- Good health, especially good eyesight (as you will be tested for clear vision without the aid of spectacles or contact lenses).

Most prospective cadets apply during their final year at school, typically in October/November when they are in a position to give their expected exam results, to start training the following November. The average cadetship lasts four years and includes experience both in college and at sea with continual practical and academic assessment. So, presuming you are accepted by a cruise line as an Officer Cadet at the age of 17 and you get through each stage of the course – not to mention all the jobs that no one else wants to do – you could be a Third Officer with a Class III Certificate by age 21.

You would then continue gaining practical experience at sea until, say, the age of 24, when you could go back to college for a year to gain your Class II Certificate and return to sea as a Second Officer.

By the age of 27 and a further two months of intensive college study, resulting in the acquisition of your Class I (Master Mariner) Certificate, known as your Master's Ticket, you might resume work at sea as a First Officer. From then on promotion through the ranks is very much 'dead man's shoes'.

Promotion prospects tend to be slower for Deck Officers on passenger ships than on other vessels like tankers and container ships, mainly because there are numerically far fewer passenger ships than other merchant vessels. Salaries also tend to be lower than in other areas of the shipping industry. But many cruise line officers agree that such disadvantages are outweighed by the social advantages of passenger ships, including access to public rooms and events, the facility to make a wider circle of friends and acquaintances and a generally more glamorous lifestyle.

For those who might like to consider the alternatives, however, high earnings and good promotion prospects are offered on tankers by leading oil companies. But the work is hard, the hours are long and the social life virtually non-existent. Container ships may be seen to be less demanding than tankers but, in terms of prospects and salary, may also be less rewarding. Ferries are the less exotic side of the passenger market, but the routine of returning frequently to a home port may prove attractive to officers with on-shore family or business commitments.

Training Organisations for Deck Cadets

According to NUMAST, the trade union for more than 19,000 Merchant Navy and other maritime professionals, there is a national and international shortage of skilled and experienced seafarers. However, places for sponsored training are limited to the Merchant Navy and a few private companies and charitable trusts. One of the few cruise-connected companies to sponsor cadet training at sea is Viking Recruitment (see addresses below). Further information on studying while at sea can be obtained from the Marine Society College of the Sea, 202 Lambeth Road, London SE1 7JW; ☎020-7261 9535; fax 020-7401 2537; www.marine-society. org.uk. Further details on training and careers for deck officers in the British Merchant Navy may be obtained from the Merchant Navy Training Board, Carthusian Court, 12 Carthusian Street, London EC1M 6EZ, UK; ☎0800-085 0973; www.mntb.org.uk and www.gotosea.org.uk. You can also get advice on training with the Merchant Navy at www.learndirect-advice.co.uk; ☎0800 100 900.

Information on specialist courses and training and career opportunities for Merchant Navy Deck Officers may also be obtained from the British colleges and other organisations listed below as well as the website www. seamanship.co.uk. Trinity House (Tower Hill, London EC3N 4DH; ☎020-7481-6900; fax 02007480-7662; e-mail emma.skingley@thls.org; www. trinityhouse.co.uk) awards scholarships/cadetships for nautical courses.

BP Shipping Cadet Recruitment: Breakspear Park, Breakspear Way, Hemel Hemel Hempstead, Herts., HP2 4UL; ☎01442-225768; fax 01442-223771; e-mail shipcareers@bp.com. Deck and Engineer Officer

Cadetships for candidates aged from 16 to 21+. All training costs paid as well as salary while training and sponsorship to degree level.

Blackpool & the Fylde College, School of Maritime Operations, Fleetwood Nautical Campus, Broadwater, Fleetwood, Lancashire FY7 8JZ, England; ☎01253-352352; fax 01253-356127; www.blackpool.ac.uk.

Clyde Marine Recruitment Ltd, Clyde House, 209 Govan Road, Glasgow G51 1HJ, Scotland; ☎0141-427-6886; fax 0141-427-6928; www.clydemarine.com; email recruitment@clydemarine.com. This company also has the capacity to place cadets with shipping companies.

Conway Merchant Navy Trust, Conway MN Trust, The Red House, 84 High Street, Buntingford SG9 9AJ; ☎01763-272202; e-mail cadets@conwaymntrust.info; www.conwaytrust.info. Offers full sponsorship to young school leavers wanting to become Deck or Engineer Officers.

Glasgow College of Nautical Studies, Faculty of Maritime Studies, 21 Thistle St, Glasgow G5 9XB, Scotland; ☎0141-565-2500; fax 0141-565-2599; e-mail enquiries@gcns.ac.uk; www.glasgow-nautical.ac.uk.

Liverpool John Moores University, Maritime & Transport Studies, Byrom Street, Liverpool L3 3AF, England; ☎0151-231-2021; fax 0151-231-2293; e-mail s.bonsall@livjm.ac.uk.

Lowestoft College, Maritime and Offshore Centre, St Peters Street, Lowestoft, Suffolk NR32 2NB, England; ☎01502-2312121; fax 01502-500-031; course enquiries@lowestoft.ac.uk; www.lowestoftcollege.ac.uk.

NUMAST, Oceanair House, 750-760 High Road, Leytonstone, London E11 3BB; ☎020-8989 6677; fax 020-8530 1015; e-mail enquiries@numast.org; www.numast.org. Trade union for the Merchant Navy and other professional seafarers.

National Sea Training Centre: North West Kent College, Dering Way, Gravesend, Kent DA12 2JJ; ☎01322-629600; e-mail paulrussell@nwkcollege.ac.uk; www.nwkcollege.ac.uk/nstc/index.html.

Northern Marine Management, Alba House, 2 Central Avenue, Clydebank Business Park, Clydebank G81 2QR; ☎0141-876 3000; fax 0141-941 2791; e-mail nmm.recruitment@stena.com; www.nmm-stena.com. Provides cadet training and sponsorship and a berth at sea. Cadet training opportunities for both deck crew and engineers.

P&O Nedlloyd UK Cadet Training, Beagle House, Braham Street, London E1 8EP; ☎+31 10400 7620; fax_31 10400 7616; m.cooper@ponl.com; www.ponl.com.

RMT, National Union of Rail, Maritime and Transport Workers, Unity House, 39 Chalton Street, London NW1 1JD; ☎020-7387 4771; fax 020-7529 8808; e-mail info@rmt.org.uk; www.rmt.org.uk. Trade union that represents seafaring ratings, ABSs, mechanics, cooks and stewards employed on all types of merchant vessels.

School of Maritime and Coastal Studies, Southampton Institute, East Park Terrace, Southampton, Hampshire SO14 0RD, England; ☎023-8031-9736; fax 023-8031-9739; www.solent.ac.uk/maritime.

Ship Safe Training Group Ltd, 135 High Street, Rochester, Kent ME11 1EW; ☎01634-405252; 01634-405242; e-mail recruitment@sstg.org; www.sstg.org. Recuitment and training company for entrant deck and engineer officer cadets and other categories of personnel as required.

South Tyneside College, Nautical Studies & Marine Engineering, St. George's Avenue, South Shields, Tyne & Wear, NE34 6ET England; ☎0191-427-3585/3585; e-mail info@stc.ac.uk; www.stc.ac.uk. Or the Marine and Mechanical Faculty at the same address as above (☎0191-427 3900; fax 0191-427 3644; e-mail mmeng.stc.ac.uk).

Trinity House SCTC, c/o Chiltern Maritime Ltd., The Red House, 84 High Street, Buntingford, Herts; e-mail ChilternMaritime@compuserve. com; www.trinityhouse.co.uk. Awards scholarships/cadetships for courses but not actual courses.

Viking Recruitment Ltd, Cadet Training Department, Aycliffe Business Centre, Archcliffe Road, Dover, Kent CT17 9EL; ☎01304-240881; fax 01304-240882; info@vikingrecruitment.com; www.vikingrecruitment. com. Offers Deck and Engine Room cadet training sponsorship on vessels of the Windstar and Holland America lines.

Warsash Maritime Centre, Newtown Road, Southampton, Warsash, Hants. SO31 9ZL, England; ☎01489-576161; fax 01489-573988; www. solent.ac.uk/wmc/ and www.warsashcentre.co.uk; e-mail wmc@solent. ac.uk.

American readers can obtain further information from:
Maine Maritime Academy, 66 Pleasant Street, Castine, Maine 04420-5000, USA; ☎207-326-2206; e-mail admissions@mma.edu; www. mainemaritime.edu).
United States Merchant Marine Academy, 300 Steamboat Road, Kings Point, New York NY11024-1699, USA; ☎516-773-5391800/732-5390 (toll- free); fax 516-773-5390; www.usmma.edu.

Royal Navy

Finally there's the Royal Navy (RN). Passenger cruise ships, as well as tankers, container ships and ferries are classed as Merchant Vessels. The Royal Navy is a totally separate maritime body with distinct ways of operating and training. Although some Merchant officers might have received RN training and may even be in the Royal Navy Reserves, the RN offers a very different and more military career structure.

Anyone wishing to pursue a career with the Royal Navy should contact the Armed Forces Careers Office, Royal Navy and Royal Marines, Palace Barracks, Holywood, Co. Down BT1S 9RA (☎0800-7833222; www. royal-navy.mod.uk) or any regional office.

Do not overlook the Royal Fleet Auxiliary Service, which is a fleet of over 22 ships, staffed by civilians whose main role is to supply the Royal Navy at sea with food, ammunition, spares and fuel needed to maintain their daily operations. It offers Deck and Engineering Officer cadetships to young people with good GCSE results including at least a B in Maths. Training is given for an HND which leads to jobs at sea as Third Officer. Further information from RFA Bureau (Recruitment), Room F4, Lancelot Building, HM Naval Base, Portsmouth PO1 3NH; ☎023-9727 6023; fax 023-9272 6021; e-mail rfarecruit@gtnet.go.uk; www.rfa.mod.uk.

Security at Sea

A specialised unit of the deck department is the security division, headed by a *Chief Security Officer*. Security Officers hold responsible positions, covering all aspects of security from issuing and checking identity papers to enforcing fire and safety regulations and carrying out regular clock patrols. In keeping with modern anti-terrorist techniques, the Chief Security Officer on high-profile ships may even be from a military background and fully trained in bomb disposal. Princess Cruises make great play of the fact that they use ex-Gurkhas (about six at a time on board) on some ships. Security measures for US waters were considerably tightened post 9/11 but ports in Europe have had anti-terrorism measures in place for many years. Most ships now operate automated systems, which enable security personnel to know who is on board at any given moment and all baggage going on the ship is X-rayed. This is to ensure that no unaccompanied bombs are left on board by a bomber (who then flees the vessel in any port. Security is potential employment for mature applicants with an appropriate career background. On US cruise lines this may mean ex-Federal agents, police or military. Candidates with British naval experience or (especially) ex-Marines might do well to contact a company which supplies security personnel to various cruise lines, including International Cruise Services, 36, Midlothian Drive, Glasgow G41 3QU; ☎0141-649 8644; fax 0141-636 1016; info@cruiseservices.co.uk; www. cruiseservices.co.uk. Falck IMS, Uglviggaardsvej 3, Denmark 6705 Esbjerg, Denmark (in the UK contact Falck IMS, The Garden House, Little Chilmington, Great Chart, Ashford, Kent TN23 3DN; ☎01233-643805; fax 01233-635290) offers courses and recruitment for ship security officers; also look at their website www.falckmaritime.com.

Security Officers are usually assisted by lesser-ranking members of the deck department, such as quartermasters and/or *Security Petty Officers* (a rank mid-way between officer and crew member).

Security personnel earn anything between $600 and $3,500 (£400 and £2,350) per month, subject to status, service and (it has to be said) nationality.

Finding a Job in the Deck Department

There are various worldwide agencies which specialise in finding placements for deck officers, engineers and ratings. For some of the addresses, refer to the end of the section *Technical & Engineering*.

It is useful to note that cruise lines tend to employ deck officers of the same nationality as the company itself, even if the non-officer staff are multinational. It is therefore important, if only for linguistic reasons, that aspiring deck staff are aware of the nationality bias of prospective companies before applying to join their deck department (this information is provided in the Cruise Ship Listing). For example Royal Olympic Cruises uses mainly Greek officers, Costa Cruises employs mostly Italians, American nationals are sought by Clipper Cruise Lines, and Norwegian Cruise Line hires mainly Norwegian deck officers. Possibly the best bet in terms of work opportunities for prospective British deck officers is P & O Cruises, as they also have a strong ferry division.

In the Words of a Deck Officer

I'm the junior First Officer onboard a passenger ship in the Mediterranean. There are actually three First Officers on this particular ship and I'm the junior, not because of my age (I'm 31) but because

I was promoted to this position more recently than the other two. As the junior, I get the raw deal when it comes to duty times, as I'm on the 12.00 to 4.00 watch. This means I hardly ever get ashore, since I'm always sleeping in the mornings and working in the afternoons, and I can't even enjoy a few drinks in the evening when I know I'm due to start work at midnight. One of the other First Officers is going on leave at the end of next cruise though, and I'll take over his 4.00 to 8.00 watch, which will suit me better.

I suppose of all the jobs on the ship, ours is one of the most insular. During the night there's usually only myself and the quartermaster here on the bridge and even in the daytime I don't have much contact with other employees. Occasionally we'll have bridge visits when I'll explain the workings of the radar and controls to any passengers who might be interested in that sort of thing. But in general, my work is navigation and does not involve the public at all.

Of course, the social side is there if that's what you want. All officers are encouraged to attend the major cocktail parties and the 'Old Man' and 'Staff' both host tables in the passenger restaurant, even though they admit that the small talk can sometimes be an effort. Some deck officers might enjoy that aspect of the job but, for most of us, the organised functions are a bit of a bore and, especially since I've become a dad, I'm not that bothered about socialising.

My wife (who was a ship's purser before we married) and baby daughter actually spend several weeks a year onboard the ship with me. They may travel free of charge, as long as they occupy my cabin, which is no problem as I have a double bed and a cot can be provided. I am also entitled to about three months paid leave, so I do get to see quite a lot of them.

I must say that although my personal terms of employment are really quite good (they include medical cover and a pension scheme), several of the major cruise lines seem to be introducing contractual changes that will mean less security for deck officers in the future. As for my personal future, who knows? I have my Master's Ticket and eventually it would be good to be based at home working as a harbour pilot, but such jobs are hard to get. If I'm honest, I suppose I would like to be Captain one day, although on passenger ships it's a slow process. If I were working on cargo vessels I would probably be Master in my own right by now, and earning a lot more than my current $40,000 (£22,000) a year. But

> *in my opinion even the captain of a container ship is underpaid when you consider what a commercial airline pilot can make.*
>
> *If money had been my main objective I would definitely have looked to the skies. But like so many of my colleagues I have always loved the sea and love working on the sea. There's nothing quite like the view from the bridge as we're sailing into the sunset or the freedom of seeing ocean for miles on every side. For me, that's what it's all about.*
>
> **Peter Morton (age 31)**

All Hands on Deck

Let's suppose a career as an officer isn't for you and that you're looking for more casual or manual work opportunities within the Deck Department. These include positions as an unskilled *Ordinary Seaman (OS)*, skilled *Able Seaman (AB)*, *Deck Carpenter, Quartermaster* (an AB who assists the deck officers with navigation) and *Bosun* (a senior AB who acts as supervisor and link between the lower ranking seamen and the deck officers, a sort of naval equivalent to a military sergeant).

The fact is your quest for a non-officer position on deck may be frustrating. Openings for deck 'ratings' (non-officers) on passenger ships are extremely limited and, nowadays, companies tend to fill even AB positions with workers from countries with low-wage economies, particularly Ukraine and the Philippines. But if swabbing the deck has always been one of your ambitions, by all means try your luck by writing to the cruise lines direct. Try also yacht charterers, cargo ships and ferry companies, as they often have more general opportunities for seamen and might be prepared to sponsor the training.

British applicants fortunate enough to receive sponsorship are normally expected to attend a three-month course, which generally culminates in the Department of Transport Efficient Deck Hand (EDH) examination or AB Certificate and pre-sea training. In the UK courses are offered at the National Sea Training Centre (North West Kent College, Dering Way, Gravesend, Kent DA12 2JJ, England; ☎01322-629-600; fax 01322-629-682; www.nwkent.ac.uk). The Publisher Witherbys (www.witherbys.com) publishes a range of textbooks to do with seamanship.

If the Deck Department doesn't sound quite as promising as you had hoped, never fear. Most newcomers do not find jobs on the bridge, but rather in one of the many departments which combine to turn a cruise ship into a floating hotel. And that's where we'll be looking next.

Hotel Department

The Hotel Department houses by far the most employees on the average cruise ship and therefore offers the most job opportunities to newcomers. It operates in much the same way as a large hotel on land, with various departments (depending on the size of the ship) including food and beverage, restaurants, bars, public rooms and housekeeping, each with their own managers and various assistant managers, all under the overall command of the Hotel Manager who is Head of Department. Needless to say, the managerial jobs are senior positions attracting annual salaries from $40,000 (£21,000), and are generally filled by internal promotion or offered to those with appropriate shipboard experience. The more basic jobs, by contrast, tend to be paid very badly at about £500-£1,500 per month.

On the American model, most of the earnings for service-related jobs come from tips.

Some Tips On Tips

There is an old joke amongst cruise line employees that at the end of the voyage the Captain climbs onto his moped and the waiter drives home in his Rolls. While this may be an exaggeration, it is certainly true to say that a high earning potential exists for anyone in the direct service sector (such as waiters, bar waiters, busboys and cabin stewards) providing they are prepared to endure the often long working hours.

The Captain climbs onto his moped, the waiter drives home in his Rolls

Passengers are generally given guidelines on how much they are expected to tip and, although tipping is discretionary, most passengers do follow the company's recommendations. Some passengers may have already pre-paid gratuities at the time of booking, in which case the company will reimburse crew members accordingly. This may not be such a bad thing as the pre-paid service charge is guaranteed and often passengers will tip a little extra as well.

Recent tipping recommendations given to guests by the following cross-section of major cruise lines may serve as a guide to the type of gratuity-making potential to expect, bearing in mind that cabin stewards, waiters and busboys may serve between fifteen and thirty passengers per day. Note that those companies, which discourage tipping, invariably pay staff a higher basic wage to compensate. Note also that the service charge percentage added to bar bills is generally the same as that added to restaurant wine bills, etc. Figures are given in US dollars, the shipboard currency of most passenger vessels ($1 = approximately 54 pence).

Previously recommended gratuity rates per passenger per day: liable to change.

Carnival Cruise Lines: automatic gratuity programme on most of its sixteen ships of $9.75 per day. 15% added to bar bills.

Celebrity Cruises: $3 for cabin steward, $3 for waiter, $1.50 for busboy, 15% added to bar bills.

Clipper Cruise Line: pooled tips of $8 per passenger per day.

Costa Cruises: $3 for cabin steward, $3 for waiter, $1.50 for busboy. All tips 50 cents less for European cruises, 15% added to bar bills.

Crystal Cruises: $4 for cabin steward, $4 for waiter, $2.50 for busboy, $4 for butler (penthouse suite only), 15% added to bar bills.

Holland America Line: no tipping policy (although tips may be accepted when offered); no service charge added to bar bills.

Norwegian Cruise Line: automatic gratuity system of $10 per day for ages 13 and older, $5 for children aged 3-12 no charge younger than 3 years. 15% added to bar bills.

P & O Cruises: $3.50 for cabin steward, $3.50 for waiter, 10% added to bar bills.

Princess Cruises: automatic gratuity system on all its ships of $10 per day and 15% added to bar bills.

Radisson Seven Seas Cruises: no tipping is expected but if staff go out of their way or are extra nice and passengers do offer tips they may be accepted (or not). This is a change to former policy which did not allow staff to accept tips. Service charges added to bar bills.

Royal Caribbean Cruise Line: $3.50 for cabin steward, $3.50 for waiter, $2.50 for busboy, 15% added to bar bills.

Seabourn Cruise Line: the company states that 'staff do not expect gratuities as they are well paid.

Windstar Cruises: like Seabourn operates a no tipping policy.

Both waiters and stewards tend to agree that shorter cruises are the best (pro rata) for gratuities, while admitting they're harder work. So if making a fast buck is one of your objectives, go for a cruise line that specialises in short party cruises of the 'fun and sun' variety, and you could be laughing all the way to the bank.

But before considering the catering, bar and housekeeping sectors of the hotel department, let's look at the types of available office jobs.

PURSER'S OFFICE

One senior manager with a specific shipboard title is the *Purser*. The Purser is chiefly responsible for the ship's accounts, although there are many aspects of the job that fall outside the realm of accountancy, including requisitioning supplies, overseeing printed matter and dealing with customs and immigration officials as well as anyone with a problem. In the days when ships were ships and not floating hotels, the Purser often assumed the role that is now allotted to the Hotel Manager. Although a few shipping companies still adhere to the increasingly-outmoded practice of referring to the head of the Hotel Department as the Purser, it is nowadays generally accepted that the Purser's position is different from and subordinate to that of the Hotel Manager.

The Purser (also known as the Chief Purser) may be aided by an *Assistant Purser* or *Hotel Purser* (to oversee all areas of passenger business), a *Berthing Officer* (to allocate accommodation) and various *Second, Third* and *Fourth Pursers*. Most ships also have at least one *Crew Purser* (and maybe *Assistant Crew Pursers* or *Clerks*) to deal specifically with crew issues and accounts. A purser with responsibility for budgeting earns about $2,300 to $3,200 per month depending on the cruise line while a chief purser's earnings are nearly double that.

Quite often the Purser's office, with its many comings and goings, is seen as the hub of the ship. It is also the perfect place for anyone with secretarial or accountancy skills to offer their services. So if you're interested in typical office work but don't want to work in your typical office, read on. The Purser's office needs *Secretaries* with good typing and basic computer skills. Previous shipboard experience is not essential although ability to work well under pressure is a must. Some temping experience would be an advantage.

The Purser's office also needs qualified *Accountants, Bookkeepers* with experience and/or qualifications, *Office Clerks*, who are eager rather than qualified, and *Receptionists* with basic secretarial skills. Often there is no actual reception area, but the front desk of the Purser's office serves this purpose. Bearing in mind that this is also the place where most passenger complaints are aired, a patient and tactful, not to say thick-skinned, disposition is also beneficial.

In applying for jobs in the Purser's office, an ability to speak at least one foreign language is a definite bonus and, in some cases, might even be a requirement. Experience or qualifications (such as a Higher National Diploma/HND in Hotel Management) would also be advantageous.

Other Office Jobs

Top secretaries are needed as *Personal Assistants* to senior officers. Depending on the size of the ship, the Captain, Chief Engineer and Hotel Manager may all have PAs. Appropriate experience is important for these positions and some specialist technical knowledge may also be desirable. Expect to earn upwards of $27,600 (£14,000) per year.

Other office-based opportunities may include work in a berthing office (allocating cabins), a manifest office (processing embarkations, etc.) or an accommodation office (attending to the servicing of passenger cabins). If this type of work appeals, you should write direct to the Head Office of the respective cruise lines or to the employment agencies listed under *Useful Addresses for Jobs in the Hotel Department.*

As with all job applications, the more you can offer, the better your chance of acceptance. Why not enrol on a short course to update your skills (or learn new ones), attend an evening class in computer studies or languages or work for a local temp agency in the meantime?

In the Words of a Fourth Purser

I started work only two months ago as a Fourth Purser onboard a mid-sized ship that normally carries about 800 passengers. I feel that I'm actually quite well suited to this type of work. I have a degree in Business Studies and I also speak reasonable French, two factors that I'm sure helped to clinch the job, even though I never use either. I also have experience in several related areas. I've worked in Greece as a representative for a big holiday company so I'm used to looking after tourists and sorting out their problems. I also did a short spell in a travel agency, where I had to use a computer as well as deal with the public. And I've even sold time-share, which proves I have a sense of humour!

In the winter months the ship sails around Mexico and the Caribbean and in the summer we go up the coast of Alaska. This itinerary means we get a lot of Americans onboard. Being from Scotland, I've had to really concentrate on speaking clearly as, initially, none of the passengers could understand me!

Communication hasn't been my only problem. On my first couple of days I had to enter the list of passenger names (the manifest) into a computer in a small back office. Unfortunately, we had unusually bad weather at the time and I felt really ill. Quite a lot of the passengers were sick too, but that was no consolation. I was literally green, staring at the computer screen in this moving, windowless room while trying to create a good first impression at the same time. In the end, I went to the nurse and she gave me some medication. This cured the sea sickness but made me feel so drowsy that I fell asleep at the keyboard. Some first impression!

My other teething problems concerned clothes or rather the lack of them. As a junior purser, I am a one-stripe officer and wear uniform for work during the day (which I had to buy myself). Longer-serving officers are also expected to keep a more formal uniform (including full-length skirts for the women) to wear at social functions and on particular evenings. As a newcomer, however, I was told I could wear my own clothes if I wished to attend the Captain's Cocktail Party. Since I had assumed I would be in uniform most of the time, I hadn't packed any suitable dresses and had to wear a lycra mini skirt that had seen better days. It certainly got me noticed, but not in the way I would have liked. Neither had I been told that I would also need white or cream shoes for work, which meant I spent my first few hours in Jamaica, searching in vain for a pair of white courts, and ended up using whitener to blanche my favourite sling-backs.

I guess for me it's still early days and I don't know yet if I'll stick it. I hate having to share accommodation with another junior purser, although with promotion I would get a single cabin. I also have bad days working on the front desk when I get sick of hearing passenger complaints. They moan about everything – the noise, the movie schedule, the service, the lack of service, the price of excursions, the price of taxis, the heat, the cold, the weather in general, the air-conditioning, the lack of air-conditioning – and it's even worse on the day before disembarkation, when they're all querying their bills and getting their luggage tags mixed up. On the other hand, I've been to a lot of places I'm sure I would never have visited otherwise and I've made some interesting friends.

Financially, my $1,900 (£870) per month is very much at the lower end of the purser's pay scale, but I find that in spite of spending a lot, I easily save over half my earnings, which is something I would miss if I went back to working onshore. And even though in all honesty I can't see myself doing this in ten years time, the last two months have been a valuable experience that I definitely don't regret and certainly won't forget.

Sarah Knight (age 26)

CATERING FOR ALL

As you might expect in an environment where guests eat around the clock, catering for hundreds of passengers (and crew) is a mammoth task that requires a huge number of staff. The person in charge of all these staff members, plus the administrative planning and budgeting, is the *Food & Beverage Manager* (or F & B Manager). The alternative title *Catering Manager* is preferred on some ships, though the responsibilities are much the same. This important department of the ship also includes the bars under the supervision of a Bars Manager.

The F & B Manager will be assisted by various under managers: *Assistant F & B Manager, Junior Assistant F & B Manager* (how about Assistant to the Assistant F & B Manager?), etc. Ships with more than one dining room may also employ a *Restaurants Manager*.

Due to the large numbers of waiting staff required, opportunities may occur more frequently in the restaurants than in any other sector of a cruise ship. Note, however, that most service personnel may be recruited *en masse* from agencies in countries with weak economies, leaving few opportunities for individual jobseekers. Western European applicants are frequently favoured for key positions such as Maître d' or Head Waiter.

If you hold an HND or OND in Hotel Management or Catering Management and have what you consider to be appropriate managerial experience in hotels or restaurants on shore, you might wish to apply for a managerial post at sea which may come with a salary of $33,000 (£18,000) and upwards. Preference will almost always be given to applicants with maritime experience as well as managerial experience. It may be worthwhile accepting a lower-ranking position than you'd prefer in order to get up the gangway as, once onboard, promotion prospects in maritime catering are generally very good.

In the Front Line: Jobs in the Restaurant

Be warned that both restaurant and bar staff work long hours on ships, generally up to 15 hours a day. Much of this time is spent standing around, and stamina is therefore an important prerequisite of the job. It is inadvisable to apply for positions in this department if you are unable or do not wish to live on your feet. Comfortable shoes are a must.

Every restaurant on every ship has its own *Maître d'Hôtel* (maître d' for short) and often *Assistant Maître d's* who are in charge of an army of waiters, wine stewards and busboys. The Maître d' is normally an experienced professional, tactful, possibly a linguist, and with a keen eye to match his earning power of $33,000-$55,000 (£18,000-£30,000) per year including tips.

Waiters should ideally be trained in silver service and have experience in a high-class restaurant. Would-be waiters without experience might do better to clinch an entry level job as a lowly paid (from about £500 per month) *Busboy* (Waiter's Assistant) in the first instance, as promotion prospects for the capable are always bright. Opportunities also exist for inexperienced *Catering Assistants* to clear tables and replenish food supplies in the buffet-style passenger restaurants.

Wine Steward/Sommeliers should possess a good knowledge of wines, obtained by an appropriate college course or work experience. As wine is becoming more popular on board (often at the expense of spirits), wine stewards, particularly those employed by Cunard and Seabourn are expected to run wine tastings and wine seminars for passengers. Note that one of the most acclaimed institutions to offer internationally recognised courses of varying lengths and levels is the Wine & Spirit Education Trust (39-45 Bermondsey Street, London SE1 3XF, United Kingdom; ☎020-7089 3800; fax 020-7089 3845; e-mail west@west.co.uk; www. west.co.uk). A useful website for catering staff is www.caterer.com where cruise ship jobs are frequently advertised.

With the exception of *Head Waiters* and *Head Wine Stewards*, basic salaries for wine stewards, waiters and busboys are low, maybe only $300/£175 per week. But with tips and commission, most restaurant staff can easily earn a weekly wage in excess of $500 (£275).

In the Words of a Waiter

I first started working at sea about five years ago when I was 32. My first ship was based in the Mediterranean and used to call at my home port of Istanbul, where at that time I was employed as a waiter in one of the main hotels. A friend who was already working onboard told me they were short of restaurant staff and managed to arrange an interview for me onboard the ship. My work experience, together with the fact that I speak reasonable English, meant I was taken on there and then.

When the company sold that vessel I was offered a job on one of their other ships, sailing out of Florida. I decided to take it even though my wife was unhappy about me working away for nine months at a time, because I knew I would be able to earn more than on land. I have always dreamed of opening my own first-class restaurant in Turkey, and I am not far from realising that goal. Of course, everything has a price and I suppose the price of my dream is not being at home to see my two children grow up. I also miss the home comforts of family life. It comes hard having to share a small cabin with three other waiters and take care of your own cleaning, bed-making and laundry after a ten hour shift in the restaurant.

Yes, we work long hours, sometimes starting at 6.30am, and this includes two sittings for breakfast and dinner or lunch and dinner most days of the week. For this I get a basic salary of (£125) per week. This may sound awful, but my real earnings come from tips. During an average cruise, my busboy and I will serve about 30 passengers each mealtime. These passengers always sit at their allocated table in my section of the restaurant so, by the end of the cruise, I know them quite well. I make a point of remembering the guests' names and chatting with them. Not only does it make the work more enjoyable but they are then more likely to tip well. The ship gives the passengers recommended tipping guidelines of $3 per passenger per day for their waiter and $2 for their busboy. Some guests may tip less but many will tip more. In an average week I clear $650 (£360) in tips and on good cruises I'll do even better. Most of that money I'll send straight home to my wife.

As for expenses, my main expense during this contract has been the cost of my airline ticket to join the ship in Fort Lauderdale, and I'll get that back. Other cruise lines work differently but my particular company always reimburses me for my outward expenses when

> *I've completed each nine-month contract and they also pay my flight home for my usual two months leave. I supply my own black trousers, white shirts and bow-tie for work, although the company supplies us with uniform jackets.*
>
> *You do, of course, have to take into account off-the-record 'expenses' such as tipping to get the food quickly in the galley. On my first day at sea I had to wait ages for each course and wondered why other waiters who put their orders in after mine kept getting their food before me. But I soon discovered that a few well-spent bucks in the galley meant my tables also got their profiteroles pronto.*
>
> *In some ways, keeping the customer happy is more important at sea than on land because a lot of emphasis tends to be placed on the comment cards which passengers fill in at the end of their cruise. If a waiter gets bad ratings it can result in a demotion to a worse station (section of the restaurant) or a reduction in his number of tables, which will of course affect his earning power. Some of the passengers can be demanding but most of them have saved hard to come on their dream cruise and are just out to have a good time. Personally, I enjoy keeping them happy. It's a two-way thing – I help them live their dreams, they help me buy mine.*
>
> **Hassan Kaya (age 38)**

Behind the Scenes: Jobs in the Kitchen

The standards of cuisine vary from ship to ship but on the whole are in mainstream banqueting-style (see the accompanying sample lunch and dinner menus, typical of a mid-range cruise ship). As in the kitchens of any large hotel, a cruise ship employs numerous chefs under the overall charge of an *Executive Chef* and/or *Head Chef* or *Chef de Cuisine*. Nowadays, these roles are largely administrative and he/she is more likely to be found at a computer than surrounded by steaming saucepans.

The actual food preparation is done by a team of *Sous Chefs, Chefs de Rang, Chefs de Partie, Chefs Entremetier, Chefs Saucier, Pastry Chefs, Commis Chefs* and *Vegetable Chefs*. The team will also include trained *Butchers* and, especially, *Bakers*, as many ships bake their entire bread requirements onboard.

Most vessels offer a self-service option as an alternative to waiter-service at breakfast and lunchtimes, together with a regular late night buffet and an occasional special Gala Buffet. *Buffet Chefs* are, therefore, required to prepare salads and other dishes for these culinary spreads. Rafael Mantas, a buffet chef from the Philippines, explains one of the more unusual aspects of his work:

Alongside my salad-making duties, I carve sculptures out of fruits and vegetables for display in the restaurants. For the Gala Buffets, I also carve featured centrepieces out of huge blocks of ice. I have never had formal training in this art but, like many children in the Philippines, I learnt from an early age how to carve in wood, and the skills required are very similar. Each cruise I give vegetable and ice-carving demonstrations for the passengers and these are usually well attended. I enjoy doing the sculptures as I can carve more or less what I like and it gives me the chance to be creative.

For all senior galley positions, relevant qualifications (such as a City & Guilds Cookery 706 or Baking & Confectionery 120/121) and experience are a must. Indeed, some ships can even boast international chefs who are members of the celebrated *Confrérie de la Chaîne des Rôtisseurs*. An international gourmet society based on the ancient French order of goose roasters, which was formed by royal charter in 1248. At the upper end of the catering pay scale, top chefs can expect to earn upwards of $63,000 (£35,000) per annum. At the bottom end, a junior vegetable chef may be lucky to make $18,000 (£10,000).

If you are a trained and experienced chef, butcher or baker you should apply direct to the catering department of the cruise lines or to the catering companies listed under *Useful Addresses for Jobs in the Hotel Department*. Keep your eye too on specialist trade publications such as *The Caterer & Hotel Keeper*, as job vacancies at sea are occasionally, albeit rarely, advertised. The specialist website, *Rolling Pin International*, (www.rollingpinjobs. com) which calls itself 'the internet magazine for job seekers,' is linked to international cruise lines and carries adverts for cruise ship vacancies.

Courses for *Catering Ratings* (as opposed to senior chefs, who assume officer status) and *Catering Assistants* may be undertaken at the National Sea Training Centre (North West Kent College, Dering Way, Gravesend, Kent DA12 2JJ, England; ☎01322-629600; fax 01322-629687; www.nwkcollege.ac.uk). Note, however, that these courses are almost exclusively part of sponsorship programmes for merchant shipping companies rather than cruise lines (which are almost never prepared to fund the training of new recruits). For organizations that sponsor ratings at sea, see *Training Organisations for Cadets* addresses.

Positions do exist for unqualified *Galley Assistants* (or is it slaves?) to do general cleaning and preparation duties, and *Dishwashers* to operate commercial dishwashing machines, but don't apply for either if you are seeking big bucks or job satisfaction. You should be warned that many unskilled jobs on ships offer exploitative salaries, long working hours and poor living standards. Cruise companies assume that most Western Europeans and North Americans will not endure such conditions, and so tend to consider only applicants from developing countries for these types of positions.

Tracey Pardoe, an assistant catering manager from Canada, remarks:

When I joined my first ship I was shocked by the blatant racism onboard. I couldn't believe the discrepancies (monetary and otherwise) between the ranks and the apparent exploitation of sectors of the crew. I've since learned to live with it, but I still can't accept it.

Frank Kohl, a sous chef from Austria, responds to this comment:

Sure, it's unfair. Life's unfair. But everything's relative. Those guys may work round the clock for a fraction of my earnings, but they can live like kings for that in their country. My salary will barely pay the rent in mine. Some of them have worked at sea for years and no one's making them do it. If they don't like the heat, they can always get out of the kitchen.

Eduardo Santos, from the Philippines, agrees:

You have to understand that even as a college graduate I can earn more money, making sandwiches in the galley than I ever could as a government official in Manila. When you have a young family to support, income is very important.

Catering Concessionaires

Many cruise lines do not employ catering staff directly but rather lease the whole concession to a specialist maritime catering organisation. As company policies are subject to frequent change it is advisable to check with their respective head offices before applying as to which concessionaire (if any) they currently use. Some of the main independent employment agencies and catering companies to the cruising industry are listed under *Useful Addresses for Jobs in the Hotel Department* at the end of this chapter.

SAMPLE MENUS

LUNCHEON

APPETISERS

Devilled Eggs with Cornets of Ham

Gravlax

Salmon marinated in honey, dill and crushed pepper and served with a mustard-dill sauce

SOUPS

Cream of Spinach with Nutmeg

Beef Consommé with Tomato Bread Croutons

Chilled Strawberry and Vanilla Soup

EGG DISH

Mushroom Omelette with Watercress Garnish

ENTREES

Sautéed Fillet of Hake

with tomato concasse, served with saffron sauce

Breaded Pork Chops

Golden-fried, served with apple purée

Spaghetti al Pesto

with a pesto sauce of olive oil, pine nuts and basil, served with parmesan cheese

VEGETABLES

Carrots, Green Beans, Roast and Boiled Potatoes

CHEF'S HEALTHY OPTION

Beef Consommé

❖

Poached Fillet of Hake

served with steamed vegetables and boiled potatoes

❖

Fresh Fruit Salad

Luncheon cont'd

SANDWICH OF THE DAY

Tuna and Avocado Toasted Triple-decker

with mayonnaise, served with salad garnish and salsa

SALAD OF THE DAY

Chicken Caesar's

Freshly tossed Caesar's salad with strips of lean chicken, served with parmesan cheese

FROM THE GRILL

Grilled Ham and Cheese Toastie

served with french fries, coleslaw and green pickles

DESSERTS

Double Chocolate Cake

with chocolate sauce and vanilla ice cream

Blueberry Yoghurt Cream

with crushed blueberry sauce

Pecan Pie with Vanilla Ice Cream

ICE CREAMS

Vanilla, Chocolate, Neopolitan or Frozen Cherry Yoghurt

DESSERT SAUCES

Chocolate, Vanilla, Strawberry, Raspberry

ASSORTED FRESH FRUITS AND CHEESES

BEVERAGES

Full Roast or Decaffeinated Coffee,
Tea or Herbal Tea (Camomile, Mint, Rosehip)

DINNER

APPETISERS
Brazilian Hearts of Palm, served with Mustard Mayonnaise

Lobster and Crab Cocktail, served with Sauce Cardinal

Macedoine of Citrus Fruits in Grand Marnier

SOUPS
Cream of Cauliflower 'Dubarry'

Chicken Consommé with Vegetable Julienne

ENTREES
Sautéed (Boneless) Rainbow Trout 'Meuniere'

Prime Rib of Beef 'Bouquetiere'
served with horseradish sauce

Roast Turkey
served with chestnut dressing, giblet sauce and cranberries

Penne alla Puttanesca
*Pasta in a sauce of garlic, tomato, capers, olives, peppers and oregano,
served with parmesan cheese*

VEGETABLE ENTREES
Vegetable Quiche baked with Herbs and Gruyere Cheese

VEGETABLES
Carrots 'Vichy', Brussels Sprouts

Roast, Baked, Mashed and Parsley Potatoes

SALADS
Salad 'Aida'
Iceberg lettuce, artichoke, egg and peppers in a Dijonnaise dressing

Garden Salad
Lettuce, cucumber, tomato and carrot in a vinaigrette dressing

Dinner cont'd

CHEF'S SUGGESTION
Brazilian Hearts of Palm
Cream Soup 'Dubarry'
Roast Turkey
Apple and Raisin Pie

LEAN AND HEALTHY OPTION
Chicken Consommé
Penne alla Puttanesca
Sugar-Free White Chocolate Eclair

DESSERTS
Apple and Raisin Pie, served with Vanilla Ice Cream
Warm Ricotta Cheese Crepes, served with Raspberry Sauce
Creme Caramel garnished with Exotic Fruits
Selection of Ice Creams and Dessert Sauces

Tonight's Flambéed Speciality
Cherries Jubilee served with Vanilla Ice Cream and Cinammon

DIABETIC DESSERT
Sugar-Free White Chocolate Eclair

SELECTION OF CHEESES AND BISCUITS

SELECTION OF FRESH FRUITS

BEVERAGES
Full Roast or Decaffeinated Coffee,
Tea or Herbal Tea (Camomile, Mint, Rosehip)

AFTER DINNER MINTS

BEHIND BARS

It is a well-known fact that a lot of alcohol gets consumed on cruise liners. However, styles of drinking seem to have polarised dramatically over the last decade with binge drinkers on one hand and discerning imbibers on the other. These days, on many cruises there is increasing emphasis on the quality of the drink, rather than the quantity consumed. Many cruise lines have themed bars which stock connoisseur ranges of whiskies, champagnes, etc. and wine lists have also been expanded and are constantly revised with the new ranges promoted to passengers at on board wine seminars and tastings. This is of course, partly a marketing ploy as sales of spirits on cruise ships have fallen in favour of wines.

Most passenger ships have several bars, under the charge of an experienced *Bars Manager* and *Assistant Bars Manager(s)*. Many work opportunities exist here for applicants over twenty-one years of age, including jobs for *Cocktail Waiters* to prepare cocktails, *Bar Stewards* to do general bar work and prepare drinks and *Bar Waiters* to take orders, serve drinks and clear tables.

With the exception of managerial positions, which generally assume officer status and minimum monthly salaries of $2,500 (£1,375), earnings in the bar department are often comprised of a basic salary (as low as $100/£54 per week), commission (usually 1.5%) on sales, inclusive service charge (usually 15%) and tips. This can amount to a combined earning potential of at least $2,000 (£1,100) per month, and frequently much more.

For jobs in each category, apply direct to the cruise lines or to the concessionaires listed under *Useful Addresses for Jobs in the Hotel Department* at the end of this chapter. They will invariably state that experience is essential. But a bit of homework, a good knowledge of cocktails and the ability to bluff can go a long way

In the Words of a Bartender

I live in Miami and have worked in the bar department of a Florida-based ship for the past six months. I first started working at sea on a friend's recommendation. He was already employed as a barman on ships and told me he was saving over $1,800 (£1,000) a month, going to places he'd never imagined he would actually visit and dating a different girl every cruise. This sounded pretty good to me so I applied to work on the ships too. After writing to loads of different companies and waiting about ten weeks, I was accepted *to start the following month.*

Of course, one thing my friend forgot to tell me was how long the hours can be. On my first cruise I was so tired I spent my entire free time catching up on my sleep. But after a while I got used to the shifts and now I find it quite easy. I would say to anyone embarking on their first ship to give it at least a month. When you first get onboard, everything's hard because it's all new. You're trying to learn a new job, remember names and faces, find your way around the ship; all this is exhausting enough. It can also be lonely because you're miles from home and you don't know anyone and, because everyone's so busy, it seems no one has time for you. But as you find your feet, you realise this isn't the case and you start making friends and having a laugh. After a few weeks you feel so at home that you can't imagine how you stuck your old routine on land for so long. But you've got to give it time. If you decide on your first day that it's not for you and you disembark at the next port, you've really not given ships – or yourself – a chance.

The other reason for sticking it is that the longer you've been on board, the better your chances of being promoted to the better jobs. For example, I've just been made a bartender which is less hours for the same money as a bar waiter. But, on this ship anyway, you have to start off as a bar waiter. Even though I'd already gained a lot of experience working behind bars on land, including a spell as relief bar manager in a nightclub, I still had to spend the first few months clearing tables and taking orders. That's just the way it works. There's also a certain amount of luck as to which bar you get allocated to work in, as some are obviously busier than others and this makes a difference to your commission and tips. But we work to a rota, so even if I'm stuck in a quiet bar one week, I'll probably be given a good 'earner' the next.

Surprisingly enough, considering I have a large apartment in Miami, I've even got used to sharing a cabin with two other guys. It's quite cramped but we get on OK and, to be honest, we're hardly ever there at the same time. And as for what my friend said? It's all true, believe me, it's true.

Miguel Lopez

And Don't Forget the Crew

Nearly all cruise ships have separate dining facilities for those who work onboard. The Officer's Mess, Staff Mess and Crew Mess will require chefs, waiters and catering assistants. The Ward Room (i.e. Officers' Bar) and, if applicable, Crew Bar will also need staff. These areas are often a good starting block for personnel with little experience and provide a great opportunity for getting to know fellow crew members. Employees are recruited through the same channels as for passenger areas (see *Useful Addresses for Jobs in the Hotel Department* at the end of this chapter).

KEEPING THE SHIP SHIP-SHAPE

The housekeeping sector of the Hotel Department is responsible for the general upkeep of the ship's interior and the provision of certain passenger services, under the supervision of the *Chief Steward* and/or *House-keeper* and *Assistant/s*. Larger ships may also have an administrative centre, under the direction of an *Accommodation Service Manager* (or similar sounding title) to deal with all aspects of maintaining and servicing cabins.

These senior positions with minimum annual salaries of around $50,000 (£26,000) do, of course, require appropriate experience and are often filled by internal promotions. But jobs for the inexperienced newcomer still abound in this division of the ship, so if you can make a bed or mop a floor, read on.

Opportunities in Housekeeping at Sea

No experience? No skills? No matter. *Cleaners* are required for work in all sectors of the Hotel Department, including both passenger and crew areas. The work is often unrewarding and cleaners' salaries are amongst the lowest on the ship (maybe as little as $200/£100 per week). But looking on the bright side, cleaners at sea have little or no overheads (unlike their counterparts on land). And what better place to soak your housemaid's knee than the waters of some balmy tropical shore? Note, however, that cleaning and general maintenance vacancies are often filled by workers from low wage countries. Unskilled Western European or North American job-seekers might do better to apply for other jobs in the Housekeeping Department, such as cabin or pantry steward.

Pantry Stewards are individually responsible for their allocated pantry, one of several small kitchens strategically situated in the passenger accommodation areas. These pantries are often not fully-equipped kitchens, but rather a place for making beverages and snacks. Stewards are expected to keep the pantries clean and take orders for Room Service, which they then prepare and sometimes deliver. Tips can easily treble their very low basic salary.

Cabin Stewards are the maritime equivalent of bedroom stewards in a hotel. Their duties include making beds and general light cleaning, replenishing toiletries and supplies, transferring laundry and delivering food and drinks (Room Service) to their allocated cabins while on duty. They may be supplemented by lower-ranking *Assistant Stewards*, who undertake the collection of cleaning and toiletry supplies for an entire section of cabins from the ship's stores, together with tasks such as furniture removal and deep-cleaning of carpets and upholstery. The basic salary is subject to the number of occupied cabins (up to twenty doubles) in a steward's charge each cruise, but may be as low as $500 (£275) per month. This is not as dire as it sounds since it is possible for them to make more than $2,000 (£1,103) per month in gratuities.

Laundry Masters are required to supervise the handling of all the ship's laundry. Considering the huge amount of cleaning involved, including officer and crew uniforms, passenger clothes, evening dresses, upholstery, tablecloths and napkins, bedlinen, etc., the task is enormous. It is not surprising then that the Laundry Master is aided by numerous *Laundry Assistants*. What may be surprising is the difficulty newcomers experience in landing a job in this field. There are two reasons: firstly, candidates need to be familiar with the machinery and cleaning techniques involved in commercial laundry work; secondly, in keeping with seafaring tradition, many ships employ only laundry workers of oriental (usually Chinese) origin. For most of these employees, the laundry, situated deep in the bowels of the ship, is not merely a workplace but an eating place (and often where they cook their own choice of food) and place of relaxation. Chinese videos may be playing on the TV, and Cantonese may be the only language spoken. In other words, the laundry is a self-contained community, more than any other section of the ship. So unless you happen to be from an appropriate cultural background, you might as well forget the idea of working in the laundry sector.

Medium to large-sized vessels may also require an *Upholsterer* and/or a *Tailor*, with proven practical ability in these areas. But salaries tend to be low and again oriental workers are frequently hired for such positions.

Note that cleaners, cabin stewards and sometimes even restaurant staff may be expected to assist as porters and baggage handlers at times of embarkation and disembarkation. Cleaners, baggage handlers, porters and pantry stewards may also be required to work night shifts.

On-the-spot job opportunities are most frequently found in the cabin servicing as well as catering sectors of the ship. These departments can provide a great way in, as in the case of Sylvia Vujinovic from Croatia:

I took a job as a cabin stewardess because I could not get work as a qualified teacher in my home country and I needed to earn some reasonable money. I had been at sea about five months when the position of Purser's Clerk was advertised internally. I asked to be considered and was offered the job. Although I actually earn less now than I did as a stewardess, the work is more interesting and the promotion prospects are excellent. In time, I could even end up as Chief Purser.

In the Words of a Cabin Steward

I work as a Cabin Steward on a ship that often calls in Jamaica where I come from, so I get to go home quite often. I first got hired through a friend of a friend (it always helps if you know someone who's already working on a ship). I've been at sea for three years now, so I guess I must enjoy the lifestyle.

My daily hours are from 9am till 1pm and from 5pm till 9pm, although I often have collection or preparation duties outside of these times. These hours actually suit me fine, as I always have time after lunch in the mess to go ashore or take a nap. After 9pm I usually work out in the crew gym before meeting the guys in the crew bar. I'm also a member of the ship's soccer team and about once a week we'll arrange to play against some local club or other. When I'm not lifting weights or (hopefully!) scoring goals, my job helps to keep me fit. As any housewife will tell you, cleaning and making beds, especially if it's 25 a day, is physical work. When I first come back from vacation I always get tired, but you soon get geared up to it again. It's what you get used to.

We each have our own station of between 11 and 16 cabins and on my ship these are allocated by the Chief Steward. Of course, some stations are better than others and everyone wants the most number of passengers for the tips. Usually, the more experienced *stewards get the best deal, but we change stations every other cruise, so even newcomers can get a good section once in a while. Naturally, we all prefer it when the ship is full. On a good week, I can make $800 (£441) in tips alone, that is if I have 15 occupied cabins, with maybe 12 of them doubles, and the tips average the company's recommended $3 a day. Of course, if half my cabins are empty and two of them have single occupancy, I may only make $300 (£165). I suppose on average I earn about $550 (£305) in weekly tips, most of which I manage to save as I have no onboard expenses.*

Apart from servicing the cabins and making the beds, I also take the towels and sheets and any garments the passengers want to be cleaned down to the laundry. Then, during my early evening shift, I deliver the next day's programmes, turn down the bedding and do my 'Tooth Fairy' routine of leaving a chocolate on each pillow.

Passengers can order Room Service around the clock, and if it's during my hours I'll deliver it to them. Outside my hours, the duty pantry assistant delivers the orders. It's like this: I work hard when I'm on duty, but when I'm off duty, I don't even think about the job. When I'm off, my time's my own.

Winston Edwards

OTHER JOBS IN THE HOTEL DEPARTMENT

A huge variety of other kinds of work are subsumed by the Hotel Department, including openings for Baggage Masters and Stores Managers (also known as Stores or Provisions Masters). These specific positions normally warrant the status of Petty Officer, a rank midway between officer and crew member. On this subject, however, it should be noted that the status and salary attached to a particular job can vary enormously from company to company and even between ships within the same company. So if you're not happy with the deal you're offered, do shop around.

Baggage Masters supervise the handling and storage of suitcases, trunks and other items. On smaller ships this may be undertaken by staff from the Housekeeping sector or the Purser's Office, whereas larger ships may employ specific personnel for this responsibility. The salary is generally about $1,500 (£825) a month.

Stores/Provisions Managers are needed to deal with the ordering, logging and storing of all provisions and supplies. This has become an increasingly administrative position, requiring appropriate skills. Larger ships may also have openings for *Yeomen* (bookkeeping assistants with computer skills) and *Stores Assistants* (to help with the more manual aspects of the job). Earnings for managers and assistants may be approximately $2,000 (£1,100) and $1,500 respectively per month.

Garbage Handlers assist with the collection and disposal of the mountains of rubbish that is continually generated. Cruise ships are notorious for waste and the garbage handlers have an unenviable task. While food and other degradable waste can be legally dumped at sea, specialist garbage barges in ports assist with the removal of additional trash (although some shipping lines have been guilty, inexcusably, of dumping non-degradable waste such as plastics into the oceans). Training and experience are not required but earnings can be as low as $180/£100 per week and positions tend to be monopolised by workers from low-economy countries.

Concierges are employed to attend to specific passenger needs, such as arranging tickets and transportation, making onshore theatre or hotel reservations and acting as a general liaison. This position does not exist on all ships, but is confined to the more exclusive luxury vessels. Good organisational skills and a tactful manner are important assets and previous experience in public relations would definitely be useful. Average earnings here may range from $1,500 to $2,500 (£825 to £1,368) and upwards per month.

Carpenters and *Joiners* do far more than carpentry and joinery. In fact, the Hotel Carpenter/Joiner is often more of a general Handyman who must be able to do anything from making a new notice-board to repairs to a damaged chair. Obviously, relevant qualifications, such as a City & Guilds Certificate, would be advantageous. Be warned, however, that many ships have a tendency to fill such positions with workers from countries such as the Philippines or Indonesia, and for salaries as low as $150 (£82) per week.

Porters and *Bellmen* may be required, especially on larger ships, although many of their typical duties, such as baggage handling on embarkation days, may be undertaken or supplemented by other crew members or shoreside workers. Weekly wages will range from $100 and $150 plus tips.

USEFUL ADDRESSES FOR JOBS IN THE HOTEL DEPART-
MENT

The following companies offer employment opportunities in the Hotel
Departments of cruise ships, including positions for chefs and galley
personnel, pursers and secretarial staff, cabin stewards/esses and other
housekeeping personnel, bar and restaurant personnel:

Apollo Ship Chandlers Inc. 1775 NW 70th Avenue, Miami, FL 33126, USA;
☎305-592-8790; fax 305-593-8335; e-mail services@apolloships.
com; www.apolloships.com.

Cruise Placement, 129-2 Suite 19 Brighton Beach Av., Brooklyn, NY
11235, USA; ☎718-670 7079; fax 718-670 7307; www.cruiseplace-
ment.com.

Cruise Service Center Ltd, Palme & Associates, 9 Crown Lofts, Marsh
Street, Walsall WS2 9LB, UK; ☎+44 01922-722 356; www.cruis-
eservicecenter.com.

CTI Recruitment and Placement Agency, 1535 SE 17th Street, The Quay
Suite 206, Fort Lauderdale, Florida 33316-1737,USA; ☎+01 954 728
9975; www.cti-usa.com. Has ten offices worldwide.

IHRM Informations GmbH, Innsbrucker Bundesstr. 47a; 5020 Salzburg,
Austria; ☎+43 662 8867 110; fax +43 662 8867 119.

Innovative Cruise Services, 36 Midlothian Drive, Glasgow GAl
3OU, Scotland; ☎0141-649 8644; fax 0141-636 1016; e-mail
info@cruiseservices.co.uk; www.cruiseservices.co.uk.

International Cruise Management Agency A/S, Jembanetorget 4B, PO
Box 95, Sentrum, N-0101 Oslo, Norway; ☎+47 23 35 79 00; fax +47
23 35 79 01; www.icma.no. Subsidiary of NYK Line and recruits for
NYK and Crystal Cruises. Oslo office handles over 1700 employees
worldwide.

International Services, Marc Chetrit, 11 rue du Commerce, Saint Pierre
du Perray; e-mail infos@internationalservices.fr; www.internation-
alservices.fr.

Miray International Cruise, Cumhuriyet Cd 129/7, 80230 Elmadag, Istanbul, Turkey; fax +90 212 231 8870; e-mail mirayint@superonline.
com.

*Oceania Cruises, Inc.,*8120 NW 53rd Street, Miami, Florida 33166;
☎305-514-2300; www.oceaniacruises.com.

Rolling Pin Jobs, 1825 Ponce de Leon Blvd, No 493, Coral Gables, Florida 33134, USA; ☎305 576-0300; fax 305 468-6406.

Royal Caribbean Cruise Line, 1080 Caribbean Way, Miami, Florida

33132, USA; fax +1 (305) 5393938; www.royalcaribbean.com.

Sea Chefs Cruise Services, 555 South San Rafael Avenue, Pasadena, CA 911905-1544, USA; ☎626-4414330; fax 626-4415211; e-mail contact.USA@seachefs.com; www.seachefs.com.

Sealife Crewing Services, 19/23 Canute Road, Southampton, Hants S014 3FJ; ☎023-8022 3546; fax 023-8022 8446; www.sealifecrewing. co.uk. Hotel manning, recruitment and short course training.

Sea Sources Vermittlungs GmbH, Innsbrucker-Bundesstr. 28/5/20, A 5020 Salzburg, Austria; ☎+43 662 827002; fax: +43 662 849210; e-mail: seasources@utanet.at.

Star Clippers, Ermanno Palace 27, Blvd. Albert 1er, 98000 Monaco; fax +377 93 508080.

Triton Cruise Services, 1007 N. America Way, Suite 407Miami, FL 33132, USA; ☎(305) 358 7860; fax (305) 374-3931; www.cruise-catering.com.

V-Ships, Gate House, 1 Farringdon Street, London EC4M 7NS; ☎020-7489 0088; fax 020-7329 2788; www.vships.com.

VIP International, 17 Charing Cross Road, London WC2H 0QH, England; ☎020-7930 0541; fax 020 7930 2860; e-mail vip@vipinternational. co.uk; www.vipinternational.co.uk. Recruits for all major cruise lines.

Other Unusual Jobs at Sea

SPECIALIST OPPORTUNITIES

While you may already be aware of the more obvious job categories discussed above, work opportunities exist in areas that you may not even have considered. For example, did you know that there is so much greenery on the *Sun Princess* that the ship carries a full-time gardener? Or that the *QE2* has its own onboard florists to cope with its huge floral requirements? Boat Blossums (www.boatblossums.com) is a Florida-based, wholesale florist to the marine hotel industry and to major cruise lines including Carnival, Cunard,, Holland America, Costa and Radisson and also supplies on board florists. Cunard also employs trained kennel staff to care for passengers' pets on QE2's transatlantic voyages, and two full-time professional librarians in charge of its books. The books (but not the staff) are supplied by the maritime library concessionaire, Ocean Books; www.oceanbooks.com. For further information on these jobs contact Cunard direct.

Admittedly, such positions are very rare (animals are generally disallowed and most ships' libraries and plants are tended by the social and housekeeping staff respectively). But they do exist, as do the following categories of work.

Computer Technicians are in increasing demand, often to work throughout a company's fleet, modifying data and educating shipboard personnel. Appropriate experience and/or qualifications and the ability to work unsupervised and under pressure are essential requirements, but annual earnings can exceed $60,000 (£32,000).

Printers are needed on many vessels, and very large ships may have a well-equipped print room employing half a dozen staff members. They are responsible for churning out hundreds or even thousands of daily programmes (giving updated information on entertainment, activities, opening times, etc.), world news-sheets, menus, party invitations, letterheads, printed cards and more. Smaller ships may off-load much of their requirements to shoreside printers, leaving little more than the daily programme and news sheets to be done by a single onboard *Desktop Publisher*. But there are enough larger vessels afloat to allow reasonable work opportunities for suitably qualified and experienced applicants. Expect to earn about $1,400 (£767) a month.

Opportunities also exist for *Journalists*, especially on larger ships, to compile magazine-style programmes and fact-sheets. This can be a rewarding job, with an annual earning potential of $25,000 (£14,000) for self-motivated individuals with flair and experience.

Butlers may be required on large vessels and ships at the more luxurious end of the market where passengers in certain suite rooms receive the services of a private butler. Appropriate training and/or experience is essential for such work. The Guild of Professional English Butlers (e-mail butlersguild@butlersguild.com) offers advice on training and recommends a training course at the International Butler Academy Foundation in Holland (☎+31 (0)344 673937; fax +31 (0)344 673933; e-mail butlerschool@butlersschool; www.butlerschool.comwhich offers an eight-week course with full board and accommodation and a reimbursement of half your airfare to the Netherlands for €12,500 (£8,384, $15,292) a cost you can quickly recoup if you land a job on a cruise ship paying £3,000-£4,000 per month including gratuities). Job openings may be limited, largely because existing butlers often retain their positions for years. However, on the plus side, new cruise liners are built all the time and will need additional butlers. Many cruise lines employ butlers including Crystal, Holland America, P&O, Radisson Seven Seas and Silversea. Although the nature of the job allows little free time, gratuities are generally excellent, often exceeding $800 (£450) per week.

From Teaching to Preaching

As the name implies, *Port Lecturers* are employed to give talks, slide shows and, especially, shopping information on the various ports of call. Although he/she may work closely with the excursion office staff and Cruise Director (even doing a job often associated with the Cruise Director), the Port Lecturer is frequently under contract to an independent company and may make substantial commission from recommended retail outlets – potentially in excess of $1,000 (£550) per week – subject to the allocated ship and itinerary. Note, however, that as payment is generally on a commission-only basis, the reverse side of the coin is that it is also possible to make nothing at all. Some experience of the retail sector, a solid background knowledge of the respective ports of call and the ability to bluff when the questions get tough is a definite bonus.

The following companies specialise in supplying Port Lecturers to cruise ships:

Page & Moy Cruises, 136-140 London Road, Leicester L32 1EN, England; ☎0870-010-6212; fax 0870-010-6211; www.page-moy.com.

Panoff Publishing Inc. 7100 Commercial Blvd., Suite 106, Fort Lauderdale, FL 33319-2124, USA; ☎954-746-5554; fax 954-746-5244; www.ppigroup.com.

An increasingly popular off-shoot of port lecturing is the unlikely-sounding cruise job of *Art Auctioneer* which consists of selling prints of works of art and original paintings on the ships themselves. Art auctioneers with a strong background in retail are generally recruited through the same channels as port lecturers, with equally variable commission-earning potential. Art is provided by companies such as Fine Art Wholesalers (www.fineartwholesalers.com) in Florida, and Park West Gallery (www.parkwestgallery.com) in Michigan. The latter signs up artists to contracts thus alllowing them exclusive rights to their art allowing them to form collections, which are sold in cruise ships. Some cruise lines also employ wine auctioneers. In 2005, Carnival launched the cruise industry's first wine club aimed primarily at past and regular cruise passengers who can enjoy exclusive wines mailed to their homes or take part in wine tastings and events on Carnival ships and on land. There are possible openings for oenologists (wine experts) to offer their services to Carnival.

Another sales job with a difference is that of *Cruise Sales Manager*. Employed directly by the cruise line, he/she is responsible for booking advance cruises (often with generous incentives) to regular passengers while they are still enjoying the current one. A basic salary of $300 (£165) and upwards per week may easily be doubled by commission for preaching to the converted.

And talking of preaching, a job that is rarely thought of but often exists on bigger ships and longer cruises such as those of Celebrity, Holland and America, Carnival and Royal Caribbean lines, is that of *Priest* or Minister of Religion. Although religious services may be conducted by the Captain, many large ships will have an onboard chapel or even a synagogue, together with a resident priest or rabbi, who is there as much for the benefit of the crew as for the passengers. These positions are usually of a short-term unsalaried nature (a sort of all-expenses-paid working holiday) and terms and conditions for clerics, as for medics (see *Medical Department*), vary enormously from ship to ship. Some cruise lines may only recruit priests for the duration of the main Christian festivals such as Easter and Christmas. The worldwide Catholic organisation, the Apostleship of the Sea has a membership system for priests who volunteer for on board ministry to those in the maritime industry, Catholic or otherwise. They used to operate mostly in ports, but as many crews now spend less and less time in port, the organisation is adapting to provide on board priests. Further details from the Apostleship of the Sea USA National Office, 3211 4th Street, NE Washington, DC 20017 or call 202-541-3226; e-mail aosusa@stellamaris.net. Other countries will have their own branches of this organisation. US-based RentAPriest.com/CITI Ministries, (www. rentapriest.com) a Catholic lay organisation that calls married Catholic priests back to the ministry also supplies cruise lines with priests for 'holiday sacramental services'. An interesting lifestyle may be enjoyed by suitably qualified theologians who 'have cassock, will travel'!

Couriers and Group Escorts

If you have previous experience of the travel industry or public relations, are sociable, responsible and have good organisational skills, then you might wish to consider applying to independent tour operators and travel organisations to be a *Courier* or *Group Escort* on their cruise ship holidays. Many travel companies employ individuals (and sometimes couples) to escort their passengers on cruises. Conditions vary: some companies pay very respectable salaries to their group escorts and others offer little more than a subsidised holiday. But all escorts are normally entitled to full passenger status, together with perks such as free shore excursions.

Naturally, companies paying a professional wage will expect a professional level of service, which should include organising cocktail parties (if appropriate), providing information, manning a hospitality desk and being generally available. This type of work is particularly suited to mature people (usually, though not invariably, female) who prefer intermittent employment to a full-time working commitment. If this is you, write direct to independent travel companies that offer cruise holidays, not the cruise lines themselves.

Companies include:

Cruise Holidays of Portland Group Services, 13611 NW Cornell Road, Portland, OR 97229, USA; ☎503 641-5225; 1-866 786-7447; www. cruzholidays.com.

Grand Circle Travel, 347 Congress Street, Boston, MA 02210, USA; ☎617-350-7500; fax 617-346-6700; www.gct.com.

Holland America Line Westours, 300 Elliott Avenue West, Seattle, Washington 98119, USA; ☎206-281-3535 (job line 206-286-3496); fax 206-298-3899; www.hollandamerica.com. Also provides shore excursion personnel for the Holland America fleet.

Page & Moy Cruises, 136-141 London Road, Leicester LE2 1EN, England; ☎0870-010-6212; fax 0870-010-6211; e-mail cruisecollection@pagemoy.com.

Princess Cruises, Fleet Personnel Department, 24844 Avenue Rockefeller, Santa Clarita, CA 91355-4999, USA; e-mail careersatsea@princesscruises.com. Accepts applications in writing only.

Saga Holidays, The Saga Building, Enbrook Park, Folkestone, Kent CT20 3SE, England; ☎01303-771111; fax 01303-221638; www. saga.co.uk.

Sawtelle Travel Service & Cruise Desk, 3469 Vestal Parkway, East Vestal, New York 13850-2020, USA; ☎607-729-6300; 0800-295-2222; e-mail vacations@sawtelletravel.com. Always looking for suitably qualified escorts for future cruises.

Vantage Deluxe World Travel, 90 Canal Street, Boston, MA 02114-2031, USA; ☎1-800-322-6677 (toll free); fax 1-617-878-6154; www.van-

tagetravel.com.
Voyages Jules Verne, 21 Dorset Square, London NW1 6QG, England; ☎020-7616-1000; fax 020-7723-8629 ; www.vjv.co.uk.

Of course, *Travel Agents* and *Cruise Consultants* with tour operators frequently get discounted holidays or free 'working trips' (i.e. escorting clients) on cruise ships. For those who enjoy the lifestyle but don't necessarily want the full-time commitment of an on-board contract, working for a travel company could provide the answer. Request the list of member agencies from the UK organisation PSARA (Passenger Shipping Association of Retail Agents, Walmar House, 4th Floor, 288-292 Regent Street, London W1R 5HE, England; ☎020-7436-2449; fax 020-7636-9206; www.psa-psara.org) or from Cruise Lines International Association in the United States (500 Fifth Avenue, Suite 1407, New York, NY 10110, USA; ☎212-921-0066; fax 212-921-0549; www.cruising.org).

Opportunities for Foreign Exchange Cashiers

Anyone who currently works in a bank or foreign exchange and wants to work in a similar capacity at sea will be pleased to learn that there are opportunities for foreign exchange cashiers at sea. *Bureau de change* on cruise ships are usually part of the Purser's Office. Interested candidates should apply to the cruise lines direct. Although previous relevant experience is a general requirement for work on ships the Purser's department of any ship will also welcome those with other types of banking experience.

In the Words of a Cashier

I work as a bank cashier onboard a mid-sized cruise ship in the Mediterranean. The Med offers more opportunities for cashiers than most other itineraries because we provide a Bureau de Change. Although the US dollar is internationally accepted, passengers in Europe still need various currencies besides euros.

Although I had little experience of dealing in foreign exchange when I joined my first ship, I had worked as a cashier for a major bank in London, and I'm sure that gave me the edge when I applied to work at sea. Initially, I was on a bigger ship with two other cashiers, but now I work alone.

I enjoy my job because, in spite of working closely with the Purser's office, I am basically my own boss and one of the few people on the ship to work relatively normal hours. Of course, I sometimes end up working late, especially towards the end of the cruise, when accounts are being settled and figures printed out. But, in general, I'm free in the evenings to do as I please.

Occasionally that means a drink in the officers' bar (I'm a one and a half stripe officer) or the public rooms, but usually I just like to relax in my cabin. Like a lot of employees onboard, I hire movies from video shops in our regular ports of call or from the crew bar, which has a small video library. My boyfriend, the stores manager, often joins me for a quiet night in with a good movie, a few beers and an extra large bag of popcorn. So it's just like being at home really.

Alison Fitzpatrick (age 29)

Entertainment

The entertainment division of the hotel department is one of the most diverse, incorporating singers, cabaret dancers, DJs, musicians of all kinds, guest lecturers and specialist experts, hosts and hostesses, stage and TV technicians, fitness and sports instructors, children's counsellors, and so on. The people in charge of organising the social programme are called Cruise Staff.

On land, the head of such a department would probably assume the title of Entertainments Manager or head of the Social & Entertainment Department. At sea, he/she is known as the *Cruise Director* (commonly abbreviated to CD). By tradition, Cruise Directors come from an entertainment background and may even be a featured act or entertainer in their own right. They are generally very experienced in the maritime leisure industry and assume a high profile position on the ship, compering shows, organising events, giving port lectures and information. Although their role is becoming increasingly administrative and many of the perks of the job are less in evidence, the position of Cruise Director can still offer a very attractive lifestyle and salary (sometimes in excess of $70,000/£38,000 per year) to those with the appropriate skills, aptitude and experience.

Cruise Staff

The Cruise Staff sector provides some of the most interesting work on a ship. Anyone with an outgoing nature who enjoys the social side of life may well find their niche here. An ability to entertain is a distinct advantage and some companies require cruise staff members to have the capacity to perform in shows or do a featured act. For this reason, people with a theatrical background are attracted to this type of work. Fluency in foreign languages is also advantageous and will almost certainly give you an edge over other applicants. But the main requirements are personality, versatility and the ability to keep smiling even on a cold gangway at 7 'o'clock in the morning.

If you wish to apply to join the Cruise Staff in any of the varied capacities outlined below, you should contact the Head of Entertainment at the head office of the respective cruise lines or try one of the agencies listed under *Addresses of Cruise Staff Employers* later in this section.

Note that in the United States, competition for cruise staff work is so intense that two ex-cruise directors formed an institute to provide courses for aspiring social/entertainment staff. The original Cruise Career Training Institute is now called the Keiser Career Institute (KCI) and is based in Florida (Lake Worth Campus, 1926 10th Avenue North, Lake Worth, FL 33461, USA; ☎561-547-5472; fax 561-547-6609; www.keisercareer.com).

Depending on the size of the ship, the Cruise Staff will include some or all of the following members. The *Deputy Cruise Director* or *Assistant Cruise Director* is the CD's right hand man/woman, sharing the workload of programming events and overseeing the smooth running of the department. Traditionally, this is a responsible position, with a general earning capacity of between $2,500 and $4,000 (£1,350 and £2,350) per month. But the title is frequently abused by certain cruise lines, who bestow it upon almost anyone in the social sector, irrespective of ability and experience.

Some ships may also employ a *Social Director* (with comparable earning potential to the Assistant CD) to assist with specific areas such as organising major events, duty rotas and the working schedules of the Gentlemen Hosts (described later).

The *Social Hostess* (or *Social Directress*) has potentially the most glamorous job on the ship. At the forefront of the social scene, she is the one making sure all those parties go with a swing. She will direct many of the onboard activities and one of her tasks may be to greet and introduce hundreds of passengers to the Captain at each welcoming cocktail reception. Monthly income here may vary between $2,000 and $3,500 (£1,100 and £1,920).

The position of Social Hostess is possibly the only job on the ship, which is invariably allocated to a woman. Females are generally under-represented in most departments but have the greatest opportunities in the hotel division, especially the entertainment/social department where they may be found in top positions.

Larger ships may have several Hostesses, all participating in general cruise staff duties and possibly incorporating individual specialities such as childcare or language skills. Depending on the cruise, the number of hostesses employed and the status given to the job, earnings may range between $1,800 and $3,000 (£1,000 and £1,650) per month. It is very rare for hostesses or any member of the cruise staff to receive tips but there are often privileges and perks (such as drinks allowances) attached to this type of work.

If you are fluent in at least one language other than English, and preferably more, you may wish to apply your skills as an *International Host(ess)*, for similar earnings to the above. In this capacity you would translate information such as menus and daily programmes, make appropriate broadcasts and announcements, escort tours and generally assist the non-English speaking passengers onboard. Even if you do not wish to specialise in this way, linguistic ability is always a bonus on ships, so don't forget to mention any languages you speak and to what level when you apply.

There are also job opportunities for general Cruise Staff Members, who may be viewed as the maritime equivalent of Red Coats/Blue Coats/ *animateurs*. They have a high profile onboard, assisting with the many games, activities and scheduled events, embarkation/disembarkation and escorting the organised tours. Salaries vary considerably and are subject to age and experience, but $1,000 to $2,500 (£650 to £1,450) per month should serve as a guide.

If you have secretarial/computer skills and the desire to work your way for $1,800 (£1,000) and upwards per month, you may also like to consider a very specialised type of job in the cruise staff sector, that of *Programme Coordinator*. The main responsibility of the Programme Coordinator is to lay out the format for the ship's daily programme on computer prior to it being printed. If you are good at English and with an artistic flair this position could be for you, particularly if you enjoy working behind the scenes. Unlike most other jobs in the department, the Programme Coordinator is office-based and may even be required to double up as secretary to the Cruise Director. Sometimes the Daily Programme is undertaken by a desktop publisher or will take on more of a newspaper format, in which case a journalistic background may be a requirement (see the earlier chapter *Unusual Jobs at Sea*).

Childcare Positions

Children's Counsellors and *Youth Counsellors* (together with *Nursery Assistants* and/or *Nannies*) are often required, especially on larger ships such as P&O's Oriana, where there may be a separate programme of children's events. It is normally the counsellors who are directly responsible for devising the programme of activities, in conjunction with the Cruise Director. These cater to different age groups, for example two to four, five to eight, nine to 13, and older teenagers of 14 to 19.

Appropriate qualifications (such as the widely-recognised NNEB nanny diploma) and/or training in child education or child psychology will certainly lend weight to an application, but a genuine interest in working with children or teenagers is the vital key to success in this field. Companies such as Carnival Cruise Lines, Thomson Cruises and Disney Cruise Line may have more openings in this sector than most since they specialise in the family market. Approximate monthly salaries of $1,800-$2,400 are paid, subject to the age and experience of the applicant. Seefar Associates Ltd (7 Berkley Crescent, Gravesend, Kent DA12 2AH; ☎01474-329990; fax 01474-329995; e-mail seefarassociates@btclick. com; www,seefarassociates.co.uk) recruit children's activity counsellors and nursery assistants for Disney Cruise Line.

Sports and Fitness Instructors

Frequent opportunities arise for *Fitness Instructors, Water Sports Instructors* and *Sports Directors* to work in the cruise staff department (as distinct from the spa/gymnasium concessionaires, described later in *Spas and Fitness Centres*). It should be pointed out that the standard is generally high and applicants should be suitably qualified and experienced in coordinating fitness programmes, aerobics classes and/or specialist activities. Expect to earn about $1,700-$2,400 per month.

SAMPLE DAILY PROGRAMME OF CHILDREN'S ACTIVITIES

TODDLERS CLUB (Ages 2 - 4)

10.00am - 10.30am	Fun with Balloons	Playroom
10.30am - 11.00am	Let's Colour it in!	Playroom
11.00am - 11.30am	Making Handprints	Playroom
11.30am - 12 noon	Let's Learn our ABC!	Playroom
2.00pm - 2.30pm	Fun with Bricks	Playroom
2.30pm - 3.00pm	Nursery Rhymes with Bobby Bear	Playroom
3.00pm - 3.30pm	It's Cartoon Time!	Playroom
5.00pm - 6.00pm	Let's Jump in the Fun Pit!	Playroom
7.00pm - 8.00pm	It's Video Time!	Playroom
8.00pm - 9.00pm	Teddy Bears Party - Bring a Furry Friend!	Playroom
9.00pm - 9.30pm	Storytime	Playroom
9.30pm	Babysitting Begins (Parents, please sign up before 5.00pm)	Playroom

JUNIOR CRUISERS (Ages 5 - 8)

10.00am - 11.00am	Let's Make a Mobile!	Playroom
11.00am - 11.30am	Potato Prints	Playroom
11.30am - 12 noon	Buttons, Badges and Brooches	Playroom
2.00pm - 2.30pm	Bingo! Win Fun Prizes!	Playroom
2.30pm - 3.00pm	Start Making Your Shell Box	Playroom
3.00pm - 3.30pm	It's Cartoon Time!	Playroom
5.00pm - 6.00pm	Find the Pirate's Treasure!	Playroom
7.00pm - 8.00pm	It's Video Time!	Playroom
8.00pm - 9.00pm	Indoor Beach Party (wear your beach gear)	Mega-disco
9.00pm - 9.30pm	Let's Limbo!	Mega-disco
9.30pm	Juniorsitting Begins (Parents, please sign up before 5.00pm)	Playroom

CADET CLUB (Ages 9 - 13)

10.00am - 10.30am	Early Bird Bingo	Teen Club
10.30am - 11.30am	Make a Puppet Pirate!	Teen Club
11.30am - 12 noon	Let's Write a Puppet Show!	Teen Club
2.00pm - 2.30pm	Crazy Word Search. Whoever finds the most words wins the prize!	Teen Club
2.30pm - 3.00pm	Tell Us A Joke!	Teen Club
3.00pm - 3.30pm	Round-the-Ship Scavenger Hunt	Teen Club
5.00pm - 6.00pm	Kite Flying	Lido Deck
7.00pm - 9.30pm	Let's Watch a Movie!	Teen Club
9.30pm	Cadetsitting Begins (Parents, please sign up before 5.00pm)	Playroom

TEEN CLUB (Ages 14 - 17)

10.00am - 10.30am	Ping Pong Tournament	Sports Deck
10.30am - 11.00am	Shuffleboard Tournament	Sports deck
11.00am - 12 noon	Splash Out at our Pool Games!	Poolside
2.00pm - 3.00pm	2nd Round of our Scrabble Tournament	Teen Club
3.00pm - 3.30pm	Quiz! Quiz! Quiz!	Teen Club
3.30pm - 5.00pm	See you at the Pool!	Poolside
5.00pm - 6.00pm	The Dating Game - Team Fun!	Teen Club
7.00pm - 9.30pm	Let's Watch a Movie!	Teen Club
9.30pm - 10.00pm	'Name That Tune' - Chart Quiz	Mega-disco
10.00pm - 11.00pm	Pig-out on Pizza Party!	Mega-disco
11.00pm - 12 midnight	Teens-only Disco	Mega-disco

Water Sports Instructors should be qualified dive instructors preferably with qualifications from two internationally recognised examining bodies, principally PADI (Professional Association of Diving Instructors) or SSI (Scuba Schools International). Additional experience and qualifications in related areas such as water-skiing, jet-skiing, Zodiac-driving and parasailing are advantageous. Instructors are usually also responsible for the maintenance of scuba and other equipment.

Smaller upmarket vessels, sailing ships and coastal cruisers in areas such as Australasia or the Caribbean are particularly worth a try for Water Sports Instructors, together with the bigger ships of Princess Cruises, Royal Caribbean International (RCI) and Norwegian Cruise Line (NCL). NCL also operates extensive 'Sports Afloat' theme cruises, featuring specialist celebrity speakers.

Technical Staff

Most medium-sized ships will have a *Stage Manager* to take care of all the technical aspects of the entertainment programme, from setting up microphones for visiting lecturers to handling the sound and lighting requirements of sophisticated production shows. Larger ships may employ several *Stage Technicians* for this purpose, including specific *Sound and Lighting Engineers*. If the ship has its own onboard TV station, as the bigger ships do, there are even opportunities for a *Television Station Manager* to take charge of broadcasting its extensive programme of videos, satellite TV and other programmes, including regular in-house interviews and features filmed onboard the ship. Appropriate qualifications and experience are a general requirement for all jobs of this nature, with earning potential in excess of $3,000 (£1,645) per month.

Addresses of Cruise Staff Employers

As well as applying directly to the Head of Entertainment of your chosen cruise line, try also entertainment agencies which supply the cruise industry and the following agencies:

Blue Seas International Cruise Services Inc, www.jobxchange.com. Runs the employment agency International Seafarers Exchange. A registration fee is payable to become a member of this internet-only based agency.

Cast-a-Way Cruise and Resort Hiring Agency, POB 145, Birchwood, Warrington WA3 7AS; e-mail info@cast-a-way.co.uk; www.cast-away.com. Canada address: 3539 Blvd. St Charles, Suite 218, Kirkland, Quebec, Canada W9H 3C4. Montreal office: ☎514694 1194;f fax 514-694 9606; e-mail castaway@total net. Vancouver office: ☎250 760 1020; fax 250-7601231. Canadian agency with a UK office. Applicants can also apply online.

Cruise Job Line, 1076 S Brightview Drive, Glendora, California 91740, USA; e-mail jobs@how2immigrate.net; www.cruisejobline.com. Offices in USA and Brazil. Recruits and places new personnel with most of the major cruise lines.

Excellent Entertainment Ltd, Suite 2, The Business Centre, 120 West Heath Road, London NW3 7TX; ☎020-8458 4212; fax 020-8458 4572; e-mail theagency@excellententertainment.biz; www.excellententerntainment.biz Cruise staff and showbiz agent.

Global Ship Services, Bayside Office Center, 245 SE 1ˢᵗ Street, Suite 332 Miami, Florida 33131; ☎305-374 8649; fax 305-374 4342; e-mail personnel@globalshipservices.com; www.globalshipservices.com. Specialist employment agency for cruise and cargo ships worldwide.

Openwide International, 7 Westmoreland Hse, Cumberland Park, London NW10 6RE, England; ☎020-8962-3409; fax 020-8962-3440; e-mail sharvey@openwideinternational.com; www.openwideinternational.com. Not a dental practice (despite the unfortunate name) but an agency for various cruise lines and affiliated companies.

Seafar Associates Ltd, 7 Berkley Crescent, Gravesend, Kent DA12 2AH; ☎01474-329990; fax 01474-329995; e-mail seefarassociates@btclick.com; www,seefarassociates.co.uk. Recruits cruise staff for the Disney Cruise Line.

In the Words of a Social Hostess

Although I am currently working as the Social Hostess on a passenger ship cruising in the Baltic Sea, I am frequently transferred to other vessels within the fleet. I quite enjoy moving around since you meet more people that way and discover new itineraries. Interestingly enough, my job also differs quite a lot from ship to ship, so flexibility is important. During a typical day at sea, I might be expected to host a get-together for single passengers, organise a general knowledge tournament, give a scarf-tying demonstration, narrate a cookery demonstration, attend several cocktail parties, and be generally on the go till late at night. Days in port are obviously easier as most of the passengers will be ashore.

I suppose most crew members see the world in their twenties and then settle down to have a family. As a divorced parent of a grown-up son, I'm doing it the other way around. The fact that most of my colleagues tend to be younger than me, especially the female ones, means suitable companionship can be a problem on occasions. But in general I enjoy the lifestyle. I feel my maturity lends a certain credence to the job, and older passengers prefer a hostess to whom they can easily relate. It is also to my advantage that I am not prepared to accept conditions that I might have put up with 20 years ago, and the company knows this. It gives me stronger bargaining power.

As the only hostess on this ship, I earn $3,000 a month. I have a spacious single cabin with steward service, free drinks allowance and laundry services. Most evenings I eat in the passenger restaurant, I often go free on any excursions that interest me and I have full public rooms privileges. However not everyone gets this sort of deal. I would say, as a general rule, the more hostesses a vessel has, the worse conditions are offered. I know of ships employing up to fifteen hostesses, each allocated separate tasks from office work to childminding and even security. In circumstances like these, the employees are nearly always in their early twenties, are expected to share cabins and are paid between $800 and $1,200 per month.

If I'm honest, I suppose the hardest aspect of my job is finding time for myself. Even ashore, passengers recognise me and engage me in conversation. Being nice to people twenty-four hours a day, seven days a week can wear you down. Even the continuous round of social functions, such as the Captain's private parties, becomes humdrum after a while, although it does give me an excuse to indulge in my passion for clothes. On an average cruise we might have three 'formal' evenings, four 'informal' ones and three 'casual' evenings, labelled according to the suggested evening dress code. Nowadays there is a trend towards less formal wear for cruising, but of course much depends on the ship and the itinerary. As the hostess on a recent World Cruise, I got through twenty different evening gowns – and that was travelling light!

Margot Lawton (age 48)

In the Words of a Cruise Director

I first started on ships about ten years ago as an entertainer in an international musical act. When the act disbanded I was offered the position of Social Directress for a major cruise line and since then I've done most jobs in the social and entertainment sector.

My average day frequently includes a series of meetings: with the Captain, the Hotel Manager or other Heads of Department; continuous e-mails to and from our shoreside offices; and scheduling each day's entire programme of activities and events, including checking the proofs of the Daily Programme from the printer. I also present lectures on the ports of call and onboard procedures such as disembarkation, together with introducing the nightly shows and other activities and attending every major cocktail party.

Above all, I am in charge of a department of about 25 people, including the musicians, entertainers, children's counsellors, fitness instructor, DJ and cruise staff members. I am also responsible for a floating (pardon the pun) staff of guest lecturers and clergy members, gentlemen hosts and short-stay headlining cabaret acts.

The downside of this hectic schedule is that I'm constantly in demand – my phone rings even in the middle of the night – and being in the midst of the passengers most of the day can be extremely tiring. I also seem to spend a lot of time attempting to resolve the professional and sometimes, personal problems of members of my department. Occasionally, I have had to fire people, which is never easy.

Fortunately, there are also many perks attached to my position. I have senior officer status and appropriate benefits such as a top-grade cabin and generous entertaining allowance, a worldwide circle of interesting friends and associates, including international entertainers and celebrity speakers, and an annual income that I would find hard to match on land. I am also frequently entertained by shoreside agents and tour operators, which gives me the perfect opportunity to indulge in my hobby of discovering good restaurants.

My advice to aspiring Cruise Directors would be to learn how the department runs and get an inside perspective by working in as many areas of the Cruise Staff/Entertainment sector as possible. It is such a specialised job that relevant shipboard experience is vital. I would also say that management skills and the ability to handle people effectively are more important than academic quali-fications (although many cruise directors, including myself, do have degrees, though often in quite unrelated subjects).

As one of a minority of female cruise directors, I must also agree with the theory that women at sea sometimes have more to prove than their male counterparts in order to achieve the same promotion. Certainly, females don't tend to be taken as seriously when it comes to long-term careers and, in many ways, it's a Catch 22. They don't get promoted and so they quit, and because they keep quitting, they don't get promoted. I see this particularly in areas such as the Purser's Office, where young women come and go, before you've had time to learn their names.

Yes, I suppose the price of working on ships can be higher for women than men, and not all females are prepared to pay that price. Motherhood and a career at sea are definitely incompat-ible. Because few continue seafaring beyond the age of about 40, a lack of suitable companionship can be a problem for more mature women. Furthermore men may be intimidated by higher-ranking females (even if they don't admit it) which can limit romantic pos-sibilities. But for women seeking both social and financial indepen-dence, a career on cruise ships can be very rewarding.

From a personal point of view I, like many of my colleagues, have several onshore business interests which allow me the finan-cial freedom to choose not to stay on ships if I wished. But like many of my colleagues, I always say I'm not coming back to do yet another six-month contract, and after two months on leave, I always do!

Christine Little (age 34)

Showbusiness

While theatres close down and venues on shore feature less live entertain-ment, the expanding cruise industry provides performers with an increas-ingly valuable floating platform for their talents and probably a reliable source of employment for a few years to come. Most ships present a varied programme of daily and nightly entertainment, including music for dancing, production shows and featured musicians and cabaret acts.

Some cruise lines, such as P&O Cruises, Royal Caribbean International and Crystal Cruises, mount their own elaborate theatrical productions in-house, while others utilise external production companies to provide a programme of non-stop musical shows.

Either way, various opportunities exist for all-round *Actor/Singer/ Dancers* as well as occasional work for *Choreographers* and *Musical Directors*. There are also many openings for *Show Dancers* (especially female). It should be noted, however, that it is commonplace for dancers and production show artists to be expected to assist with general cruise staff duties as well as performing on stage.

Featured Entertainers such as headlining cabaret acts and solo musicians on the other hand are generally not expected to assist with cruise staff or any other duties beside their featured shows (although it must be said that this is gradually changing). Musical, magical and visual speciality acts are particularly popular with cruise lines, due to their international appeal and ability to cut across language barriers.

Ballroom Dance Couples are an attraction on many ships, to teach group classes as part of the activity programme and perform occasional featured routines during the course of each cruise. Some general cruise staff duties may also be expected and, at the artists' discretion, freelance dance lessons given for a privately negotiated fee.

Cruising is still one of the few areas of showbusiness to offer regular employment to **Dance Band Musicians**. Most ships will have at least one or two live bands offering different styles of music from jazz to ballroom and the latest in rock & roll and pop. Main lounge/theatre showband members should also be good sight readers as they may frequently be requested to back headlining acts and production shows.

Lounge Bar Musicians and *Cocktail Pianists* are particularly in demand, as even the smallest ships may require a talented pianist or duo for their intimate lounge or piano bar. A resident pianist would be expected to have a repertoire of about 400 tunes and be adaptable in suiting them to the circumstances of the moment (including the weather) whenever possible. Above All Entertainment, Excellent Entertainment, Elite Artiste Management, Gary Parkes Music and Key Signature International (see addresses below) are among the agencies that regularly recruit solo cocktail pianists with vocals. Subject to a ship's itinerary, speciality musical groups such as jazz, tribute or calypso bands, may also be required.

Self-contained *Featured Musicians* (such as harpists, accordionists, xylophonists and even zither players) are occasionally required on larger vessels. *Opera Singers, Concert Pianists* and other *Classical Musicians* (e.g. string quartets) may be employed to give recitals and concert performances, especially during themed Classical Music and World cruises. Openings here are fairly limited, however, and trained singers may find more regular work as part of a shipboard production show.

Many opportunities exist for professional disc jockeys. Note, however, that salaries and conditions vary enormously from company to company and ship to ship, and often the DJ will be expected to assist with other aspects of the entertainment programme, including cruise staff duties.

Addresses of Entertainment Agencies

For work as a musician, ballroom dance couple, DJ or headlining act, contact the entertainment department of the respective cruise lines or the many theatrical and musical agencies, which specialise in booking for ships. It is also worth consulting theatrical newspapers, particularly *The Stage* (www.thestage.co.uk) in the UK.

Salaries, as in all areas of show business, will be individually negotiated and can range from $550 (£300) per week for a youthful dancer to $2,000 (£1,350) and up for an established featured act. Agents move in and out of favour, so it is worth checking with the cruise lines which ones they are currently using before applying. The following is just a selection of the agents and producers active in the cruise ship market. A fuller list of ships' entertainment agencies can be found at www.cruiseshipentertainment. com and also check out www.showcall.co.uk.

Above All Entertainment, 15 Eastport Lane, Lewes, East Sussex BN7 1TL; ☎01273-486622 or 01273 472931; fax 01273-486633. Specialises in cruise lines.

Basa Productions, 1 Furness Avenue, Dunstable, Bedfordshire LU6 3BN; England; ☎01582-475263; fax 01582-475263; e-mail info@basa productions.com; www.basaproductions.com; .

Blackburn International, Le Montaigne, 7 Avenue de Grande Bretagne, Monte Carlo, MC98000, Monaco; ☎(377) 93 30 67 98). Also has a UK office at 63 Rosemary Lane, Blackwater, Surrey GU17 0LS, England; ☎01276 517106.

Bramson Entertainment, 630 Ninth Ave., Suite 203, New York, NY 10036, USA; ☎(212)265-3500; fax (212)265-6615; www.bramson.com.

Cabaret World UK, 7 P O Box 2734, London W1A 5AD; ☎07092-336596; fax 07092-342376.

Cambrian, 24 Titan Court, Laporte Way, Luton, Bedfordshire LU4 8EF; ☎015282-488888; 01582-488877; e-mail mailbox@Cambrian.tv; www.forliveartistes.com.

Chancery Cruising, 2-3 Cursitor Street, Chancery Lane, London EC4A 1NE; ☎020-7405 7506; fax 020-7405 0903; e-mail holborn@dial. pipex.com; www.chancerycruising.com. Specialises in musical (big band, jazz, classical and fusion) cruises for the likes of Crystal, P&O, Norwegian Cruise Lines and Radisson.

Elaine Avon, 127 Westhall Road, Warlingham, Surrey CR3 9HJ, England; ☎01883 622317. One of the longest established and best known cruise entertainment consultants that supplies top end cruise lines with professional and up-coming new artists and acts from all over the world.

Elite Artiste Management Ltd., 2 Fieldsway House, Fieldsway Crescent, London N5 1QA; ☎020-7619 0220; fax 020-7619 0330; e-mail info@elite-artistes.com; www.elite-artistes.com. Musicians that can sight read, lounge artistes, solo piano/vocalists, light classical trios. Clients include Holland and America and Windstar.

Excellent Entertainment, Suite 2, The Business Centre, 120 West Heath Road, London NW3 7TU; ☎020-8458 4212; fax 020-8458 4572; e-mail the agency@excellententertainment.biz; www.excellententertainment.biz. Supplies musicians and other cruise staff to cruise lines, including Disney Cruises.

First Class Entertainment, 483 Ridgewood Road, Maplewood 07040-2136 NJ, USA; ☎973-763 0591; fax 973 763 0570; e-mail talent@gotofirstclass.com. Supplies musicians and entertainers to most of the big American cruise lines including Carnival, Crystal and Norwegian Cruise Line.

Garry Brown Associates, 27 Downs Side, Cheam, Surrey SM2 7EH, England; ☎0208 643 3991; fax 020 8770 7241; gbaltd@btconnect.com. For many years GBA specialised in supplying Cunard Cruises (now part of Carnival) and has widened his range to other cruise lines.

Gary Musick Productions, 885 Elm Hill Pike, Nashville, TN 37210; ☎615 259 2400; fax 615-259 2457; www.garymusick.com. Major US producer of corporate events with a theatrical basis that also provide show productions for Celebrity Cruises.

Gary Parkes Music, 172 Haverstock Hill, London NW3 2AT; ☎020-7794 1581; fax 020-7431 5537; gary@garyparkes.com; www.garyparkes.com. Supplies musicians (bands, duos, classical, pianist/singers) to major cruise lines.

Key Signature International. Suite 550, Andover House, George Yard, Andover, Hants. SP10 1PB; ☎01264-335344; e-mail piano@keysignature.co.uk; www.keysignature.co.uk. International entertainment agency for musicians supplying American most other cruise lines worldwide.

KMC Agencies, PO Box 122, 48 Great Ancoats Street, Manchester M4 5AB; ☎0161-237 3009; fax 0161-237 9812; e-mail casting@kmcagencies. co.uk; www.kmcagencies.co.uk. Specialises in actors and dancers and supplies cruise lines including Cunard and Seabourn.

Live Business Productions, 6 Calico Row, Plantation Wharf, Battersea, London SW11 3UF; 020-7924 5550; fax 020-7924 6270; info@livebusiness.co.uk; www.livebusiness.co.uk. Supplies nine cruises lines with entertainers (Mediterranean and the Black Sea).

Micha Bergese Productions, 16 Onslow Gardens, London N10 3JU; ☎020-8374 6866. Produces shows for P&O's Ocean Village.

Roger Kendrick Cruising Entertainment, Suite 201, St. Anne's House, Wood Street, St. Anne's-on-Sea, Lancs FY8 1QG; ☎01253-726046; fax 01253-712125; roger.kendrick@btinternet.com. Supplies Costa Lines and has also found acts for P&O, NYK, Abou Merhi and Easy Cruise.

Mirage Shows & Productions Ltd, The Annex, Ravinia House, King Row, Shipham, Thetford Norfolk IP25 7RW; ☎01362 820323; e-mail info@mirageshows.com; www.mirageshows.com.

Openwide International, 7 Westmoreland House, Cumberland Park, London NW10 6RE, England; ☎020 8962 3418; fax 020 8962 3440; e-mail sharvey@openwideinternational.com; www.openwideinternational.com.

Partnership Events and Entertainment (PEEL), North Barn, Broughton Hall, Skipton, North Yorkshire BD23 3AE; ☎01756-796176; enquiries@peelcruise.com; www.peelcruise.com. Provides entertainment artistes for Thomson's three ships Celebration, Destiny and Spirit.

Pepperpot Promotions, Suite 20b, 20-20 Orde Hall Street, Holborn, London EC1N 3JW; ☎020-7405 9108; e-mail chris@pepperpot. co.uk. Provides top guest bands for P&O cruise ships (now owned by the American company Princess Cruises).

Proship Entertainment, 5253 Decarie Blvd, Suite 308, Montreal, Quebec, Canada H3W 3C2; ☎514-485-8823; fax 514-485 2675; e-mail info@proship. Provides musicians, entertainers and technical personnel for the cruise industry.

Resident Entertainers, P.O. Box 142, Ellesmere, Cheshire, CH66 4WP; ☎/fax 0151-339 1100; e-mail recruit@residententertainers.com. Only places entertainers on cruise ships.

Saga Cruises, Entertainment Office, Saga Shipping, Middleburg Square,

Folkestone, Kent CT20 1AZ; ☎01303-771111. Saga's two cruise ships, Saga Rose and Saga Ruby. Solo artists and groups can apply direct to the Entertainment Office at the above address.

Shoreline Entertainments, 7 P O Box 236, Barnstaple, N Devon, EX31 4ZJ; ☎0870 751 7632; fax 0870 751 7633; www.shorelineagency. co.uk.

Showbiz International, Rossall Point, 83 Princes Way, Fleetwood, nr Blackpool, Lancashire FY7 8DX, England; ☎01253-771000; fax 01253 777711. showbizinternational@internet.com. Specialises in supplying artistes and bands to cruise ships.

Showstoppers Worldwide Entertainments, Unit 4, Waterside Mill, Macclesfield, Cheshire SK11 7HG; ☎0870-2432024; www.showstoppers-worldwide.com. ·

The World, c/o ResidenSea Ltd, 5200 Blue Lagoon Drive, Suite 790, Miami, FL 33126 USA; www.aboardtheworld.com. The World is a timeshare apartment ship that goes round the world. The management company ResidenSea organises an Enrichment and Entertainment programme aboard, which includes guest entertainers and musicians. Prospective acts and musicians can apply direct by email to enrichme ntdirector@theworld.cc.

For work as a singer, actor or dancer, try the following production companies. The website www.getgigs.com carries regular postings of cruise ship auditions. British performers should note that many American-based companies also hold regular auditions in Great Britain.

Jean Ann Ryan Productions, 308 SE 14th Street, Ft Lauderdale, FL 33316, USA; ☎954 523 6399; fax 954 523 5407; jarjobs@aol.com and jarinc2@aol.com; www.jeanannryanproductions.com. Large-scale top end productions at sea, mainly for Norwegian Cruise Lines, including circus.

KMC Agencies, P O Box 122, 48 Great Ancoats Street, Manchester M4 5AB; ☎0161-237 3009; fax 0161-237 9812; e-mail casting@kmcagencies. co.uk; www.kmcagencies.co.uk. Specialises in actors and dancers and supplies cruise lines including Cunard and Seabourn.

PGT Entertainments, 1353 N. Courtenay Parkway, Suite Y, Merritt Island, Florida FL 32953 USA; ☎321 453-2313; fax 321 453-6511. Large scale productions currently for Costa and Radisson. Holds regular auditions in London.

Ray Kennedy Production Company, 244 South Academy St., Mooresville, North Carolina 28115, USA; ☎704-662-3501; fax 704-662-3668.

SAMPLE DAILY PROGRAMME

Sunrise: 5.50am   Sunset: 5.39pm

 AT SEA   **Thursday, 11th January, 1996**   **AT SEA**

FITNESS WITH OUR INSTRUCTOR, LIZ

8.00am	Good Morning Stretch Class - Spa	2.00pm	Beginners Aerobics - Spa
8.30am	Walk a Mile - Jogging Track	3.00pm	Below the Belt! (Hips & Thighs) - Spa
9.15am	Step Aerobics - Spa	5.30pm - 7.30pm	B.C.A./Personal Training - Spa

9.00am - 11.00am Eye Openers! Screwdriver, Bloody Mary - $2.50 — Pool Bar, Deck 8

9.00am Jigsaw Mania continues! — Outside the Calypso Bar, Deck 5

9.00am Daily Quiz is available. Post your answers in the box - earliest top score — Library, Deck 7
wins a prize! (Answers posted tomorrow)

9.30am Bridge players meet your lecturer, Bill — Card Room, Deck 8

9.30am   **EARLY BIRD TEAM TRIVIA** — Showtime Lounge, Deck 5
with the Cruise Staff

10.00am Napkin Folding Demonstration with the Restaurant Staff — Neptune's Lounge, Deck 5

10.00am Ping Pong Tournament with the Cruise Staff — Sun Deck, Deck 8

10.00am Junior Cruisers' Treasure Hunt with Children's Auntie, Janice — Rainbow Playroom, Deck 8

10.00am Spanish for Beginners with our International Hostess, Renata — Calypso Bar, Deck 5

10.00am Handwriting Analysis with your lecturer, Bertha — Stardust Disco, Deck 8

10.30am   **WHAT TO SEE, WHERE TO GO** — Showtime Lounge, Deck 5
with your **Cruise Director, Tom,** and **Tour Manager, Leslie.**
Lecture on the forthcoming ports of call, including useful hints and advice plus a review of the
Shore Excursions on offer.
(This lecture will be broadcast on Channel 16 at 1.00pm and 2.30pm today)

11.00am Service Club Meeting (Lions, Kiwanis, Rotarians, etc.) — Library, Deck 7

11.00am Arts and Crafts with your lecturer, Noreen — Neptune's Lounge, Deck 5

11.15am   **THE MATCH GAME!** — Stardust Disco, Deck 8
Join your Cruise Staff for this hilarious game show!

11.15am MILEAGE POOL! Guess the distance travelled since leaving port — Pool Bar, Deck 8
till noon today - $2 per guess. Meet your Cruise Staff

11.30am Shuffleboard Tournament with the Cruise Staff — Sun Deck, Deck 8

11.30am   **GRANDPARENTS GET-TOGETHER** — Calypso Bar, Deck 5
with your **Hostess, Sally** - bring your photos!

11.30am How to play Blackjack - with our Casino Staff — Casino, Deck 5

11.30am Make-up Seminar. Handy hints from our onboard Beauticians — Beauty Salon, Deck 8

11.45am - 1.30pm Lunchtime melodies with our pianist, Alistair — Atrium, Deck 4

12 noon Midday navigational information will be broadcast from the bridge

| 2.00pm | **CATCH THE SCENT**
A Perfume Seminar
presented by our onboard **Duty Free Shops** | Showtime Lounge, Deck 5 |

2.00pm	Bridge Tournament with Bill	Card Room, Deck 8
2.00pm	Scrabble Tournament with your Cruise Staff	Calypso Bar, Deck 5

2.15PM	ICE CARVING DEMONSTRATION with our Chefs	Poolside, Deck 8

2.15pm	Arts and Crafts with Noreen	Neptune's Lounge, Deck 5
2.15pm	LINE DANCING with your Hostess, Sally	Stardust Disco, Deck 8
2.30pm	Kids meet Janice!	Rainbow Playroom, Deck 8

| 2.45pm | **HORSE RACING**
with your Cruise Director, Tom
Have a flutter at our Whacky Races!   Big Cash Prizes! | Showtime Lounge, Deck 5 |

2.45pm	Materials and ideas for tomorrow's Fancy Dress Competition are available from the Cruise Staff	Atrium, Deck 4
3.00pm	NAME THAT TUNE! Musical Quiz with our DJ, Paul	Stardust Disco, Deck 8
3.00pm	Deck Quoits Tournament with our Cruise Staff	Sun Deck, Deck 8

| 3.00pm | **POOL-ING AROUND!**
Fun and Games with our Production Show Team! | Poolside, Deck 8 |

3.15pm	Oriental Cookery Demonstration with our Chefs	Neptune's Lounge, Deck 5
3.30pm	American Roulette lessons with our Croupiers	Casino, Deck 5
3.30pm	Wine & Cheese tasting (nominal charge of $5.00 per person)	Calypso Bar, deck 5

| 3.30pm | **JACKPOT BINGO**
More Cash Prizes to be Won! | Showtime Lounge, Deck 5 |

4.00pm	AFTERNOON TEA is served until 5.00pm	Palm Court Café, Deck 7
4.30pm	Chess Tournament with the Cruise Staff	Card Room, Deck 8

| 4.30pm | **LIAR'S CLUB!**
Join your **Cruise Director** and **his Staff** for this fun-filled **Game Show!** | Showtime Lounge, Deck 5 |

5.00pm	HAPPY HOUR! Two drinks for the price of one! (until 6.30pm)	Calypso Bar, Deck 5
5.00pm	Early evening melodies with Alistair at the piano	Calypso Bar, Deck 5

| 5.30pm | **SINGLES MINGLE**
Travelling Solo? Join your Hostess, Sally, and fellow guests | Neptune's Lounge, Deck 5 |

| 5.30pm | **Dance to the Big Band Sounds**
of the **Mike Davidson Orchestra** | Showtime Lounge, Deck 5 |

| 7.15pm - 8.30pm
9.30pm - 10.30pm | **MUSIC FOR DANCING**
with the **Dave Peters Trio** | Neptune's Lounge, Deck 5 |

| 7.45pm | **FASHION SHOW** | Showtime Lounge, Deck 5 |

FASHION SHOW Showtime Lounge, Deck 5
**Our Gift Shop Manager and Staff model Clothing
and Accessories from our onboard Duty Free Shops**

8.45pm - 1st Sitting   Showtime Lounge, Deck 5
10.30pm - 2nd Sitting

 SHOWTIME

starring

The Comedy-Magic of
DANNY & DENISE

and

 # The Multi-Musical Talents of
PIETRO BARROLI

Accompanied by The Mike Davidson Orchestra

Thank you for not smoking during the performances. Videotaping is not permitted

10.00pm **DANCE UNTIL THE EARLY HOURS** Stardust Disco, Deck 8
with our DJ, Paul

9.30pm - 1.00am **MUSIC FOR DANCING** Neptune's Lounge, Deck 5
with
MOOD INDIGO

7.45pm - 8.45pm **EVENING COCKTAIL MELODIES** Calypso Bar, Deck 5
9.45pm - 11.00pm **with our pianist, Alistair**

11.45pm - 12.30am LATE NIGHT BUFFET is served!   Trident Restaurant

TODAY'S MOVIES

CHANNEL 15   Broadcast of this morning's Port and Travel Talk at 11.00am and 2.30pm

CHANNEL 16   **BATMAN BEGINS** (action adventure featuring Christian Bale – 12A).
7.30am, 10.00am, 4.00pm, 6.30pm and 11.30pm

CHANNEL 28   **MADAGASCAR** (computer animated comedy featuring Ben Stiller, Chris Rock – U)
7.30am, 9.30am, 11.30am, 2.00pm, 4.00pm, 6.00pm, 8.00pm, 10.00pm
and 12 midnight

ONBOARD DINING

Breakfast	7.00am - 7.30am	Early risers coffee and pastries in the Palm Court Café
	7.00am - 9.00am	Open Sitting Breakfast in the Trident Restaurant
	7.30am - 10.00am	Breakfast Buffet in the Palm Court Café
Snack	10.30am - 11.15am	Hot Bouillon and Crackers in the Palm Court Café
Lunch	12 noon	1st Sitting Lunch in the Trident Restaurant
	1.30pm	2nd Sitting Lunch in the Trident Restaurant
	12.30pm - 2.30pm	Buffet Lunch in the Palm Court Café
	4.00pm - 4.45pm	Afternoon Tea in the Palm Court Café
Dinner	6.00pm	1st Sitting Dinner in the Trident Restaurant
	8.30pm	2nd Sitting Dinner in the Trident Restaurant
Buffet	11.45pm - 12.45pm	Late Night Buffet in the Trident Restaurant

BAR HOURS

Calypso Bar	9.00am - Close
Pool Bar	9.00am - 6.00pm
Neptune's Lounge	5.00pm - Close
Showtime Lounge	7.30pm - Close
Stardust Disco	10.00pm - Close

DEPARTMENT HOURS AND TELEPHONE NUMBERS

Purser's Office, Deck 5 - Tel: 0	Open 24 Hours
Shore Excursion Office, Deck 5 - Tel: 5423	11.00am - 2.00pm and 7.00pm - 8.30pm
Hospital Surgery Hours, Deck 2 - Tel: 5000	9.00am - 11.00am and 5.30pm - 6.30pm
Gift Shops, Deck 5 - Tel: 5682	9.00am - 12 noon, 2.00pm - 6.00pm and 8.00pm - 10.00pm
Duty Free Liquor Shop, Deck 8 - Tel: 5121	9.00am - 12 noon, 2.00pm - 6.00pm and 8.00pm - 10.00pm
Beauty Salon, Deck 8 - Tel: 5480	8.00am - 8.00pm
Spa and Gymnasium, Deck 8 - Tel: 5771	8.00am - 8.00pm
Photo Gallery, Deck 4 - Tel: 5232	11.00am - 12 noon and 4.00pm - 5.00pm
Casino, Deck 5 - Tel: 5569	9.00am (Slots) and 2.00pm (Tables) - Close

Photo Gallery: To order photos, fill out an order form (available at the Photo Gallery) with your name, cabin number and the code number of the displayed photo(s) of your choice. Drop the form in the Photo Order Box and your photos will be delivered to your cabin by the end of the cruise. 35mm film can also be processed on board. Ask our photographer for details.

Gift Shops: Take a look at our loose gemstones -amethyst, Citrine and Blue Topaz. Only $10 per carat and all with certificates from the Gemological Board of Trade.

Stadium Theatre Company, c/o P & O Cruises, Richmond House, Terminus Terrace, Southampton, Hants. SO14 3PN, England; ☎: 01703-534200.

Entertainment, 18295 La Cienega Blvd. Inglewood, California CA 90301, USA; www.stilettoentertainment.com/cruiseship_entertainment. Provides casts and production shows (singers and dancers) mainly for Holland America line. Auditions are usually held in the USA.

In the Words of a Dancer

I'm a dancer in a shipboard production show, along with seven other performers, four female and three male. Four of us are from different parts of the United States, one is Canadian and two are from Great Britain, so we're quite an international cast. Although our company is based in Florida, dancers from Europe and Britain in particular have such a good reputation that a lot of American producers audition in cities such as London, Manchester and Paris, as well as in the US. My two colleagues from England attended an audition in London. We all met up for the first time in Fort Lauderdale where we spent three weeks rehearsing before joining the ship. Of course, our company paid for our flights and provided our food and accommodation, together with a rehearsal salary, during this time.

There's a lot of competition for work as a dancer on ships and most companies like you to be able to sing as well. All seven of us are good all-rounders, but the two principals are trained singers who can move, rather than great dancers. All the vocals are performed live and the band accompanies us by following a 'click-track', so the tempos are the same for every show.

On each cruise we do three different shows with two performances of each show (for first and second dinner sittings). This week we've also been rehearsing a lot for a new fourth show. It can sometimes be difficult to schedule practice times because the show lounge is also used for other activities, so we may have to rehearse at lunchtimes or even midnight. This can be hard if we then have to get up early the next day to help with cruise staff duties, even if the tasks are fairly easy like decorating for theme nights or assisting with games and activities.

My contract is for six months but I will probably accept an offer to extend it, mainly to be with my boyfriend, Carlos. He is from

Panama and works as the head bartender in the main lounge where we do our shows. I like him because he's different from most of the other straight guys on this ship. In fact, he's the only bartender who didn't make a pass at me in my first week. As a girl dancer, you get a lot of attention from the men onboard which can be flattering at first. But you soon realise that most of them only see you as 'fresh meat' and as soon as other girls come on the scene, they quickly lose interest. The three guys in our show are all gay so they're not interested in us anyway.

Some entertainers may think that working at sea is inferior to performing on land, but I disagree. Many ships now have full-scale theatres onboard, complete with all kinds of special lighting and sound effects, and shipboard production shows are becoming more and more sophisticated, often rivalling shows on Broadway or in London's West End. Besides, so many of my colleagues on land are struggling for work that I feel lucky to be here. Who wants to starve in Manhattan when you can be paid to perform and travel the world at the same time?

Mandy-Jo Murphy (age 19)

Opportunities for Experts

Do you have any special skills, hobbies or unusual claims to fame? And would you be able to pass on your knowledge or expertise to other people? If the answer is yes, you might like to consider applying to be a *Guest Lecturer* at sea. Don't be put off by the academic-sounding title; some cruise lines use the less formal term of *Enrichment Provider*. You don't need teaching qualifications to do this, simply the ability to do something well and the confidence to tell or show an audience of passengers how you do it.

There is a hitch, however: you don't get paid. What you do get is a free or substantially-reduced cruise for yourself and a companion with full passenger status and accommodation in return for just a few hours of work. Neither is there an upper age limit. Many guest lecturers are retired and some 'work their passage' several times a year.

The most common specialist subjects are contract bridge, arts and crafts (including portraiture and caricatures) arts appreciation, astronomy, computers, dance, earth and marine science, finance, fortune-telling (including palmistry and tarot cards), genealogy, graphology (handwriting analysis), health and nutrition, history, photography, self-improvement

Scope for Fortune-Telling

(positive thinking, health and beauty, how to combat stress, improve your memory, etc.) and world affairs. Leading exponents in a particular field may also give celebrity lectures. Airline pilots, media personalities, mountaineers, archaeologists, antiques and gardening experts have all found an audience among cruise passengers. Golf professionals are recruited by Elite Golf Cruises, LLC (www.elitegolfcruises.com; fax 954-382-5398) based in Florida as guest instructors using both an onboard simulator and golf courses en route in return for a free cruise and additional revenue via rentals, product sales and gratuities.

Check through holiday brochures for companies that offer theme cruises that may be relevant to your area of work or interest – and don't forget operators of specialist and 'explorer' cruises, for instance geologists, explorers and naturalists are needed on expedition cruises from the Arctic to the Amazon basin by organizers such as Abercrombie & Kent, Hapag Lloyd, Condor Journeys (www.condorjourneys-adventures.com/antartica_cruise2.asp), Norwegian Coastal Voyage Inc. (www.coastalvoyage.com), Orient Lines *'Marco Polo'* (Antartica), Voyages of Discovery (info@voyagesofdiscovery.com), Cruise West (www.cruisewest.com) among others. Holland and America are experts in Alaska travel and their ships include an onboard naturalist and a native artist in residence.

If you contact the cruise lines direct, do enquire about their policies regarding guest lecturers (as their requirements are subject to change) before bombarding them with samples of your work. Bear in mind too the feasibility of your chosen topic, considering you will be expected to provide and transport any materials or photographic slides that you intend using (and this includes materials for your pupils if you intend to give classes in an art or craft).

Often, cruise companies use employment agencies that specialise in supplying guest lecturers to ships. The head office of the respective lines should be able to tell you which agents (if any) they use for your specific line of expertise. But don't forget, if you obtain work through an agency they will charge you a placement fee which, on top of other expenses such as the cost of flights to join the ship, may make your working holiday more expensive than you had envisaged.

The following agencies all recruit guest lecturers and experts:

Bramson Entertainment, 630 Ninth Ave., Suite 203, New York, NY 10036, USA; ☎(212)265-3500; fax (212)265-6615; www.bramson.com.

International Voyager Media, 11900 Biscayne Blvd, Suite 300, Miami, FL 33181, USA; ☎305 892 6644.

Lauretta Blake, The Working Vacation Inc, 12544 West 159 St., Homer Glen, Illinois 60491-8378, USA; ☎708-301-7535; fax 708-301-6202; www.theworkingvacation.com).

Lectures International, P O Box 35446 Tucson, AZ 85740, United States of America; ☎520 297 1145.1

Panoff Publishing, 7100 Commercial Blvd., Suite 106, Fort Lauderdale, FL 33319-2124, USA ☎954-746-5554; fax 954-746-5244; www.ppi-group.com.

Posh Talks Inc, 160 Luring Drive, Palm Springs, California 92262 USA; ☎760-323-3205; e-mail poshtalks@aol.com.

Program Experts Inc, P O Box 510, Cresskill, NJ 07626-0510 USA; ☎210 569 7950.

Semester at Sea, Institute for Shipboard Education, University of Pittsburgh, 811 Willaim Pitt Union, Pittsburgh, PA 15260 USA; ☎800-854-0194.

To Sea with Z, 19195 Mystic Pointe Drive, Tower 100, Suite 2007, Aventura, Florida 33180, USA; ☎305-931-1026; fax 305-931 1132; e-mail zammel@aol.com; www.toseawithz.com.

The World, c/o ResidenSea Ltd, 5200 Blue Lagoon Drive, Suite 790, Miami, FL 33126 USA; e-mail enrichmentdirector@theworld.cc; www.aboardtheworld.com. The World is a timeshare apartment ship that goes around the world (a ship that you can literally call home). The Enrichment and Entertainment Department organises guest lecturer programmes and potential candidates can apply direct to the management company ResidenSea above.

Jobs for the Boys: Gentlemen Hosts

Cruise lines are in need of older gentleman (age range 45-72) who are smart, articulate, well-travelled, well-read, good conversationalists, preferably single and, above all versatile dancers (ballroom, swing, Latin, and rock'n'roll). Don't be fooled into thinking that an occasional glide round the dance floor will suffice. The emphasis will be more on work than on holiday. According to one gentleman host the job is 60% dancing and 40% socialising. This is because the number of female passengers on the

Gentleman hosts are in demand

average cruise invariably outweighs the number of males and a highlight for many of the ladies is the chance to dance the night away. Gentlemen Hosts are therefore in great demand as companions and especially as dancing partners, in return for a free, or subsidised, cruise on much the same terms as the Guest Lecturers.

If you have poise, charm and a strong pair of dancing shoes, the larger ships at the more upmarket end of the industry may be particularly interested in hearing from you. Try especially Cunard Line, Crystal Cruises, Celebrity Cruises, Holland America Line, Radisson Seven Seas, Orient Lines and World Explorer. Skills of the job come with experience and there are rules: although gentleman hosts are obliged to dance with any ladies who request a dance (though singles get special attention) they should not ask the same woman for a dance twice in a row and they should not ask an escorted woman to dance even if her escort is not in sight. They have to treat the ladies with kid gloves and professionalism as not much has changed since the 18th century when the proverb 'hell hath no fury like a woman scorned' was coined. The number of gentleman hosts on board ranges between two and eight.

The following agencies specialise in recruiting gentlemen hosts and dance instructors and Crystal Cruises have their own host department:

Crystal Cruises, 2049 Century Park East, Suite 1400, Los Angeles CA 90067; e-mail shoffman@crystalcruises.com.

Karp Enterprises Inc, 16056 Brier Creek Drive, Delray Beach, Florida 33446 USA; ☎561 637-1700; e-mail applicants@karpenterprises. com; www.karpenterprises.com.

Lauretta Blake, The Working Vacation Inc, 12544 West 159 St., Homer Glen, Illinois 60491-8378, USA; ☎708-301-7535; fax 708-301-6202; e-mail info@theworkingvacation.com; www.theworkingvaca-tion.com).

Sixth Star Entertainment & Marketing, 21 NW 5th Street, Fort Launder-dale, Florida 33101, USA; ☎954-462-6760; fax 954-462-0737; www. sixthstar.com.

Shore Excursions: Work in the Tour Sector

On some ships, the sale and marketing of organised shore excursions may fall under the umbrella of the cruise staff department, while on others the Shore Excursions (Tour) Office is a separate department under the direction of an experienced *Shore Excursions Manager* (or similar-sounding title). By liaising with pre-allocated tour operators in each port of call, the Shore Excursions Manager will ensure the smooth running of the whole programme of optional or included tours, from the reservation of coaches and local guides to the sale of tickets. Although Tour Office personnel frequently escort excursions, there are no real opportunities for Tour Guides at sea as local guides are generally used in the various ports of call.

Shore excursion work is an interesting job, socially as well as professionally. An added perk is that local tour company personnel are often eager to entertain and reward you for bringing business their way.

Opportunities also exist for *Shore Excursions (Tour) Office Assistants*, especially on larger ships where a whole team of staff may be employed in this capacity. Experience is not necessarily a requirement here, although previous work in the travel industry would be helpful.

Monthly salaries before range from $1,800 (£980) for assistants to $3,000 (£1,650) and upwards for managers, and there may be commission-making opportunities to add to this. For newcomers to ships who are interested in the tourism and excursion angle, a job as a Tour Office Assistant can be an excellent starting point.

For work in this sector, apply directly to the cruise lines. One exception is Holland America Line which has its own affiliated company (Westours) at the same address which recruits tour staff: Westours, 300 Elliott Avenue West, Seattle, Washington 98119, USA (☎206-281-3535; fax 206-298-3899; www.hollandamerica.com).

Concessionaires

Cruise lines frequently make use of specialist companies and agencies to supply some of the services and staff needed on their vessels. This means that many, if not most, of the employees in the Hotel Department of a ship might work for a company other than the cruise line itself. This company will have an onboard concession, and is therefore known as a 'concessionaire'. Catering has already provided us with a good example of this (see section *Catering Concessionaires*). But, outside the restaurant, concessionaires may also operate the onboard gift shops, photographic services, beauty salons, spas, fitness centres and casinos.

Catering and housekeeping apart, the people who work in the various concessions usually fall into the classification of staff, as distinct from officers and crew. They are paid directly by the company which hired them, although they are bound by the rules and conditions of the ship. In a minority of cases, unlike people employed directly by the cruise line, they may be required to contribute towards their living expenses. They do, however, get more free time in port than those working in other capacities. This particularly applies to staff whose work is affected by customs regulations, such as the on-board duty-free shop and casino.

SHOPS

Why be a *Shop Assistant* in town, when you can be a shop assistant all over the world? Good *Sales Staff* and experienced *Shop Managers*, are in demand on ships, especially those who speak more than one language. Salaries are generally comparable with shoreside retail earnings and include incentives. If you have retail experience, especially in the duty-free or department store sector, there could be openings here for you.

There are virtually no opportunities for *Window Dressers* to work on a ship for more than a couple of days (or even hours) at a time. But concessionaires may employ staff specifically to travel between ships, changing and updating displays during the few hours that a liner is in port. This affords exciting travel opportunities for experienced window dressers who are able to be creative under pressure and still meet seemingly impossible deadlines. Bear in mind, however, that such openings are extremely limited.

For general sales positions, the outlook is much more optimistic. All reasonably-sized ships have at least one retail outlet onboard and large ships may have whole shopping arcades, selling a vast range of duty-free goods, clothes, cosmetics, necessities and gifts. Sometimes these shops are run by famous High Street companies. Obviously anyone who is already employed by such a company has an advantage. But others can consider approaching the relevant personnel officer and asking about vacancies in the firm's branches at sea.

The most promising cruise lines to approach directly for this kind of work are P & O Cruises, Princess Cruises, Carnival Cruise Lines, Louis Cruise Lines (a Cyprus-based company with several ships and a duty-free shopping chain), and Norwegian Cruise Line. Don't forget to also consider ferry companies, such as DFDS Seaways (www.dfds.co.uk), Caledonian MacBrayne (www.calmac.co.uk), Irish Ferries (www.irishferries.ie), and Fjord Line (www.fjordline.co.uk).

Addresses of Shop Concessionaires

The following companies place retail staff on various lines:

Apollo Ship Chandlers Inc, 1775 NW 70th Avenue, Miami, Florida 33126, USA; ☎305-592 8790; fax 305-593 8335; e-mail Services@apolloships.com; www.apolloships.com.

Blue Seas International Cruise Services Inc., 1033 Tyler Street, Hollywood, Florida 33019, USA. Vacancies registered throughout the hotel department, including beauty salons and gift shops. Their new International Seafarers' Exchange (www.jobxchange.com) undertakes to match cruise ship vacancies with qualified staff who pay a membership fee.

Harding Brothers, Avonmouth Way, Avonmouth, Bristol BS11 8DD, England; ☎0117-982 5961; fax 0117-982 7276; e-mail info@hardingbros. co.uk; www.hardingbros.co.uk.

Starboard Cruise Services, Doral Concourse, 8400 NW 36th Street, Suite 600, Miami, Florida 33166, USA; ☎305-845 7300; fax 786-845 1119; e-mail hrships@starboardcruise.com; www.starboardcruise.com.

VIP International, VIP House, 17 Charing Cross Road, London WC2H 0QW, England; ☎020-7930 0541; fax 020-7930 2860; e-mail vip@vipinternational.co.uk; www.vipinternational.co.uk.

In the Words of a Gift Shop Assistant

For the past year and a half I've been employed as a gift shop assistant onboard a Caribbean-based cruise ship. Like most retail staff on ships I work for an independent concessionaire rather than for the cruise line itself and, because of this, I personally have to contribute about $60 (£42) per week towards the cost of my board, which I pay direct to the Crew Purser on the ship.

When I originally applied for this position I was already working on the cosmetics counter of a large department store in my home town of Manchester. I'm sure it was mainly because of this practical experience that I was offered the job, since at that time I'd never even set foot on a ship and didn't really know what to expect.

I must admit, when I first saw my cabin I couldn't believe how small it was. I now realise that I'd packed far too many clothes, especially as my company provides me with a uniform for work and I only wear casual summer clothes ashore. I have to share the cabin with one of the other 'shoppies' and fortunately we get on really well, in spite of the fact we'd never met before. It helps that her boyfriend is an engineer with his own cabin, so I often have the place to myself.

We are allocated a steward, who cleans and makes our beds each day, but we have to take our uniforms to the laundry ourselves. Our uniforms are cleaned free of charge and there are also free washers and dryers in the crew areas but the machines are in such demand that it's often quicker to rinse things out by hand and hang them in our shower to dry.

Although my cabin is in a crew area, I do have 'public rooms privileges' (as most gift shop assistants do), which means I can use passenger facilities such as the pool and the gymnasium (at off-peak times) and the passenger lounges and bars. I often join other staff members and officers in the passenger disco after work, as it's a nicer option than the crew bar and we get a good discount on drinks.

I suppose my bar bills and taxi fares to the beach are my only real expenses at the moment, which is why, for the first time in my life, I'm able to save money. I earn a basic of $200 (approximately £135) per week plus commission if we make our sales target. On 'target' weeks I'll treat myself to something special onshore. On that subject, I do get quite a lot of time off in exotic places.

Of course it's not all palm trees and cocktails. On days at sea the shops are open from early in the morning till late at night. I dread certain tasks like stocktaking and the arrival of new supplies on embarkation days. I also hate the weekly crew safety drill as I'm sometimes asked to help lower a lifeboat. But in the main, I enjoy my job and prefer it to working on land. Yes, there are times when I get homesick but after a few days on leave I get sick of home.

Andrea Gordon (age 24)

HAIR & BEAUTY SALONS

Most cruise ships will have their own onboard Hair and Beauty Salon and some may even boast a sophisticated Health and Beauty Centre, equipped with the very latest technology. *Salon Managers, Hairdressers, Beauticians/Manicurists, Masseurs* and *Masseuses* are therefore in great demand and larger vessels may also have openings for *Chiropodists* and *Physiotherapists* (see also the sections *Spas & Fitness Centres* and *Medical Department*).

If you wish to apply for any type of work in this sector you should be qualified and experienced before climbing the gangway, as there are generally no openings for trainees in shipboard salons. As with all applications, the more versatile you appear to be, the greater your chance of acceptance. Beauticians who can manicure, masseuses who can make-up, hairdressers who can style both the normal and the very formal, these are the types of people employers are seeking.

A salon manager can earn $2,500 (£1,365) to $3,800 (£2,075) a month while a hair stylist earns around $2,200 (£1,200) to $2,900 (£1,582). There is also potential for making reasonable tips, not to mention the appeal of doing a blow-dry in Bali rather than a blue rinse in Balham.

Major salon concessionaires include Steiner, Canyon Ranch and Mandara Spa (recently acquired by Steiner); see the next section *Spas and Fitness Centres* for the addresses. Note that Steiners tends to offer lower salaries than some others but, with its London-based training school (*Steiner School Of Beauty Therapy*, 193 Wardour Street, London W1V 3FA, England; ☎020-7434 4534) and high staff requirements, also offers more opportunities for newcomers.

SPAS AND FITNESS CENTRES

Spas are becoming an increasingly popular feature of luxury cruise ships, with many modern liners possessing highly sophisticated hydrotherapy, fitness and sauna facilities. Sometimes the spa operates in conjunction with the beauty salon and is run by the same parent company. In other cases it is operated by a separate concessionaire. Some ships' gymnasiums are affiliated to the spa, while others are controlled by the cruise line itself. Needless to say, this can become rather confusing and it is worth checking to whom you should apply before sending off your details.

As a generalisation, positions exist for experienced *Spa Managers*, qualified *Masseurs/Masseuses, Spa Assistants* with a good working knowledge of the latest hydrotherapy, relaxation and detoxification techniques, qualified *Gymnasium Supervisors, Fitness and/or Aerobics Instructors* who can offer personal health and fitness programmes (see also *Entertainment* chapter), and qualified and experienced *Physiotherapists*. Salaries are generally comparable to those in land-based health and fitness facilities.

Addresses of Beauty & Fitness Concessionaires

Canyon Ranch Spa Club, 8600 E Rockcliff Road, Tucson, Arizona 85750, USA; ☎520-749 9000; fax 520-749 7759; www.canyonranch.com.

Harding Brothers, Avonmouth Way, Avonmouth, Bristol BS11 8DD, England; ☎0117-982 5961; fax 0117-982 7276; e-mail info@hardingbros. co.uk; www.hardingbros.co.uk.

Mandara Spa-Cruise Ship Division, 8125 NW 53rd Street, Suite 116, Miami, Florida 33166, USA; ☎305-471 9553; fax 305-471 9501; www.mandaraspa.com.

Steiner Leisure (USA), 770 South Dixie Highway, Suite 200, Coral Gables, Florida 33146; USA ☎305-358 9002; fax 305-372 9310; www.steinerleisure.com.

Steiner Leisure (UK), The Lodge, 92 Uxbridge Road, Harrow Weald, Middlesex HA3 6BZ, England; ☎020-8909 5016; fax 020-8909 5040; www.steinerleisure.com.

In the Words of a Fitness Instructor

During the two years that I have worked as a fitness instructor at sea, I have worked on three different ships and have cruised Alaska, South America, the Bahamas, and now the Caribbean. And yes, I really enjoy the life. Before I came to sea I was working in a private health club near my home in Essex, and also acting as a coach at a local sports centre. This experience, together with about fifteen related Health and Fitness qualifications, definitely helped me to get the job. Qualifications are important and any British instructors wishing to teach fitness at sea should at least have passed the RSA (Royal Society of Arts) Exercise to Music, be qualified in NABA (National Association of Bodybuilders and Athletes) personal training programmes, including BCA (Body Composition Analysis), and be fully trained in CPR and First Aid.

On the ship, I'm responsible for my own programme of classes, which I try to make as balanced as possible. I also have to gear my classes to the variable standard of the students, remembering that cruise ship passengers are generally older and less active than the fitness students I teach onshore. The morning 'walk-a-mile' around the deck is really popular and a surprising number of passengers come to the daily stretch class. I also get a mixture of active younger passengers, especially those who work out regularly at

> *home, who want me to devise personal training programmes for them. Although use of the spa and gymnasium is free, I charge for consultations, and this can make a big difference to my $220 (£150) weekly 'basic'. The money is actually worse than I could make on land, but it's a great way to see the world. The concessionaire I work for pays for my flights and expenses, and I manage to save far more than I ever did at home. But I would advise would-be instructors who are offered a choice between working directly for a cruise line as a member of cruise staff or working for a spa concessionaire to go for the cruise staff option as the money and conditions are usually better and you're not bound by the rules and hours of the spa and beauty salon.*
>
> *I suppose the thing I find the hardest about my job at sea is keeping up with the fitness industry itself. It's easy to get isolated in your own little floating gym and get out of touch with the latest equipment and techniques. For this reason, I get my family to send me copies of trade magazines and, when I go back on leave, I always enrol for a few classes and refresher courses. I believe that passing on knowledge and acquiring it go hand in hand. A good instructor never stops learning.*
>
> **Lesley Davey-Jones (age 25)**

CASINOS

If you are over 21 years old and a trained dealer with previous experience you could be onto a winner at sea. Ships' casinos have a high requirement for all kinds of staff: *Managers, Assistant Managers, Pit Bosses, Inspectors, Croupiers, Cashiers* and *Casino Technicians.*

All casinos at sea will have a Manager and possibly even an Assistant Manager, while only the ones with large casinos need Pit Bosses and Inspectors. The latter, however, may have the opportunity of being promoted to managerial positions on smaller ships.

Technicians must be able to maintain and repair slot machines and other gaming devices. Cashiers should have appropriate experience, although not necessarily casino experience.

Croupiers must be able to handle both Blackjack and Roulette, while experience of other games like Punto Banco, Poker or Craps is a bonus. A minimum of two years dealing experience is preferred, although exceptions may be made if, for example, the applicant has passed a college course in gaming.

As with all casinos, working hours are anti-social. But there are compensations, including the fact that, due to international gaming laws, casinos on ships are closed (and therefore the staff are off) in every port of call.

Salaries are frequently lower than those paid by onshore casinos (particularly British ones), but incentives may be offered and tips – often in the form of chips – are not only accepted but expected. Dealers should therefore earn at least $1,900 (£1,035) to $2,400 (£1,310) per month, managers can generally expect $2,800 (£1,530) to $3,600 (£1,965), and a cashier can take $1,400 (£764) to $2,000 (£1,090).

Useful Contacts for Casino Work

At www.ukcroupiers.com you will find a list of a number of companies who specialise in cruise ship casino work. Another useful website for job-seekers is www.gamingfloor.com, a good place to find industry info and vacancies, while *The British Casino Association* (38 Grosvenor Gardens, London SW1W 0EB, England; ☎020-7730 1055; fax 020-7730 1050; e-mail enquiries@britishcasinoassociation.org.uk; www.britishcasinoassociation.org.uk) can help with a description of the working conditions for persons considering starting in the business. Their website also lists UK casinos, training schools and agencies.

Carnival Casinos, Carnival House, 5 Gainsford Street, London SE1 2NB, England; ☎020-7378 4699; fax 020-7378 4698; www.oceancasino-jobs.com.

Casinos Austria International (HQ), Dr. Karl Lueger Ring 14, A-1014 Vienna, Austria; ☎1-534 40504; fax 1-532 9207; www.casinos.at.

Century Casinos, 1263 A Lake Plaza Drive, Colorado Springs, CO 80906, USA; ☎719-527 8300; fax 719-527 8301; www.centuryca-sinos.com.

Games Plus, 154 Court Farm Road, Newhaven BN9 9HB, England; ☎01273-611378; e-mail info@croupier.net; www.croupier.net. Exclusive UK representative for Norwegian Cruise Line. Applications via e-mail only.

Greater Atlantic Casinos Ltd, 1050 Lee Wagner Boulevard, Suite 303, Fort Lauderdale, Florida 33315 USA; ☎954-359 0001; fax 954-491 9924; www.casinoatsea.com.

International Casino Monitoring (UK) Ltd, PO Box 195, Hythe, Kent CT21 6GZ, England; ☎01303-260108; fax 01303-260114; e-mail

intcasmon@intcasmon.ndirect.co.uk; www.intcasmon.ndirect.co.uk.
IMC Inc (USA), 440 E Front Street, Florence, New Jersey 08518, USA; ☎609-499 7378; fax 609-499 7379; www.intcasmon.ndirect.co.uk.
Norwegian Cruise Line (NCL), recruits direct through its website www. ncl.com/news/shipboard – emp/shipboard – index.htm.
Princess Cruises, Fleet Personnel Department, 24844 Avenue Rockefeller, Santa Clarita, California 91355, USA; e-mail careersatsea@pri ncesscruises.com; http://employment.princess.com.
Seefar Associates, 7 Berkley Crescent, Gravesend, Kent DA12 2AH, England; ☎01474-329990; fax 01474-329995; www.seefarassociates.co.uk,
Star Cruises, PO Box 288, Pulau Indah, Pelabuhan Barat 42009, Pelabuhan Klang, Selangor Darul Ehsan, Malaysia; ☎3-3109 2445; fax 3-3109 2098; e-mail hnsim@starcruises.com.my; www.starcruises.com. Star Cruises operate a continuous recruitment drive for casino (and other) staff.
SunCruz Casinos, 647 East Dania Beach Boulevard, Dania Beach, Florida 33004, USA; ☎954-929 3880; fax 954-929 3830; www.suncruzcasino.com.

In the Words of a Croupier

I work as a dealer on a cruise ship based in the Bahamas. Our ship specialises in three and four-day party cruises and the passengers are really out to have a good time. They play hard, both in the casino and in the bars, so it tends to be one long party for us too.

We work late, usually until at least 2am, although this depends on how busy we are. Most of the dealers then go to the disco until it closes at 4am. Fortunately, we don't open the tables until the afternoon, so we also get a lie-in. But I would warn newcomers to casinos, and especially casinos at sea, of the danger of getting into a nocturnal lifestyle, whereby you eat breakfast at lunchtime, never see daylight and never get off the ship because you're sleeping through the day. It's easy to lose track of time and, to wake up not knowing whether it's night or day (since most crew cabins don't have portholes). Quite recently, one of our dealers woke at 6 o'clock and, thinking he had overslept for the evening shift, threw on his tuxedo and ran to the casino, only to find it was 6am and his only customer was the night cleaner.

I personally tend to take advantage of the fact that casino staff

I see, so its 6am not 6pm!

don't have to work in port, by getting off the ship as much as possible. I'm a keen scuba diver so this itinerary in the Caribbean is perfect for me. I dive whenever I have the chance since I am currently working towards my Master Diver Certificate. When I'm not in the water, I go to the onshore casinos, particularly in Nassau, where I'm friendly with some of the local dealers. It may seem strange to want to spend my free time at the tables, but we're not allowed to gamble in our own casino, and it can be quite refreshing to be a punter for a change.

My advice to would-be dealers is, first of all, get trained. Either approach your local casino and ask if they are recruiting or enrol at a reputable croupier training school. Once you have two games such as roulette and blackjack under your belt and some experience, you are in a position to apply to the cruise lines and casino concessionaires. Since working on ships I have also made a point of learning how to deal dice and stud poker, as the more games you can deal, the better your chances of being accepted by other

companies, if and when you need a change.
As a dealer, the world's your oyster and not just on the ships. I
have friends who trained at the same casino as I did in London who
are now working in Sun City (South Africa), the Bahamas, Australia and the Far East. But for me, cruise ships offer the most exciting
lifestyle, and without the expenses of working on land. When I go
back home and see my family and friends, everyone seems so hard
up. It's as if whatever they earn gets swallowed up by the cost of
living. But at sea you're in a continual holiday atmosphere and it's
easy to forget about the hard realities. If you're looking for travel,
glamour, romance and the chance to save a bit of money, working
as a croupier on ships is definitely the answer. It's a great life.

Allan Hicks (age 30)

SAY CHEESE: OPPORTUNITIES FOR PHOTOGRA-PHERS

Professional *Photographers* will find plenty of opportunities on cruise ships, which may have anything from a small single-handed operation to a six or seven-person team under the direction of an experienced *Chief Photographer*. Applicants should possess a high standard of photographic skills, combined with practical ability and experience in printing and developing. Processing work, together with the selling of photographs, is often an integral part of the job.

One factor that you should take into account before applying to be a ship's photographer is that you are likely to be working against much tighter deadlines than on land. Thousands of split-second shots of passengers – shaking the Captain's hand, posing for portraits, on the gangway, in the restaurant, from port to port and party to party – all have to be snapped and processed against the clock. And if the photos aren't on the display board by the end of the cruise, you've lost the sale and therefore the commission that forms the bulk of your income. A photographer's salary is commissison-based and can range from $300 (£165) to $1,000 (£545) a week depending on experience. This is also one of the 'fun' jobs on the ship, in the midst of the social scene and with plenty of free time in port.

MARITIME PHOTOGRAPHIC EMPLOYERS

While some cruise operators, most notably Carnival Cruise Lines, hire their photographers direct, most employ the services of concessionaires. Anyone interested in this type of work should keep an eye on trade publications and specialist magazines for cruise job advertisements or get in touch with the following companies. Who knows? Your next shoot could be on location.

Image Photo Services, Beacon Centre, Suite A, 2085 NW 87th Avenue, Miami, Florida 33172, USA; ☎305-476 3666; fax 305-476 3663; www.imageservices.com.

Neptune Photographic, 202 Fulham Road, London SW10 9NB, England; ☎020-7351 7181; fax 020-7352 5014.

Ocean Images (UK), Unit 7, Home Farm Business Centre, Lockerley, Romsey, Hampshire SO51 0JT, England; ☎01794-341818; fax 01794-341415; www.ocean-images.com. Ocean Images (UK) also uses *Shipboard Services Ltd*, ASL House, 12-14 David Place, St. Helier, Jersey JE2 4TD, Channel Islands, as recruiting agents.

Shoreside Florida Inc, Atlantis Building, 2800 SW 4th Avenue, Bay 5, Fort Lauderdale Florida 33335, USA; ☎954-523 2308; fax 954-527 4262; www.shoresideflorida.com, is the USA representative of Ocean Images (UK).

Trans-Ocean Photos Inc, 40 Lydecker Street, Nyack, New York 10960, USA; ☎1-845-727 0001; e-mail info@transoceanphotos.com; www.transoceanphotos.com.

In the Words of a Ship's Photographer

I've worked as a Chief Photographer on ships for so long (about seven years) that I've almost forgotten what it was like to do photography on land, even though I started off with a local studio in England doing the usual rounds of weddings, barmitzvahs and 'Bonny Baby' portraits.

On the ship I'm on now, I'm in charge of two other photographers. One is a 20 year old newcomer to cruising and the other has worked with me on two previous ships. The main advantage of being the 'number one' is that I get a better sales percentage than they do. Also I have a cabin to myself, whereas they have to double up. The disadvantage is that I'm responsible for everything to do with the photographic department, including my guys being late for the early morning shots because they are still hung over from the night before.

To be a good ship's photographer is not just a matter of taking a good picture. Although related qualifications, such as a college degree in photography, are certainly advantageous, we are not looking for artistic individualists. Rather, we need flexible all-rounders, people who can work as a team. I stress this because we are living and working together in such confined conditions for such long periods that team spirit and the ability to get along with people is essential. If someone is really technical it's a help, and every team member should be able to develop films, using a Fuji (or similar) lab processor. Our photographers need also to be adept at handling professional-quality cameras by makers such as Nikon, Leica and Hasselblad. I always use my own personal Nikon FM2, and although our company supplies us with additional cameras, I find most of my colleagues also prefer to use their own models.

We operate a rota system of selling the prints, so retail experience is always handy, and we each earn a percentage of the overall sales. This varies between 3% and 7% according to status and length of service with the company. I personally have made over $1,500 (£1,000) per week on some ships, especially on seven to ten-day cruises with interesting itineraries. But every group of passengers is different and on a bad week I may only end up with $400 (£250). You also have to take into account the fact that most photographic concessionaires do not pay your travel expenses to and from the ship, so you are personally responsible for your own flights and this can knock your earnings back. For this reason I always do contracts of at least six months and sometimes nine.

If I'm honest, I think some of the cruise lines are getting greedier at the expense of the concessionaires and, indirectly, the photographers themselves. There is a trend for the lines to operate their own in-house photographic departments, which usually means they cut out the middle-man but pay the staff the same as (or less than) before. Even cruise lines that still use independent companies may expect to take 60%-70% of the revenue, which means the concessionaires then reduce our percentages too.

But in spite of this, cruising can still be both financially and socially rewarding for photographers who want to travel the world in a party atmosphere. Most ships' photogs are in their twenties or thirties and definitely single. But I've also known a few girlfriend/

boyfriend teams who have successfully worked together on ships and, assuming both partners are of a good professional standard, it can be a nice option for a couple.

Of course, the one thing you'll need more than anything else is patience with the passengers. You just have to get used to them ignoring you when you're trying to organise a series of shots and, occasionally, they can be downright rude. Gangways are often the hardest. You get sick of saying 'OK folks, let's get a picture. Stand a bit closer, next to the sign. No, this sign. That's it, now look at me... I'm over here, madam...big smile, that's great. OK folks, let's get a picture.' You say it so many times, you repeat it in your sleep. And no matter how polite you are, there are several predictable things that passengers complain about every cruise: the weather, the air-conditioning – and the photographers. If we're always around, we get accused of pestering. If we leave them alone, they say that they can never find a photographer when they need one. Either way, we can't win. I've now resigned myself to the situation and am concerned only with the sales figures. But if, when the cruise evaluation forms come in, we rate better than the air-conditioning, then I guess it's been a good cruise.

Steven Callaghan

Technical &
Engineering

The Engineering Department covers most aspects of the ship's maintenance and workings, including the main and auxiliary engines, the generators, plumbing and sanitation, electrical systems, water desalinisation systems, air conditioning, heating, ventilation and refrigeration.

The hub of activity is obviously the Engine Room itself. But gone are the days of grimy stokers with sweat-drenched torsos. Computer expertise is nowadays as important as the ability to wield a hammer, and in order to facilitate promotion and to ensure the continuing education of their officers, cruise lines frequently finance college courses for engineers alongside their work onboard (see information on training courses below).

Officers

The *Chief Engineer* (almost invariably referred to simply as 'The Chief') is in charge of this department. As the engineering equivalent of the Captain, he has a highly responsible position and is assisted by the *Staff Chief Engineer* (his second-in-command) and *Chief Electrician.*

The *Ship's Service Manager* (otherwise known as *Hotel Engineer* or similar-sounding title) is directly responsible for areas such as air conditioning, heating, refrigeration and plumbing systems. The SSM/ Hotel Engineer will usually be of First Engineer rank and, like all senior engineers, is likely to have already gained a Class I HND in Marine Engineering, otherwise known as his 'Chief's Ticket' (the engineering equivalent of a navigator's Master's Ticket). Below the rank of First Engineer are *Second, Third* and *Fourth Engineering Officers,* at appropriate stages of their training and careers.

But the journey through the ranks begins as an *Engineering Cadet.* Cadets should be between 16 and 22 years of age and are frequently recruited direct from school. Potential cadets should apply to the cruise lines for sponsorship during their final academic year and, once accepted by a company, will undergo an intensive three- or four-year training programme. This should combine both practical and theoretical education, leading to an HND in Marine Engineering.

The requirement for entry to the four-year course is at least five GCSE passes (preferably including physics and maths). To complete the course in three years, at least two A-level passes (including physics or maths) are needed. The first year is spent at college, the second year at sea, and the third (and fourth) years back at college. For further information contact the Coordinating Agent, Merchant Navy Training Board, Carthusian Court, 12 Carthusian Street, London EC1M 6EB, England; ☎020-7417 2800; fax 020-7726 2080; e-mail enquiries@mntb.org.uk; www.merchantnavy.com).

Electrical Engineers can pursue a similar career route, although obviously their speciality is the maintenance and repair of the ship's electrical systems. Most ships will have a *Chief, First* and *Second Electrician*, perhaps assisted by a Third and Fourth Electrician. Opportunities also occasionally exist for independently trained and suitably qualified electricians. These are usually recruited through maritime recruitment agencies (for contact details, see Recruitment Agencies below).

Increasingly, opportunities also exist for *Technical Engineers* with a strong computer background (generally to degree level) and

Communications Engineers, whose responsibilities may include the maintenance of the ship's internal telephone system (see also *The Radio Room*).

All these positions assume officer status and annual salaries of approximately $30,000 (£20,000) and upwards per annum.

Ratings

Various positions for *Ratings* (non-officers) exist in the technical, engineering and electrical sectors, including *Engineering* and *Electrical Assistants, Motormen* and *Plumbers,* but cruise lines almost invariably fill such posts with workers from countries such as Indonesia, Eastern Europe or the Philippines.

Should you be lucky enough to find a company to sponsor you, you could attend a three-month course for ratings at the National Sea Training College in Gravesend (address listed below). During this period you would gain instruction in ships' propulsion, auxiliary systems and machinery, with a view to becoming a Motorman.

Note, however, that as the workings of ships become increasingly sophisticated and automated, it is the jobs at the more manual end of the scale that are rapidly being reduced. The sweating 'donkeymen' with their grease-soaked vests and soot-stained neckerchiefs are nowadays seen only in old movies.

Training

The following colleges offer specialist courses for those wishing to pursue a nautical career in engineering.

Glasgow College of Nautical Studies, 21 Thistle Street, Glasgow G5 9XB, Scotland; ☎0141-565 2500; fax 0141-565 2599; e-mail enquiries@gcns.ac.uk; www.glasgow-nautical.ac.uk.

Liverpool John Moores University, Roscoe Court, 4 Rodney Street, Liverpool L1 2TZ, England; ☎0151-231 5090; fax 0151-231 3462; www. ljmu.ac.uk.

National Sea Training Centre, North West Kent College, Dering Way, Gravesend, Kent DA12 2JJ, England; ☎01322-629600; fax 01322-629682; www.nwkcollege.ac.uk.

South Tyneside College, Faculty of Electrical & Electronic Engineering, St. George's Avenue, South Shields, Tyne & Wear NE34 6ET, England; ☎0191-427 3500; fax 0191-427 3535; e-mail info@stc.ac.uk;

www.stc.ac.uk.

Southampton Institute, School of Maritime and Coastal Studies, East Park Terrace, Southampton, Hampshire SO14 0RT, England; ☎023-8031 9039; fax: 023-8022 2259; e-mail enquiries@solent.ac.uk; www. solent.ac.uk/maritime.

University of Greenwich, Maritime Greenwich Campus, Old Royal Naval College, Park Row, London SE10 9LS, England; ☎0800-005 006; fax 020-8331 8145; e-mail courseinfo@gre.ac.uk; www.gre.ac.uk.

University of Plymouth, Drake Circus, Plymouth PL4 8AA; ☎01752-232137; fax 01752-232014; e-mail admissions@plymouth.ac.uk; www.plymouth.ac.uk.

Recruitment Agencies

If you already possess relevant marine engineering, technical or electrical engineering skills and qualifications, contact the cruise lines direct or the following specialist agencies. Note that these companies have placements for deck officers and ratings, as well as for engineering officers and ratings. Occasionally vacancies in the hotel department are also registered with them. Conversely, companies such as *BlueSeas International Cruise Services,* (www.jobxchange.com) which are listed as hiring hotel staff may also recruit deck and engine personnel (see *Useful Addresses for Jobs in the Hotel Department*).

Trade newspapers provide information and job advertisements relating to all areas of maritime engineering. One particularly useful publication is *The Telegraph* published by NUMAST (National Union of Marine & Aviation Shipping Transport). See *Further Reading* at the end of the book for details.

CTI Group Inc, 3696 Federal Highway, Suite 303, Fort Lauderdale, Florida 33308, USA; ☎954-568 5900; fax 954-568 5888; e-mail CTI-USA@cti-usa.com; www.cti-usa.com.

Crewfinders International, 404 & 408 SE 17th Street, Fort Lauderdale, Florida 33316, USA; ☎954-522 2739; fax 954-761 7700; e-mail crew@crewfinders.com; www.crewfinders.com.

Delta Marine Personnel Services Ltd, Office Suite 2, Lockside Marina, Navigation Road, Chelmsford CM2 6HF, England; ☎01245-251377; fax 01245-495583; e-mail crewdept@deltamarine.co.uk; www.deltamarine.co.uk.

Döhle (IOM), Fort Anne, South Quay, Douglas, Isle of Man IM1 5PD, UK; ☎01624-649649; fax 01624-673717; e-mail info@doehle-iom.

com; www.midocean.co.im.

Humber Ship Services (Recruitment Agency), Carlisle House, Carlisle Street, Goole, North Humberside DN14 5DS, England; ☎01405-767229.

International Cruise Services, 36 Midlothian Drive, Glasgow G41 3QU; ☎0141-649 8644; fax 0141-636 1016; www.cruiseservices.co.uk.

International Marine Manning Services, Larkfield House, 14 River Road, Lambeg, Lisburn, County Antrim BT27 4SD, Northern Ireland; ☎028-9062 6215; fax 028-9062 6610; www.internationalmarine.co.uk.

Marine Recruitment Co, Riverside Business Centre, Riverside Road, Lowestoft, Suffolk NR33 0TQ, England; ☎01502-537188; fax 01502-531199; e-mail info@marine-recruitment.co.uk; www.marine-recruitment.co.uk.

Martinoli Consulting Monaco, 7 rue du Gabian, MC-98000, Monaco; ☎9205 0280; fax 9205 4938.

Sealife Crewing Services, 19-23 Canute Road, Southampton, Hampshire SO14 3FJ, England; ☎023-8022 3546; fax 023-8022 8446; www.sealifecrewing.co.uk.

Seamariner Ltd, 114-118 Hampton Lane Blackfield, Southampton, Hampshire SO45 1WE, England; ☎023-8089 0432; fax 023-8089 0449; e-mail recruitment@seamariner.ltd.uk; www.seamariner.com.

V-Ships UK, 5th Floor, Skypark, 8 Elliot Place, Glasgow G3 8EP, Scotland; ☎0141-243 2435; fax 0141-243 2436; e-mail vships.glasgow@vships.com; www.vships.com.

Viking Recruitment, Aycliffe Business Centre, Archcliffe Road, Dover, Kent CT17 9EL, England; ☎01304-240881; fax 01304-240882; e-mail info@vikingrecruitment.com; www.vikingrecruitment.com.

In the Words of an Engineer

I'm a second engineer on a 70,000GRT cruise ship in the Caribbean. Maintaining such a large vessel certainly keeps us busy. No sooner do we finish at one end than we have to start again at the other. As for exercise, who needs the gym when you can walk miles just getting from deck to deck?

Needless to say, I hardly ever get off the ship. To be honest, it's not just the time, it's making the effort. When you get to my age you've been to most of the ports many times before. All I want to do when I finish work now is sit in the Ward Room (Officers' bar), have a few beers and relax.

> *Some of the younger guys spend a lot of time trying to keep up with technology and taking one exam after the other. You need those pieces of paper more than ever before and if I were trying to get my job all over again I probably wouldn't even be accepted. But I'm not bothered about promotion and I can live quite comfortably on my salary of $28,000 (£18,500) a year, all found.*
>
> *Like the navigators, we work Watches. I'm on the eight to twelve at the moment, but often things crop up that mean we have to work well over our Watch hours. There might be a problem with the air-conditioning, for example, or a flood. We don't get many burst pipes on this particular ship, but on older vessels the plumbing can be a nightmare. I've even had to help extinguish a couple of fires in my time. I was on one ship that burnt right out due to an engine room fire that blazed out of control. We got everyone off, but it shakes you up something like that. In fact, it almost made me leave the job.*
>
> *I sometimes wonder why I didn't quit. It wasn't for lack of opportunity, as engineering skills can always be used on land. I was even offered a couple of shore-based jobs around that time. Leaving the ships might have also saved my marriage. My ex-wife always wanted me to stay at home. So why didn't I? I guess it's the sea salt – it gets in the blood.*
>
> **Jim MacDonald (age 54)**

THE RADIO ROOM

The Radio Room is the ship's link to the outside world, and the station for all its radio, telex, telegraph, telephone and satellite communications. Although affiliated to Technical & Engineering, the radio room is something of an isolated unit in the overall workings of the ship. For obvious reasons, it is usually located within close proximity of the navigational bridge and this also forges a link with the deck department.

In charge of this division is the *Chief Radio Officer* who, depending on the size of the vessel, may have several assistants. The duties of the *Radio Officers* include urgent distress, weather and traffic communications, general ship's business (e-mails, calls and faxes to and from Head Office) and the personal correspondence of passengers and crew.

As with any job of this kind, discretion and confidentiality are essential. The other current requirement is a GMDSS Certificate, which has in effect replaced the higher standard MRGC (Maritime Radio General Certificate), which included elements of Morse Code operation.

On older vessels the plumbing can be a nightmare

With advancements in digital communication and the demise of the Morse Code, the role of Radio Officer is rapidly changing. Many companies are even phasing them out in favour of lesser-qualified *Radio Assistants*. But trainees still need to serve a cumulative minimum of six months at sea in order to validate their GMDSS Certificate and operate the ship's radio equipment single-handed.

Having achieved the basic GMDSS Certificate, anyone wishing to pursue a serious career in this field should aim for an HND Engineering in Electronics and Communications. This is generally a two-year course, but an OND (Ordinary National Diploma) in electronics is an entry requirement that would be considered equivalent to two years of study. It is advisable to study for both OND and HND qualifications at the same establishment in order to avoid any omissions in syllabus modules.

For employment in this field, together with a monthly earning potential of around $2,000 (£1,350) for radio assistants and upwards of $2,500 (£1,650) to $3,500 (£1,910) for radio officers, write direct to the cruise lines or contact the independent agencies listed above (under *Recruitment Agencies*).

Training

All British colleges offering courses for Radio Officers and related personnel are affiliated to the AMERC (Association of Marine Electronics and Radio Colleges, Wray Castle, Ambleside, Cumbria LA22 0JB, England; ☎01539-440218; fax 01539-440219; www.amerc.ac.uk). They include:

Jewel & Esk Valley College, 24 Milton Road East, Edinburgh EH15 2PP, Scotland; ☎0131-660 1010; fax: 0131-657 2276; e-mail info@jevc. ac.uk; www.jevc.ac.uk.

Glasgow College of Nautical Studies, 21 Thistle Street, Glasgow G5 9XB, Scotland; ☎0141-565 2500; fax 0141-565 2599; e-mail enquiries@gcns.ac.uk; www.glasgow-nautical.ac.uk.

South Tyneside College, Faculty of Electrical & Electronic Engineering, St George's Avenue, South Shields, Tyne & Wear NE34 6ET, England; ☎0191-427 3500; fax 0191-427 3535; e-mail info@stc.ac.uk; www.stc.ac.uk.

Southampton Institute, East Park Terrace, Southampton, Hampshire SO14 0RT, England; ☎023-8031 9000; fax 023-8033 4161; e-mail enquiries@ssolent.ac.uk; www.solent.ac.uk.

University of Leeds, The University, Leeds LS2 9JT, England; ☎0113-343 3999; fax 0113-343 3877; e-mail admissions@adm.leeds.ac.uk; www.leeds.ac.uk.

Wray Castle College, Bridge Mills, Stramongate, Kendal LA9 4UB, Cumbria, England; ☎01539-742740; fax 01539-742743; e-mail training@wraycastle.com; www.wraycastle.com.

Medical

Considering the hundreds or, indeed, thousands of passengers and crew on the average ship, it is hardly surprising that a reasonably equipped hospital should be a fairly standard feature. What may be surprising, however, is that sea sickness is rarely the main complaint. Medical problems of all descriptions from cardiac arrests to workplace accidents need to be swiftly treated. Although patients may later be 'landed' to shoreside hospitals, it is the members of the ship's medical team who have to cope in the interim. For this reason, a strong Accident & Emergency background is preferred for applicants to this department.

Opportunities for Medical Staff

In charge of the Medical Department is the *Principal Medical Officer* (PMO). Depending on the size of the ship, he/she may be the only doctor, although very large vessels are more likely to have two fully-qualified *Medical Officers* (Doctors). Ships' doctors, referred to as surgeons by naval tradition, tend to be general practitioners rather than specialists (although a surprising number of Soviet gynaecologists seem to find employment, most notably on ships of Greek registry!).

Doctors employed by large companies and on ships catering mainly to North American passengers, are generally licensed in the US, Canada or Great Britain. They automatically receive senior officer status (usually three stripes) together with the appropriate salary and conditions. Depending on the cruise company, ships' doctors might also retain a proportion of the treatment fees charged to passengers. Thus, the earning potential of the PMO of a busy ship's hospital could be considerably more than even the Master of the vessel. Note, however, that this situation is gradually changing and cruise lines are increasingly likely to retain 100% of treatment fees.

It has to be said that the standard of medical services and the status given to doctors varies drastically from line to line. Some companies hire medical staff from a variety of countries and disciplines and on short-term contracts amounting to little more than a working holiday. But some (notably, US) medical organisations are becoming increasingly aware of the special demands of shipboard medical practices and now operate specific divisions in cruise medicine. One of the forerunners is the American College of Emergency Physicians (ACEP) which operates a Cruise Ship & Maritime Medicine Section (CSMMS).

In most cases, ships' doctors are assisted by a team of other medical personnel. Qualified and experienced *Nurses* (RGN or equivalent), preferably with a strong Accident & Emergency or Intensive Care background, are frequently needed. Many ships employ only one nurse, but some vessels may require two or more onboard at any time, including a *Senior Nurse*. Nurses generally receive two-stripe officer status and a salary of $33,000 (£18,000) and upwards per year.

Some ships will employ one or two *Medical Orderlies* with appropriate training and experience. Medical orderlies often have Petty Officer status and an accompanying annual salary of $15,000 (£10,000) and upwards.

On smaller vessels, the nurse and/or orderly may also act as dispenser, whereas very large ships may employ a qualified *Medical Dispenser* (also a Petty Officer) on a full-time basis.

Two other positions found only on larger vessels are those of a qualified and experienced *Physiotherapist* and *Dentist*. Qualified dentists with a minimum of two years' experience can earn from \$4,800 (£2,600) to \$7,000 (£3,800) a month. On most ships the doctor will administer emergency treatment or pain-killers until a suitable appointment can be made for the passenger or crew member to consult a shoreside dentist or physiotherapist. Only on larger ships (and even then, only on longer cruises) can the luxury of an onboard dentist or physio be accommodated, which is why these professionals tend to work at sea for just several months of the year, as a supplement to their work on land.

Anyone wishing to apply for medical positions at sea should contact the cruise lines direct and compare contractual terms. *Cruise Ship & Maritime Medical Co* (4822 NW 167th Street, Miami, Florida 33014, USA; ☎305-474 5757; fax 305-474 5755; www.cruiship-maritimedical.

Most ships have a small mortuary

com) also recruits medical staff for cruise ships. *Six Star Dentistry* (2881 Leeward Way, Bellingham, Washington 98226, USA; ☎360-758 2326; fax 360-758 4231; www.seadent.com) places US-trained dentists on cruise ships on a working holiday basis.

In the Words of a Nurse

I am employed as a nurse onboard a cruise ship currently sailing the Indian Ocean. I have worked on six different ships over the past seven years, and each ship has been quite different in terms of the medical facilities it offers. These range from the well-equipped hospital with full operating theatre and isolation units to basic sick bays without even an X-ray machine. This means you really have to be quite adaptable. An ability to cope (or at least appear to cope) is an important asset, especially in what for a land-based nurse may be difficult or unusual circumstances. Rough seas, for example, can affect your duties, even though the hospital will be situated in the most stable part of the ship (towards the middle of a lower deck). Working conditions may be more cramped than is usual onshore; and you are frequently faced with medical decisions that would not be expected of a nurse in a shoreside hospital.

The amount of responsibility I had was the hardest factor for me to accept when I first started working at sea. Even with a strong background in Intensive Care and Accident & Emergency, I was simply not used to being the only trained person around when a medical emergency arose. My current ship has about 600 passengers, 300 crew members and the medical team consists of one doctor and one nurse. Outside the surgery hours (which we work together), the doctor and I work an alternating duty rota that includes days in port. This means he could be ashore at the very time the carpenter cuts an artery or a passenger has a coronary. And I then have to deal with the situation single-handed.

We operate surgery hours with different times for passengers and crew, although we may also be called out at all times of the day or night to deal with emergency and, annoyingly, non-emergency cases. That's the thing with this job. You never know what tomorrow will bring. You can be having an easy cruise when, all of a sudden, someone needs intensive care and your working hours are suddenly doubled.

Of course, if the patient is dangerously ill or in need of a major operation, the doctor may decide to land them to an onshore hos-

pital. I've known several occasions when the ship has actually changed course and altered its itinerary because of such emergencies. But naturally, considerations such as the medical standards and facilities of the country in question are taken into account. It would usually be crazy, for example, to get the ship's agents to deal with all the arrangements and legislation of landing a patient in Alexandria if the very next day the ship is due to call at Haifa.

On this subject, I'm always asked if we get many deaths on board and whether or not we have a mortuary. Naturally, with so many passengers and crew members, especially in view of the age group of many of the passengers, occasional deaths are inevitable. When they occur, however, the situation can be more traumatic for the bereaved than if it were onshore because of the unfamiliar environment. One of the hardest aspects of my job is trying to give comfort to some elderly lady, who has probably never before ventured out of Sutton Coldfield and is unexpectedly widowed on her first cruise. To see her, now faced with the prospect of being landed in, say, Mombasa with her hastily-packed cases and the body of her late husband, is heart-rending, to say the least. But, beyond sympathy, all you can do is hope the ship's agents will help her through the formalities.

Burials at sea are very uncommon nowadays because of the need for a coroner's report, and the majority of corpses are flown home for burial. Most ships have a small mortuary, situated in or near the hospital, although I did work on one vessel where lack of space meant a body was kept in a refrigerated cheese store. Needlesss to say, the crew's demand for Danish Blue hit an all-time low that week.

Apart from the job itself, which can be very rewarding, I especially enjoy the travel aspect of working on cruise ships. I have a particular interest in archaeology, so to visit places such as Chichen Itza, Giza, Ephesus and Olympia is a great bonus for me.

On the down side, ours can be a sexist department where male doctors are frequently employed in preference to female and female nurses in preference to male. Also, promotion prospects are nil. You come in as a nurse, you go out as a nurse. I have considered returning to nursing on shore, but I think I would find it boring now. On land, I might work in Outpatients, a Surgical or Intensive Care Unit or Accident & Emergency department. At sea, I work in all of them at the same time!

Carole Henderson (age 35)

Which Line?
Which Ship?

We have now considered the huge range of opportunities for employment provided by various departments of a cruise ship. But each cruise line and every ship is different, and it is worth becoming acquainted with some of these differences.

To the puzzled job-seeker thumbing through a handful of cruise brochures, the seven seas may seem truly unfathomable, such are the choices available. Add to this the frequent changes in the industry – not to mention numerous ships and companies with confusingly similar names – and one may easily feel swamped by possibilities.

Whether you go for the theory that 'biggest is best' or prefer the approachability of a smaller line; whether you like the aristocratic or the more plebeian lines, you will want to be assured that you have found the most suitable conditions and the best deal for your particular skills.

It should be noted that the cruise line industry is constantly evolving, with companies merging, expanding or sometimes going out of business.

Which Line ?

THE CRUISE LINES

The following descriptions of most of the major and many minor cruise lines (in alphabetical order) and their respective vessels may help you to distinguish between them. Contact details are listed under *Addresses of Cruise Lines and Other Companies* and additional information is included in the sections *Who Owns What?* and *Cruise Ship Listing.*

African Safari Club
This hotel and tourism group operates the tiny ship, *Royal Star* on year-round cruising in the Indian Ocean out of Mombasa. As the vessel only employs approximately 140 crew members, however, recruitment opportunities are limited. Applicants must be able to speak fluent German.

Aida Cruises
This line (a Carnival Group company) operates the *AIDAcara, AIDAvita, AIDAaura* and *AIDAblu* ships with distinctive faces painted along their bows. These ships cater for the German market so crew will need appropriate language skills.

Carnival Cruise Lines
Undisputably one of the cruise industry's current leaders, Carnival Cruise Lines operates a mammoth fleet of large, modern, high-action *fun-ships*, based mainly in Caribbean and Mexican waters. The fleet comprises some of the largest cruise ships in the world (such as *Carnival Liberty, Carnival Valor* and *Carnival Glory*), each offering job opportunities for approximately 1,000 crew members. But Carnival leads the way not only in ship size but also in cruising's design revolution. While Carnival's designs have evolved throughout the years, its vessels still feature striking interiors that provide a dramatic departure from anything else at sea.

Love or loathe Carnival's razzle-dazzle approach, the company's mainstream marketing success cannot be denied. The giant Carnival Corporation which owns Carnival Cruise Lines has also staked a larger claim on other regions of the industry. It also owns Holland America Line, Cunard Line, Seabourn Cruise Line, Windstar Cruises, Costa Cruises, Princess Cruises, P&O Cruises, P&O Cruises Australia, Aida Cruises,

Swan Hellenic and Ocean Village (job-seekers should apply directly to the individual lines).

If you are looking to work hard and play hard, then Carnival should be the company for you. As for sun, sea and the high life, it can only be assumed that these are all perks of the job in a workplace called *Ecstasy, Fantasy* or *Elation.*

Celebrity Cruises

Originally a division of the long-established Greek company, Chandris, this line is a subsidiary of Royal Caribbean International. Celebrity Cruises is one of the leaders in the upper mid-stream of cruising. The Celebrity fleet currently comprises nine large, well-facilitated, hi-tech vessels, boasting suitably evocative names (*Century, Constellation, Galaxy, Infinity, Mercury, Millennium, Summit,* and *Zenith*).

Cruising mainly in American and Caribbean waters, each Celebrity ship employs between 600 and 900 people, including mostly Greek officers. *Celebrity Xpedition* began cruising around Galapagos islands in 2004 and is the first major cruise line to do so. In 2005, the company will operate a summer cruising programme in Europe. Applicants from the UK should send a CV to Crown Recruitment UK (e-mail shipjob@aol. com; www.workonship.co.uk), Celebrity's recruitment agency.

Classic International Cruises

Four ships, *Arion, Athena, Funchal* and *Princess Danae*, sail from the eight British ports of Dundee, Harwich, Hull, Liverpool, Tilbury, Portsmouth, Rosyth and Southampton to destinations including the Norwegian Fjords, Spitzbergen and North Cape, Iceland, the Baltic and British Isles.

Club Méditerranée (Club Med)

This well-known French holiday resort specialist currently operates one of the world's largest sail-cruisers (a cross between a modern cruise ship and a sailing ship). *Club Med II* boasts huge computerised sails, an 'elegantly casual' ambience and good watersports facilities. Following the sale of her 'sister ship' *Club Med I,* she has taken over the Caribbean and Mediterranean itineraries.

Compagnie des Isles du Ponant

This French line operates the sleek, yacht-like *Le Levant,* the unusual hi-tech sail-cruiser, *Le Ponant,* and *Le Diamant* (formerly *Song of Flower)* started cruising again in 2004. *Le Ponant* is something of a cross between a small, deluxe cruise ship and a sailing ship, and has fully-automated sails (no scaling the rigging here), offering the romance of sailing without the discomfort. Be warned, however, that fluent French-speakers only are employed on these vessels and that with less than 100 crew members between them, work opportunities are limited. However, most of *Le Levant's* cruises are chartered through Tauck Tours in the USA so English-speaking guides are required.

Costa Cruises

One of the biggest and newest fleets in the world, Costa Cruises is a long-established Italian Line (Costa Crociere) that is now part of Carnival. Costa is a leader in mainstream cruising catering to a European market. The eleven ships operate in Caribbean and Mediterranean waters, North Europe and South America.

In keeping with its heritage, Costa employs many Italian officers and Italian themes prevail. This line is also a popular choice with Italian, French and other European passengers, so linguists could find their skills in demand.

Croatia Cruise Lines

This company operates a single petite vessel, the *Dalmacija,* that is marketed to mostly German-speaking passengers. It is not a major source of employment opportunities.

Crystal Cruises

If working on a deluxe cruise ship is your specific aim, you should definitely consider applying to Crystal Cruises, owners of the magnificent *Crystal Serenity* and *Crystal Symphony.* These modern vessels epitomise the changes that have taken place in passenger ship design over recent years. Once aboard, within sight of the waterfall (no less) in the spacious lobby, you could be excused for thinking you were not afloat at all, but rather in an elegant five star hotel. Bigger than most ships in this price bracket, these two 'sisters' provide job opportunities – and excellent crew accommodation – for more than 500 crew members apiece.

Cunard Line

At the long-established, traditional end of the cruising industry, Cunard Line is now part of the giant Carnival Corporation. The Cunard ships provide Carnival with a truly deluxe fleet, comprising the *Queen Elizabeth*

2 and the gargantuan new *Queen Mary 2*, the largest and most expensive passenger vessel ever built. The third queen, *Queen Victoria*, will be launched in 2005. *Queen Mary 2* has taken over the transatlantic journeys from the QE2 which now operates a UK-UK cruising programme (including two annual world cruises). Currently, however – and despite competition from all those new superships – the *QE2* is still the most famous vessel sailing the high seas. Ports as far removed as Liverpool, Hong Kong and Auckland reserve a special welcome for 'The Queen', and in Japan she is, quite simply, a superstar.

Kieran Lynch, a 25 year-old barman from Dublin, describes the ship's departure from the port of Kagoshima:
We didn't sail until late in the evening and I remember hundreds if not thousands of local people descending on the harbour to watch us leave. They were all clammering for souvenirs, and passengers were throwing postcards and beer mats down to them from the open decks. It was like something out of an old black-and-white movie. As we pulled away from the quayside, the ship sounded its horn

Tails may be worn in the evening

and 'Auld Lang Syne' started to play through the port loudspeakers. By then it was quite dark and all those on the dockside were waving little Chinese lanterns that lit up the night. Even when we were way out to sea, you could still make out those bobbing orange lights. There are so many special events during her World Cruise, but the highlight is always the 'Queen' herself.

Delphin Seereisen
The name of the cruise line and its chartered ship (*Delphin* and *Delphin Queen*), this company offers worldwide mid-budget cruises for a predominantly German-speaking clientele. Non-German-speaking job-seekers should try elsewhere.

Discovery World Cruises
A relatively new addition to the cruise market, Discovery World Cruises sail to exotic destinations, such as South Pacific, Caribbean and Galapagos in winter and Mediterranean, Iceland and Greenland in summer, onboard the 650-passenger *Discovery*.

Disney Cruise Line
The very company that leads the world in family theme parks, the giant Disney Corporation, launched the first of its ships (*Disney Magic*) in 1998, followed by *Disney Wonder*. The ships sail from Florida's Port Canaveral and package deals including the Disney World Resort and Disney's private island in the Bahamas. In 2005, *Disney Magic* will switch to Los Angeles for summer cruises to the Mexican Riviera.

The ships are classic in design, evocative of the golden age of ocean liners, but with the latest hi-tech facilities and all the familiar Disney faces. Needless to say, there are varied employment opportunities on these huge vessels for job-seekers. Children's counsellors and would-be Mickeys, Minnies and Plutos take note.

easyCruise
The 'serial entrepreneur' Stelios Haji-Ioannou, who entered the low-cost airline market with easyJet, has turned his attention to the cruise industry with the launch of *easyCruiseOne*, a small cruise liner with 54 crew. These cruises are aimed at the independently minded in their 20s, 30s and 40s and sail along the French and Italian Rivieras.

Fred. Olsen Cruise Lines

With a Norwegian heritage dating back to the mid-1800s, Fred. Olsen Cruise Lines operates four ships, *Black Watch, Black Prince, Braemar* and the latest acquisition *Boudicca*. These are vessels with a friendly, rather than sophisticated, ambience and cater mainly to mature British passengers. They offer a series of interesting worldwide itineraries and specialist theme cruises (good news for globe-trotting guest lecturers).

Hapag-Lloyd Cruises

An established leader at the upper end of the German cruise market, Hapag-Lloyd operates the deluxe mid-sized *Astra II, Columbus, Europa, and Hanseatic*. These are sophisticated ships, providing good opportunities for classical musicians and expert lecturers. They also offer unusual worldwide itineraries, one vessel (*Hanseatic*) even exploring the Arctic and Antarctic. With a mainly German-speaking clientele, however, an ability to speak German is a definite plus for work with this line.

Hebridean Island Cruises

The charming little *Hebridean Princess* and *Hebridean Spirit* employ between 38 and 65 all-British crew members for luxurious cruises around the west coast of Scotland, the Indian Ocean, Mediterranean and Baltic, the Red and Arabian Seas.

Holland America Line

A long-established leader in quality cruising, Holland America Line (HAL) has an impressive history dating back to the launch of the original *Rotterdam* in 1872. Now owned by the Carnival Corporation and catering to a predominantly American clientele, the line's Dutch heritage is still in evidence and the company continues to employ many Dutch officers.

Holland America's large fleet currently consists of mostly mid-sized, modern vessels offering a range of worldwide itineraries. In particular, HAL is a good bet for those seeking work in the Caribbean or Alaska.

Imperial Majesty Cruise Line

After the demise of Regal Cruises in 2003, Imperial Majesty Cruise Line purchased *Regal Empress* and after a total refit in 1997 she now sails regularly from Port Everglades to Nassau in the Bahamas.

Island Cruises

A UK-based joint venture between Royal Caribbean Cruises and First

Choice Holidays, this company operates two cruise liners: *Island Escape*, which cruises the Mediterranean in summer and Brazil in winter, and *Island Star* (formerly Celebrity Cruises' *Horizon*).

Kristina Cruises

A family-owned Finish shipping company operating *Kristina Regina* and *Kristina Brahe* on cruises in the Mediterranean, Baltic Sea, Norwegian fjords and sailings from Helsinki to St Petersburg. Completely Finnish crew.

Louis Cruise Lines

This Cyprus-based company (with mostly Greek officers) currently operates a fleet of older vessels on short itineraries to Egypt, Syria, Beirut and around the Greek Islands. An extension of holiday packages in Cyprus, these 'mini-cruises' are more akin to a ferry service than conventional cruising, but nevertheless there are various job opportunities here, especially in the retail sector (Louis operates its own duty-free shops).

Mediterranean Shipping Cruises (MSC)

MSC is the passenger division of the large, Italian, Mediterranean Shipping Company. It currently operates seven mid-sized, traditional ships, offering affordable all-year-round cruising in the Mediterranean, Caribbean, to Northern Europe, South America and South Africa. Two new ships are under construction, *Musica* (delivery June 2006) and *Orchestra* (2007).

With mostly Italian officers and restaurant staff and many Italians among its international mix of passengers, MSC could be especially good news for Italian-speaking linguists and pasta chefs.

Mitsui O.S.K. Passenger Line (MOPAS)

The mid-sized (often corporately chartered) vessel (*Fuji Maru*) of this line follow itineraries that include Southeast Asia, Alaska, Australia and a world cruise. As MOPAS caters for predominantly Japanese passengers, however, Japanese-speakers only should apply.

Norwegian Cruise Line (NCL)

One of the established leaders of the mid-range cruise market, Norwegian Cruise Line is, despite its name, an American-based company owned by Star Cruises. In keeping with its title and Scandinavian roots, however, the line employs many Norwegian officers and the names of many of its ships have Norwegian associations (*Norwegian Dawn, Norwegian Dream*). *Pride of Hawaii* will join the fleet in 2006, while *Pride of Amer-*

ica joined in 2005.

The NCL flagship is the famous *Norway* (formerly the *France*) – one of the last great ocean liners and still the longest cruise ship in the world. With this mature vessel as a notable exception, NCL operates a fairly modern fleet, based predominantly in the Caribbean and the Americas.

Ocean Village

A division of Carnival UK, Ocean Village offers informal holidays in the Mediterranean and Caribbean aimed at the 30 to 50 year-old age bracket on board Ocean Village. A second ship, Princess Cruises' *Regal Princess*, will be added to the fleet at the end of 2006 and renamed.

Oceania Cruises

A relatively new cruise line (formed in 2002) and based in Miami, Oceania offers traditional premium and luxury category. Its three mid-sized ships, *Insignia, Regatta* and *Nautica,* cruise to the Mediterranean, Caribbean, Scandinavia, Mexico, Black Sea, Central and South America, Russia and the British Isles.

Orient Lines

Now part of the Star Cruises group, Orient Lines operates the mid-sized *Marco Polo.* Sailing itineraries with Orient are often destination-intensive providing opportunities for guest lecturers and specialist experts.

P & O Cruises

A long-standing British company with an enviable pedigree that dates back to the early 1800s. Over the years, the line has amassed a loyal following among both passengers and crew members and is a good source of employment for British officers and staff.

P & O Cruises is part of Carnival Corporation which also includes Cunard, Princess Cruises, Ocean Village, Seabourn Cruises and Swan Hellenic. P&O's own ships are *Artemis, Aurora, Oceana, Oriana, Pacific Sky* and *Pacific Sun.* P&O's newest flagship is the 85,000-ton *Arcadia*, built in 2005, with a crew of 869.

Peter Deilmann Cruises

Alongside its nine deluxe European riverboats, this established German company operates the upmarket cruise ship *Deutschland* (new star of the television series, *Traumschiff* – the German equivalent of *The Love Boat*, replacing its predecessor *Berlin*). As Peter Deilmann Cruises caters almost exclusively to German-speaking passengers, an ability to speak German is a must for work with this line.

Phoenix Reisen
This German company markets a fleet of older styled ships (mostly under long-term charter from European companies such as V-Ships) with some unusual worldwide itineraries. Phoenix attracts predominantly German-speaking passengers. The flagship, *Maxim Gorki,* is one of the world's most easily-recognised vessels on account of its unusual funnel.

Princess Cruises
The larger, more 'American' division of the P & O Group, Princess Cruises is the company forever associated with *The Love Boat*, the television series originally filmed on the *Pacific Princess* which sold the romance of cruising to millions of viewers in almost a hundred countries. The fleet has since been upgraded and expanded in recent years to now include eight ships and three of the mammoth *Grand Princess* class (five times the tonnage of *Pacific Princess*). Despite this 'expansion' the publicity brochures ensure that the *Love Boat* lives on.

With each vessel of this large fleet requiring between 500 and 1,000 crew members, Princess is currently one of the cruise industry's major employers. It is a particularly good bet for British job-seekers and employs many British officers. Keen travellers should note that Princess also offers more diverse worldwide itineraries than many of its mainstream rivals.

Radisson Seven Seas Cruises
Floating very much at the upper end of the cruise market, this luxury fleet comprises several very different, yet equally stylish vessels. These are the Tahiti-based *Paul Gauguin*, the the deluxe medium-sized *Seven Seas Navigator,* and the larger, all-suite, all-balcony *Seven Seas Mariner* and *Seven Seas Voyager*. The latter are part of the line's long-term expansion programme.

ResidenSea
In 2004, the floating apartment block cum cruise ship *The World* converted its guest suites into 106 apartments, 40 veranda studios and 19 new studio apartments. The price of residences range from $1.3 million to $7.52 million and most are available to rent. Following a worldwide itinerary, owners and passengers onboard *The World* have exclusive access to events around the world, such as the Rio Carnival, Monaco Grand Priz, and Cannes Film Festival. The number of international crew and staff on

this luxury residential ship equal the number of owners/passengers.

Royal Caribbean International

If cruising to you means the Caribbean, this could be the company for you. Currently one of the world's biggest cruise lines, Royal Caribbean International (RCI), and its subsidiary Celebrity Cruises, has a worldwide fleet but, in keeping with its name, bases the majority of its ships in West Indian waters for at least part of the year. Large, modern and well-facilitated, RCI vessels each display a distinctive blue anchor logo as part of an easily identifiable corporate image that attracts a faithful, predominantly American, following of passengers. RCI currently operates 19 ships.

Always at the forefront of cruise ship innovation, the larger ships include 9-hole golf courses and rock-climbing facilities. To be launched in 2006, *Freedom of the Seas* will be one of the largest cruise ships ever built at 158,000 tons. Royal Caribbean International provides plenty of employment opportunities in all sectors of the industry. Applicants from the UK should send their CVs to Crown Recruitment (e-mail shipjob@aol. com; www.workonship.co.uk), RCL's recruitment agency.

Saga Holidays

Saga is a travel company for the over-50s that operates its own cruise ships, the mid-sized *Saga Rose* and *Saga Ruby*. Cruise destinations include the Baltic, Mediterranean, Canary Islands, Caribbean, New York, Boston, Quebec, and Montreal. With frequent sailings out of Dover and with predominantly British officers, this line could be of particular interest to British job-seekers.

Seabourn Cruise Line

This Carnival-owned company's fleet currently consists of three deluxe, small, yacht-like cruise ships, offering a range of unusual worldwide itineraries. Seabourn has always been a leader (many would say *the* leader) in the upper end of the cruising market and its standards of service are high. If you have the relevant experience and enjoy working in a sophisticated atmosphere, this could be the line for you.

SeaEscape

Operates the casino/party ship, *Island Adventure*, which cruises from Port Evergaldes to nowhere. It's South Florida's longest running entertainment attraction at sea.

Silversea Cruises
Competing in the luxury cruise market with a range of worldwide itineraries, Silversea operates four modern ships, *Silver Cloud, Silver Wind*
and the larger *Silver Shadow* and *Silver Whisper.* These ships offer watersports facilities and while they have cigar smoking lounges, these are for
passengers not crew.

Star Cruises
The largest cruise line in Asia-Pacific and the third largest in the world,
Star Cruises operates a modern fleet of various-sized vessels. The com-
pany has, in recent years, acquired Norwegian Cruise Line and Orient
Lines. Star Cruises offers scheduled itineraries to some of the most
exotic and exciting destinations in the region from the hubs of Singapore,
Taiwan, Hong Kong and India. Its passengers are from Asian- as well as
English-speaking countries, while the crew is international in composition. Knowledge of Chinese, Japanese or other Asian languages would be
useful when applying to this line.

Swan Hellenic
This is a British-based upscale line, offering destination-orientated cruises
aboard its single modern ship, *Minerva II.* With the emphasis on education rather than entertainment, expert lecturers on subjects ranging from
literature to marine biology could strike it lucky here. Variety acts, on the
other hand, should send their demo tapes elsewhere.

Thomson Cruises
Competing in the burgeoning family cruise market, this division of Thomson Holidays currently charters three mid-sized vessels. These are *Emerald, Thomson Celebration, Thomson Destiny* and *Thomson Spirit.* This
line might appeal particularly to British job-seekers who enjoy a 'holiday
camp'-style workplace. Opportunities here, however, are more limited
than with its rivals because Thomson does not actually own its ships.

Transocean Cruise Lines
This German company operates the *Astor* and *Astoria.* Catering to an
almost exclusively German clientele, these vessels provide affordable
cruising in Europe and the Caribbean. An ability to speak German is a
must for work on these ships.

Windstar Cruises

Windstar operates an unusual fleet of modern hi-tech motor-sail-yachts – something of a cross between a small, luxury cruise ship and a sailing ship. A subsidiary of the Carnival Corporation, the fleet currently consists of the *Wind Star, Wind Spirit* (each with approximately 90 crew members) and the larger *Wind Surf* (with a crew of 188).

With exotic island-hopping itineraries and a range of watersports facilities (instructors take note), these vessels offer a more informal style of upmarket cruise than most of their competitors. A warning, however, to any would-be mariners who long to scale the rigging – those giant sails are computer-controlled.

Ship Charterers and Marketing Agents

The following travel companies are among the vast number of operators which frequently charter ships or market cruises of other companies. They are listed here merely to avoid confusion and clarify their status in the industry. Note that charterers and marketing agents are rarely in a position to offer shipboard employment.

Abercrombie & Kent is the sales and marketing company for *Explorer II* trips to the Antarctic.

Classical Cruises is an American-based company that markets special interest cruises and charters ships such as Swan Hellenic's *Minerva II*.

Equity Cruises markets various international cruise lines in the UK.

First Choice is a British charterer of Louis Cruise Lines' *Princesa Ausonia*.

Page & Moy is the UK marketing agent and charterer for Majestic International, owners of *Ocean Majesty* and *Ocean Monarch*.

Thomson Cruises (see The Cruise Lines).

Voyages of Discovery is a British charterer, specialising in educational and special interest cruises.

Voyages Jules Verne is the UK marketing agent for various riverboat companies, Leisure Cruises and African Safari Club.

Sprechen Sie Deutsch? German-speaking job-seekers may be interested to learn that the ships of Russian, Ukrainian and other East European companies are often chartered by German cruise operators. Alongside **Phoenix Reisen** and **Transocean Reederei** (see The Cruise Lines), these include **Holiday Kreuzfahrten** which charters *Mona Lisa* for Mediterranean cruises from Genoa and the Baltic from Kiel.

WHO OWNS WHAT?

Considering that more than a thousand cruise ships are currently operating around the world, including some that are more like upmarket ferries or floating casinos than cruise ships proper, keeping up with this transient industry can prove difficult.

Vessels frequently change hands and names and companies are taken over or merged. Royal Caribbean and the P&O Princess Group tried merging into the largest cruise operator in the world but, instead, the current largest operator, Carnival Corporation, bought P&O outright. Such mergers and negotiations aside, at the time of writing there were seven major players, with a whole host of subsidiary companies, between which you will find several smaller operators trying hard to survive. Several medium-sized enterprises have gone bust, with their ships being arrested, laid up or sold on, often to leasing companies. The business is now dominated by three of the major seven companies, Carnival, Royal Caribbean and Star Cruises, who account for 80% of the market.

In addition to these changes in the number of companies that make up the industry, the number of ships you can find work on is increasing. The floating apartment block cum cruise ship *The World* has been launched and Cunard (part of the Carnival Corporation) launched *Queen Mary 2,* the tallest, widest, and longest ship ever built. Although how long she'll hold that record isn't worth betting on in this rapidly changing industry as plans for Royal Caribbean's launch of a 160,000 ton cruiser are well advanced. At the time of writing there are at least 13 new ships under construction or planned, due to enter service between 2006 and 2007.

> **Bob Williams, a seasoned ship's Hotel Manager, comments on current developments and trends in the market**
> *The whole business is changing and more rapidly than ever before. Certainly, there's less stability than there used to be. In fact, you can't pick up a trade magazine these days without reading that yet another company has gone bust or been taken over by someone else. Nobody in shipping presumes they're going to have a job in six months time any more.*
>
> *Having said that, business is booming and cruising is still very much a growth industry. There's tremendous pressure on the companies to expand and upgrade their fleets. As I see it, it's this rapid expansion and development that is the root of the problem for some lines. They need to have new ships to keep up with their rivals, but*

> *they often can't afford what they're buying. And so, quite simply, they over spend. It's particularly hard for smaller companies to ward off the competition from 'the big boys', which is why some of them are being forced out of business or taken over.*
>
> *I know that none of this is unique to cruising. Look at how small retailers are being pushed aside by the megastores. But a huge monopoly is bad for any industry and is bound to reduce the element of choice for the customer.*

Taking into account the likelihood of overnight collapses, takeovers and expansions, it is advisable to consider the durability factor of companies, before applying to work for them. What follows is an alphabetical listing of cruise companies and the ships they operate. Cruise line addresses and further information on specific vessels are given later in the book.

Bear in mind that ships are often chartered by one company from another, making it difficult to know to whom it is appropriate to apply for a job. Russian/Ukrainian companies pose particular difficulties as the same vessel may be chartered by several different (often German) tour operators.

While the list here does not pretend to be exhaustive, it does include the major cruise lines and the names of the ships that make up their fleets. Company names are in bold type, ships are in italics. Note, however, that this list does not include all of the numerous operators of riverboats, coastal vessels, non-automated sailing ships and yachts, explorer vessels and passenger-cargo ships. Information on these companies and their fleets is to be found under the relevant sections of *Which Ship?* (under *Sailing Ships & Yachts; Riverboats & Coastal Vessels; Explorer Vessels & Passenger-Cargo Ships*).

African Safari Club
Royal Star

Aida Cruises
AIDAcara
AIDAvita
AIDAaura
AIDAblu

Andrew Weir Shipping (St Helena Cruises)
St. Helena

Carnival Cruise Lines
Carnival Conquest
Carnival Destiny
Carnival Glory
Carnival Legend
Carnival Liberty
Carnival Miracle
Carnival Pride
Carnival Spirit
Carnival Triumph
Carnival Valor
Carnival Victory
Celebration
Ecstasy
Elation
Fantasy
Fascination
Holiday
Imagination
Inspiration
Paradise
Sensation

Celebrity Cruises
Celebrity Xpedition
Century
Constellation
Galaxy
Infinity
Mercury
Millennium
Summit
Zenith

Classic International Cruises
Arion
Athena
Funchal
Princess Danae

Clipper Cruise Lines
Clipper Adventurer
Clipper Odyssey
Nantucket Clipper
Yorktown Clipper

Club Med Cruises
Club Med 2

Compagnie des Iles du Ponant
Le Diamant
Le Levant
Le Ponant

Costa Cruises
Costa Allegra
Costa Atlantica
Costa Classica
Costa Concordia
Costa Europa
Costa Fortuna
Costa Magica
Costa Marina
Costa Mediterranea
Costa Romantica
Costa Victoria

Croatia Cruise Lines
Dalmacija

Cruise West
Spirit of Oceanus

Crystal Cruises
Crystal Serenity
Crystal Symphony

Cunard Line
Queen Elizabeth 2
Queen Mary 2

Queen Victoria

Delphin Seereisen
Delphin
Delphin Queen

Discovery World Cruises
Discovery

Disney Cruise Line
Disney Magic
Disney Wonder

easyCruise
easyCruiseOne

Fred. Olsen Cruise Lines
Black Prince
Black Watch
Boudicca
Braemar

Hapag-Lloyd Cruises
Astra II
Columbus
Europa
Hanseatic

Hebridean Island Cruises
Hebridean Princess
Hebridean Spirit

Holland America Line
Amsterdam
Maasdam
Oosterdam
Prinsendam
Rotterdam
Ryndam
Statendam

Veendam
Volendam
Westerdam
Zaandam
Zuiderdam

Imperial Majesty Cruise Line
Regal Empress

Island Cruises
Island Escape
Island Star (formerly *Horizon*)

Kristina Cruises
Kristina Regina
Kristina Brahe

Louis Cruise Lines
Aquamarine
Ausonia
Calypso
Princesa Marissa
Sapphire
Serenade

Mediterranean Shipping Cruises
Armonia
Lirica
Melody
Monterey
Opera
Rhapsody
Sinfonia

Mitsui OSK Passenger Line
Fuji Maru

Norwegian Coastal Voyage (Hurtigruten)
Finnmarken
Kong Harald

Lofoten
Midnatsol
Narvik
Nordkapp
Nordlys
Nordnorge
Nordstjernen
Polarlys
Richard With
Trollfjord
Vesterålen

Norwegian Cruise Line
Norway
Norwegian Crown
Norwegian Dawn
Norwegian Dream
Norwegian Jewel
Norwegian Majesty
Norwegian Sea
Norwegian Spirit
Norwegian Star
Norwegian Sun
Norwegian Wind
Pride of Aloha (formerly *Norwegian Sky)*
Pride of America
Pride of Hawaii

Ocean Village

Ocean Village
Regal Princess

Oceania Cruises
Insignia
Nautica
Regatta

Orient Lines
Marco Polo

Peter Deilmann Cruises
Deutschland

P & O Cruises
Arcadia
Artemis
Aurora
Oceana
Oriana
Pacific Sky
Pacific Sun

Page & Moy
Ocean Majesty
Ocean Monarch

Phoenix Reisen
Albatros
Alexander von Humbold (formerly *Saga Pearl*)
Amadea (formerly *Asuka*)
Maxim Gorki

Princess Cruises
Caribbean Princess
Coral Princess
Dawn Princess
Diamond Princess
Golden Princess
Grand Princess
Island Princess
Pacific Princess
Sapphire Princess
Sea Princess
Star Princess
Sun Princess
Tahitian Princess

Radisson Seven Seas Cruises
Paul Gauguin
Seven Seas Mariner

Seven Seas Navigator
Seven Seas Voyager

ResidenSea
The World

Royal Caribbean International
Adventure of the Seas
Brilliance of the Seas
Empress of the Seas
Enchantment of the Seas
Explorer of the Seas
Freedom of the Seas
Grandeur of the Seas
Jewel of the Seas
Legend of the Seas
Majesty of the Seas
Mariner of the Seas
Monarch of the Seas
Navigator of the Seas
Radiance of the Seas
Rhapsody of the Seas
Serenade of the Seas
Sovereign of the Seas
Splendour of the Seas
Vision of the Seas
Voyager of the Seas

Saga Holidays
Saga Rose
Saga Ruby

Seabourn Cruise Line
Seabourn Legend
Seabourn Pride
Seabourn Spirit

Sea Cloud Cruises
Sea Cloud
Sea Cloud II

SeaDream Yacht Club
SeaDream I
SeaDream II

SeaEscape
Island Adventure

Silversea Cruises
Silver Cloud
Silver Shadow
Silver Whisper
Silver Wind

Star Clippers
Royal Clipper
Star Clipper
Star Flyer

Star Cruises
MegaStar Aries
MegaStar Taurus
Star Pisces
SuperStar Gemini
Superstar Libra
SuperStar Virgo

Swan Hellenic Cruises
Minerva II

Thomson Cruises
Emerald
Thomson Celebration
Thomson Destiny
Thomson Spirit

Transocean Cruise Lines
Astor
Astoria

Windstar Cruises
Wind Spirit
Wind Star
Wind Surf

Who owns whom?

The current state of play for the major players can be seen from this list:

Carnival Corporation:
Aida Cruises
Carnival Cruises
Costa Cruises
Cunard Line
Holland America Line
Ocean Village
P&O Cruises
P&O Cruises Australia
Princess Cruises
Seabourn Cruise Line
Swan Hellenic
Windstar Cruises

Nippon Yusen Kaisha:
Crystal Cruise Lines
NYK Cruises

Royal Caribbean International:
Celebrity Cruises
Royal Caribbean International

Star Cruises:
Norwegian Cruise Line
Orient Lines
Star Cruises
Cruise Ferries

Which Ship?

HOW OLD?

New Ships

With most of the major, and many of the minor, companies building new ships, the race is always on for the claim to fame of owning the biggest, fastest, newest or most innovative cruise ship in the world. Generally these are large ships: Cunard's new *Queen Mary 2* is the biggest, tallest, and widest afloat (150,000 GRT – gross registered tonnage) although she carries less passengers than, for example, Royal Caribbean's *Voyager of the Seas* (137,000 GRT), obviously the intention is to provide a luxurious and uncrowded cruise experience. In May 2006, Royal Caribbean will launch its supership, a 160,000 GRT cruiser, *Ultra-Voyager,* but Carnival is already talking about going one better and looking to build a vessel of between 170,000 and 180,000 tons. Not all new cruise ships are huge, of the seven ships in build at present, all are in the XL range (70,000 GRT

New ships can have drawbacks

and over) with four over 100,000 GRT. The main rush to build is coming from Carnival Cruises, Costa Cruise Line, Holland America Line, Mediterranean Shipping Cruises, Norwegian Cruise Line, Royal Caribbean International and Princess Cruises.

For the would-be employee though, size is not always everything, for example a Star Cruises Superstar class ship (75,000 GRT) carries 1,900 passengers and between 1,100 and 1,300 crew. Whereas Royal Caribbbean's *Explorer of the Seas* (137,000 GRT) carries 1,181 crew for 3,114 passengers.

Of course, to the traditionalist, the environmentalist, and even the experienced cruiser, most of these new ships are no better than floating apartment blocks with their deckless sides and high-rise sterns to maximise internal space. Some would say that they are nothing but ugly, polluting, impractical blots on the horizon. To the job-seeker, however, they're very good news indeed.

Old Ships

In contrast to what some regard as 'modern monstrosities', many European vessels (especially Greek and Ukrainian-registered ships) are well into middle-age and possibly almost pensionable. But there can be advantages to working on an older vessel. Wine steward, Georgiou Andropoulos, explains:

I have worked on seven different ships for three different companies, and I can honestly say I prefer the older ones. Sure, the newer ships are glitzier and easier to keep clean but they don't have the atmosphere that an old ship has. Atmosphere is like a good claret, it takes time to develop and mature. I know many people who would rather work on a 'tub' with a good atmosphere than a new ship straight from the yard. If a ship is new, so is the crew, and because people may be trying to prove themselves, they tend to enforce more rules and regulations. Plus, there are bound to be teething problems. 'Shake-down' trips and maiden voyages are invariably cruises from hell.

In terms of facilities, there may be more space for the passengers on a new ship but crew cabins are often small and you just don't get the craftsmanship that you did even 20 years ago. Neither can they take the weather. Because of their shallower draft, the slightest swell and they roll all over the place (seasickness suffer-

ers take note). Older ships were built to last. It is hard to imagine any of today's megaships still working in the year 2050.

While taking into account Georgiou's enthusiasm for ships of character, one should also consider the viewpoint of senior engineer, Eddie McKenzie:

Of course older ships have character. They are also more likely to have plumbing, sanitation and air-conditioning problems, together with difficulty in complying with modern fire and safety regulations. Many of the ferries and 'tubs' floating around the Mediterranean barely meet the standards set by the IMO and might well not pass a standard US Coastguard inspection. From a servicing point of view, give me a new ship any day!

HOW BIG?

Apart from the age of a vessel, the most important factor for the nautical job-seeker to bear in mind is size, because the size of a ship can make a huge difference to the working and social conditions.

Large Ships

Larger ships with as many as 3,000 passengers and more than 1,000 crew members obviously offer wider social possibilities and, sometimes, greater earning potential for those relying on tips. There may also be better crew facilities, including sports and leisure programmes. On the downside, large ships are more likely to have to anchor (rather than dock) at the various ports of call and the use of tenders can severely restrict crew shore leave since passengers always have priority. By their very nature, large ships are bound to be more impersonal and you will be lucky to get to know even a third of the crew. They also tend to enforce more regulations. But if you are outgoing, independent and like the anonymity that working in a large workplace affords, you will want to consider Carnival Cruise Lines, Celebrity Cruises, Costa Cruises, Holland America Line, Princess Cruises and Royal Caribbean International.

It may also be worth noting that very large ships often control operations in the staff sector (production shows, casino, beauty salon, fitness and gift shops) that would be delegated to a concessionaire by smaller ships.

Small Ships have a more intimate atmosphere

Small Ships

Very small ships with less than 200 passengers and 100 crew members have advantages such as their ability to dock alongside in virtually every port and to follow unusual itineraries inaccessible to bigger ships. Naturally there will be a much more intimate atmosphere on board. On the down side, there may be fewer (if any) facilities for the crew. On the one hand, you will get to know your colleagues better. On the other, they will get to know your business better, and gossip on any ship is rife.

The other major factor about working on a very small ship is that the nature of your job may differ drastically from the same position on a larger vessel. Versatility tends to be the key and it is not unusual to find the Hotel Manager directing housekeeping or the Cruise Director acting as concierge. The programme of activities may be quite different or even non-existent. This tends to happen particularly at the 'mega money' end of the market, where passengers virtually dictate what they wish to do and when. There may even be scope for the passengers to suggest the route the ship takes. In these cases the ambience onboard may be more akin to a private yacht than a cruise ship, with the emphasis on water sports and top-class dining. Very few opportunities therefore exist in the field of entertainment, other than for musicians to play dance music and pianists with a cocktail and classical repertoire.

If you prefer a more intimate workplace off the usual tourist track and think you can cope with a wealthier and potentially more demanding clientele, apply to Seabourn Cruise Line, Radisson Seven Seas Cruises and operators of hi-tech sailing ships, such as Windstar Cruises and Compagnie des Isles du Ponant.

Note, however, that smaller vessels tend to be less stable in rough seas than their bigger counterparts. If you are prone to sea-sickness, it may be best to try working on a larger ship first.

Mid-Size Ships

Somewhere between the mainstream giants and the terribly exclusive lies the vast mid-range of ships catering to the vast mid-range of passengers. For many cruise ship employees, vessels which carry between 400 and 1,200 passengers and between 200 and 600 crew members provide the best of both worlds. They are big enough to offer reasonable facilities yet sufficiently small to be friendly and able to dock in many of their ports of call.

Companies with a good range of mid-sized ships include Fred. Olsen Cruise Lines, Hapag-Lloyd Cruises, Louis Cruise Lines, Norwegian Cruise Line, and P & O Cruises.

How to Spot Your Ship When it Eventually Comes in

In the same way that players of a soccer team wear a matching 'strip', so the ships of a cruise line may each sport the same colour and/or corporate logo on their stack (funnel). This gives uniformity to the fleet and allows each vessel to be easily identified. Some of the major cruise lines and their respective trademarks are as follows:

Carnival Cruise Lines: red, white and blue stack, shaped like a whale-tail
Celebrity Cruises: navy stack with large white 'X' (Greek for the letter 'C' as they used to be part of Chandris)
Costa Cruises: bright yellow stack with large letter 'C'
Crystal Cruises: white stack with pair of turquoise seahorses
Cunard Line: red stack with black horizontal stripes
Disney Cruise Line: red stack with Mickey Mouse's ears (what else?)
Holland America Line: white stack with ocean liner & galleon logo
Norwegian Cruise Line: navy stack with 'NCL'
P & O Cruises: pale yellow stack
Princess Cruises: white stack with blue flowing-haired 'sea witch'
Royal Caribbean International: white stack with blue crown &

anchor
Star Cruise: navy stack with yellow star

CRUISE SHIP LISTING

The following list may help to give an indication of which companies
and vessels are most likely to suit your preferences and requirements. For
each ship listed, it is possible to ascertain:

a) name of cruise line or operating company
b) date when the ship was originally launched
c) predominant nationality of officers (bearing in mind that cruise
ship complements are always international)
d) size of ship:

S   = Small (up to 10,000GRT)
M   = Medium (between 10,000 and 40,000GRT)
L   = Large (between 40,000 and 70,000GRT)
XL = Extra Large (Over 70,000GRT)

e) total complement of officers, staff and crew

Example:
Norwegian Wind – Norwegian Cruise Line
1993   Norwegian   M   610

From this example, one can ascertain that the cruise ship *Norwegian Wind* is operated by Norwegian Cruise Line. She was launched
in 1993 and her officers are predominantly Norwegian. She is a
medium-sized ship (between 10,000 and 40,000GRT) and carries
approximately 610 employees.

Please note that all figures given are approximate and for guidance only.
Inevitable changes in the cruising industry may render some entries obso-
lete within the lifetime of this book. Where a date is followed by a second
date (for example, 1974/1988) that refers to the ship having undergone
a major refurbishment or structural change, such as the insertion of an
entire prefabricated extension ('chop and stretch'). Note that vessels
mentioned in specialist sections of the chapter, *Other Options (Sailing
Ships & Yachts; Riverboats & Coastal Vessels; Explorer Vessels & Passenger-Cargo Ships)* are not included in this list.

Adventure of the Seas – Royal Caribbean International
2001   Norwegian   XL   1176

AIDAaura – Aida Cruises
2003   German   L   418

AIDAblu – Aida Cruises
1990   European   L   650

AIDAcara – Aida Cruises
1996   German   M   370

AIDAvita – Aida Cruises
2002   German   L   418

Albatros – Phoenix Reisen
1957/1993   Scandinavian   M   400

Alexander von Humbold (formerly *Saga Pearl*) – Phoenix Reisen
1996   European   M   157

Amadea (formerly *Asuka*) – Phoenix Reisen
1991   M   243

Amsterdam – Holland America Line
2000   Dutch   L   644

Aquamarine – Louis Cruise Lines
1971   Norwegian   M   400

Arcadia – P&O Cruises
2005   British   XL   984

Arion – Classic International Cruises
1965/1999   Portuguese   S   120

Armonia – Mediterranean Shipping Cruises
2001   Greek   L   711

Artemis – P&O Cruises
2005   British   L   520

Astor – Transocean Cruise Lines
1987/1997   Ukranian/Russian   M   270

Astoria – Transocean Cruise Lines
1981/2002   German   M   240

Astra II – Hapag-Lloyd Cruises
1974   Eastern European   M   200

Athena – Classic International Cruises
1948   Italian   M   260

Aurora – P & O Cruises
2000   British   XL   850

Ausonia – Louis Cruise Lines
1957/1998   Italian   M   210

Black Prince – Fred. Olsen Cruise Lines
1966   European/Filipino   M   200

Black Watch – Fred. Olsen Cruise Lines
1972/1996   Norwegian   M   330

Boudicca – Fred. Olsen Cruise Lines
2006   Norwegian   M   330

Braemar – Fred. Olsen Cruise Lines
1974/2001   Norwegian   M   312

Brilliance of the Seas – Royal Caribbean International
2002   Scandinavian   XL   859

Calypso – Louis Cruise Lines
1968/2000   Greek/Cypriot   M   225

Caribbean Princess – Princess Cruises
2004　　　　　British　　　　　XL　　　1150

Carnival Conquest – Carnival Cruise Lines
2002　　　　　Italian　　　　　XL　　　1170

Carnival Destiny – Carnival Cruise Lines
1996　　　　　Italian　　　　　XL　　　950

Carnival Glory – Carnival Cruise Lines
2003　　　　　Italian　　　　　XL　　　1170

Carnival Legend – Carnival Cruise Lines
2002　　　　　Italian　　　　　L　　　930

Carnival Liberty – Carnival Cruise Lines
2005　　　　　Italian　　　　　XL　　　1170

Carnival Miracle – Carnival Cruise Lines
2004　　　　　Italian　　　　　XL　　　930

Carnival Pride – Carnival Cruise Lines
2002　　　　　Italian　　　　　XL　　　930

Carnival Spirit – Carnival Cruise Lines
2001　　　　　Italian　　　　　XL　　　930

Carnival Triumph – Carnival Cruise Lines
1999　　　　　Italian　　　　　XL　　　1000

Carnival Valor – Carnival Cruise Lines
2004　　　　　Italian　　　　　XL　　　1170

Carnival Victory – Carnival Cruise Lines
2000　　　　　Italian　　　　　XL　　　1000

Celebration – Carnival Cruise Lines
1987　　　　　Italian　　　　　L　　　670

Celebrity Xpedition – Celebrity Cruises
2001   Ecuadorian   S   64

Century – Celebrity Cruises
1995   Greek   L   843

Century – Celebrity Cruises
2001   Ecuadorain   S   64

Clipper Adventurer – Clipper Cruise Lines
1975/1998   European   S   72

Clipper Odyssey – Clipper Cruise Lines
1989/1999   European   S   72

Club Med 2 – Club Med Cruises
1992   French   M   200
Columbus – Hapag-Lloyd Cruises
1997   German   M   170

Constellation – Celebrity Cruises
2002   Greek/International   XL   999

Coral Princess – Princess Cruises
2002   British/Italian   XL   900

Costa Allegra – Costa Cruises
1992   Italian   M   450

Costa Atlantica – Costa Cruises
2000   Italian   XL   961

Costa Classica – Costa Cruises
1992   Italian   L   650

Costa Concordia – Costa Cruises
2006   Italian   XL   906

Costa Europa – Costa Cruises
1986/2002   Italian   L   615

Costa Fortuna – Costa Cruises
2003 Italian XL 1068

Costa Magica – Costa Cruises
2000/2004 Italian XL 1068

Costa Marina- Costa Cruises
1990 Italian M 395

Costa Mediteranea – Costa Cruises
2002 Italian XL 920

Costa Romantica – Costa Cruises
1993 Italian L 650

Costa Victoria – Costa Cruises
1996 Italian XL 760

Crystal Serenity – Crystal Cruises
2003 Norwegian/Japanese L 530

Crystal Symphony – Crystal Cruises
1995 Norwegian L 530

Dalmacija – Croatia Cruise Lines
1965 Croatian S 112

Dawn Princess – Princess Cruises
1997 British/Italian XL 900

Delphin – Delphin Seereisen
1975/1993 Ukranian M 234

Delphin Queen – Delphin Seereisen
1998 Ukranian S 66

Deutschland – Peter Deilmann Cruises
1998 German M 285

Diamond Princess – Princess Cruises
2004   British/Italian   XL   1100

Disney Magic – Disney Cruise Line
1998   European   XL   945

Disney Wonder – Disney Cruise Line
1999   European   XL   945

easyCruiseOne – easyCruise
1990/2005   S   54

Ecstasy – Carnival Cruise Lines
1991   Italian   XL   920

Elation – Carnival Cruise Lines
1998   Italian   XL   920
Emerald – Thomson Cruises
1958   Greek/Cypriot   M   412

Empress of the Seas – Royal Caribbean International
1990   Scandinavian   L   685

Enchantment of the Seas – Royal Caribbean International
1997   International/Norwegian   XL   760

Europa – Hapag-Lloyd Cruises
1999   German   M   245

Explorer of the Seas – Royal Caribbean International
2000   Norwegian   XL   1176

Fantasy – Carnival Cruise Lines
1990   Italian   L   920

Fascination – Carnival Cruise Lines
1994   Italian   L   920

Finnmarken – Hurtigruten (Norwegian Coastal Voyages)
2002   Norwegian   M   150

Freedom of the Seas – Royal Caribbean International
2006   Norwegian   XL   1360

Fuji Maru – Mitsui OSK Passenger Line
1989   Japanese   M   190

Funchal – Classic International Cruises
1961/1986   Portuguese   S   155

Galaxy – Celebrity Cruises
1996   Greek   XL   843

Golden Princess – Princess Cruises
2001   British/Italian   XL   1100

Grand Princess – Princess Cruises
1998   British/Italian   XL   1150

Grandeur of the Seas – Royal Caribbean International
1996   Norwegian   XL   760

Hanseatic – Hapag-Lloyd Cruises
1993   German   S   120

Hebridean Princess – Hebridean Island Cruises
1964/1989   British   S   37

Hebridean Spirit – Hebridean Island Cruises
1991/2001   British   S   65

Holiday – Carnival Cruise Lines
1985   Italian   L   660

Imagination – Carnival Cruise Lines
1995   Italian   L   920

Infinity – Celebrity Cruises
2001   Greek   XL   999

Insignia – Oceania Cruises
1998/2004　　　European　　　M　　　370

Inspiration – Carnival Cruise Lines
1996　　　Italian　　　L　　　920

Island Adventure – SeaEscape
1995　　　American　　　M　　　800

Island Escape – Island Cruises
1982/1991　　　Scandinavian　　　L　　　500

Island Princess – Princess Cruises
2003　　　British/Italian　　　XL　　　900

Island Star – Island Cruises
1990　　　Greek　　　M　　　642

Jewel of the Seas – Royal Caribbean International
2004　　　Scandinavian　　　XL　　　859

Kong Harald – Hurtigruten (Norwegian Coastal Voyages)
1993　　　Norwegian　　　M　　　70

Kristina Brahe – Kristina Cruises
1975/1998　　　Finnish　　　S　　　24

Kristina Regina – Kristina Cruises
1960/1987　　　Finnish　　　S　　　55

Le Diamant (formerly *Song of Flower*) – Compagnie des Iles du Ponant
1986　　　European/Scandinavian　　　S　　　157

Le Levant – Compagnie des Iles du Ponant
1999　　　French　　　S　　　55

Le Ponant – Compagnie des Iles du Ponant
1991　　　French　　　S　　　30

Legend of the Seas – Royal Caribbean International
1995   Scandinavian/European   L   720

Lirica – Mediterranean Shipping Cruises
2003   Norwegian   XL   1185

Lofoten – Hurtigruten (Norwegian Coastal Voyages)
1964/1995   Norwegian   S   91

Maasdam – Holland America Line
1993   Dutch   L   571

Majesty of the Seas – Royal Caribbean International
1992   Norwegian   XL   834

Marco Polo – Orient Lines
1966/1999   Scandinavian   M   350

Mariner of the Seas – Royal Caribbean International
2003   Norwegian   XL   1185

Maxim Gorki – Phoenix Reisen
1969/1988   Russian/Ukranian   M   340

MegaStar Aries – Star Cruises
1991/1994   Asian   S   59

MegaStar Taurus – Star Cruises
1991/1995   Asian   S   59

Melody – Mediterranean Shipping Cruises
1982/1997   Italian   M   500

Mercury – Celebrity Cruises
1997   Greek   XL   770

Midnatsol – Hurtigruten (Norwegian Coastal Voyages)
2003   Norwegian   L   98

Millennium – Celebrity Cruises
2000   Greek   XL   999

Minerva II – Swan Hellenic Cruises
1998/2003   European/British   M   300

Monarch of the Seas – Royal Caribbean International
1991   Norwegian   XL   834

Monterey – Mediterranean Shipping Cruises
1952/1988   Italian   M   280

Nantucket Clipper – Clipper Cruise Lines
1984/1999   European   S   36

Narvik – Hurtigruten (Norwegian Coastal Voyages)
1982   Norwegian   S   55

Nautica – Oceania Cruises
1999/2005   European   M   370

Navigator of the Seas – Royal Caribbean International
2002   Norwegian   XL   1213

Nordkapp – Hurtigruten (Norwegian Coastal Voyages)
1996   Norwegian   M   70

Nordlys – Hurtigruten (Norwegian Coastal Voyages)
1994   Norwegian   M   70

Nordnorge – Hurtigruten (Norwegian Coastal Voyages)
1997   Norwegian   M   70

Norway – Norwegian Cruise Line
1962/2001   Norwegian   XL   900

Norwegian Crown – Norwegian Cruise Line
1988   European   M   470

Norwegian Dawn – Norwegian Cruise Line
2002   Scandinavian/Asian   XL   1112

Norwegian Dream – Norwegian Cruise Line
1992   Norwegian   L   780

Norwegian Jewel – Norwegian Cruise Line
2005   Scandinavian/Asian   XL   1000

Norwegian Majesty – Norwegian Cruise Line
1992/1997   Norwegian   L   682

Norwegian Sea – Norwegian Cruise Line
1988   Norwegian   L   680

Norwegian Spirit – Norwegian Cruise Line
1998   European/Asian   XL   1100

Norwegian Star – Norwegian Cruise Line
2001   Scandinavian/American   XL   1100

Norwegian Sun – Norwegian Cruise Line
2001   Norwegian   XL   968

Norwegian Wind – Norwegian Cruise Line
1993   Norwegian   L   700

Ocean Majesty – Page & Moy
1966/1994   Greek   M   235

Ocean Monarch – Page & Moy
1955   European   M   235

Ocean Village – Ocean Village
1989/2003   British   L   514

Oceana – P & O Cruises
2000   British   XL   875

Oosterdam – Holland America Line
2003 Dutch/British XL 900

Opera – Mediterranean Shipping Cruises
2004 Italian L 750

Oriana – P & O Cruises
1995 British L 760

Pacific Princess – Princess Cruises
1971 Italian M 373

Pacific Sky – P & O Cruises (Australia)
1984/2000 British L 540

Pacific Sun – P&O Cruises (Australia)
1986 Italian L 650

Paradise – Carnival Cruise Lines
1998 Italian L 920

Paul Gauguin – Radisson Seven Seas Cruises
1998 European/French M 206

Polarlys – Hurtigruten (Norwegian Coastal Voyages)
1997 Norwegian M 70

Pride of Aloha (formerly *Norwegian Star*) – Norwegian Cruise Line
1999/2004 American XL 950

Pride of America – Norwegian Cruise Line
2005 Scandinavian/Asian/AmericanXL 800

Princesa Marissa – Louis Cruise Lines
1966/1987 Greek/Cypriot M 185

Princess Danae – Classic International Cruises
1955/1997 European M 240

Prinsendam – Holland America Line
1988/1999   Dutch   M   460

Queen Elizabeth 2 – Cunard Line
1969/1999   British   XL   921

Queen Mary 2 – Cunard Line
2004   British   XL   1238

Queen Victoria (in build) – Cunard Line
2007   British   XL   1200

Radiance of the Seas – Royal Caribbean International
2001   Norwegian   XL   859

Regal Empress – Imperial Majesty Cruise Line
1953/1993   European   M   396

Regal Princess – Ocean Village
1991   Italian   L   630

Regatta – Oceania Cruises
1998/2003   European   M   370

Rhapsody – Mediterranean Shipping Cruises
1977/1995   Italian   M   350

Rhapsody of the Seas – Royal Caribbean International
1997   Norwegian   XL   765

Richard With – Hurtigruten (Norwegian Coastal Voyages)
1993   Norwegian   M   70

Rotterdam – Holland America Line
1997   Dutch   L   644

Royal Clipper – Star Clippers
2000   International   S   100

Royal Star – African Safari Club
1956/1990   Greek   S   140

Ryndam – Holland America Line
1994   Dutch   L   571

Saga Rose – Saga Holidays
1965/1997   British   M   350

Saga Ruby – Saga Holidays
1973   British   M   390

St. Helena – Andrew Weir Shipping (St Helena Cruises)
1990   British   S   53

Sapphire – Louis Cruise Lines
1967/1996   Greek   M   250

Sapphire Princess – Princess Cruises
2004   British/Italian   XL   1100

Seabourn Legend – Seabourn Cruise Line
1992/2000   Norwegian   S   160

Seabourn Pride – Seabourn Cruise Line
1988/2000   Norwegian   S   160

Seabourn Spirit – Seabourn Cruise Line
1989/2000   Norwegian   S   160

Sea Cloud – Sea Cloud Cruises
1931/1979   European   S   60

Sea Cloud II – Sea Cloud Cruises
2001   European   S   60

SeaDream I – SeaDream Yacht Club
1984/2002   Norwegian/Scandinavian   S   91

SeaDream II – SeaDream Yacht Club
1985/2002   Norwegian/Scandinavian   S   91

Sea Princess – Princess Cruises
1998   Italian   XL   900

Sensation – Carnival Cruise Lines
1993   Italian   L   920

Serenade – Louis Cruise Lines
1957/1999   Greek/Cypriot   M   320

Serenade of the Seas – Royal Caribbean International
2003   Norwegian   XL   859

Seven Seas Mariner – Radisson Seven Seas Cruises
2001   French   L   445

Seven Seas Navigator – Radisson Seven Seas Cruises
1999   European/Italian   M   325

Seven Seas Voyager – Radisson Seven Seas Cruises
2003   European/Scandinavian L   445

Silver Cloud – Silversea Cruises
1994/2004   Italian   M   185

Silver Shadow – Silversea Cruises
2000   Italian   M   295

Silver Whisper – Silversea Cruises
2001   Italian   M   295

Silver Wind – Silversea Cruises
1995/2002   Italian   M   185

Sinfonia – Mediterranean Shipping Cruises
2002   Italian   L   711

Sovereign of the Seas – Royal Caribbean International
| 1988 | Scandinavian | XL | 750 |

Spirit of Oceanus – Cruise West
| 1990 | American | S | 72 |

Splendour of the Seas – Royal Caribbean International
| 1996 | Scandinavian | L | 720 |

Star Clipper – Star Clippers
| 1992 | European | S | 60 |

Star Flyer – Star Clippers
| 1991 | European | S | 60 |

Star Pisces – Star Cruises
| 1990 | Scandinavian | M | 750 |

Star Princess – Princess Cruises
| 2002 | British/Italian | XL | 1150 |

Statendam – Holland America Line
| 1993 | Dutch | L | 571 |

Summit – Celebrity Cruises
| 2002 | Greek | XL | 999 |

Sun Princess – Princess Cruises
| 1995 | Italian | XL | 900 |

SuperStar Gemini – Star Cruises
| 1992/1995 | Scandinavian | M | 470 |

Superstar Libra – Star Cruises
| 2005 | Scandinavian | L | 700 |

SuperStar Virgo – Star Cruises
| 1999 | European/Asian | XL | 1125 |

Tahitian Princess – Princess Cruises

| 1999 | Italian | M | 373 |

The World – ResidenSea

| 2002 | Scandinavian | M | 320 |

Thomson Celebration – Thomson Cruises

| 1984/2005 | Dutch | M | 542 |

Thomson Destiny – Thomson Cruises

| 1982/2005 | International | M | 550 |

Thomson Spirit – Thomson Cruises

| 1983/2003 | Dutch/British | M | 540 |

Trollfjord – Hurtigruten (Norwegian Coastal Voyages)

| 2002 | Norwegian | M | 150 |

Veendam – Holland America Line

| 1996 | Dutch/British | L | 571 |

Vesterålen – Hurtigruten (Norwegian Coastal Voyages)

| 1983/1995 | Norwegian | S | 60 |

Vision of the Seas – Royal Caribbean International

| 1998 | Norwegian | XL | 765 |

Volendam – Holland America Line

| 1999 | Dutch/British | L | 650 |

Voyager of the Seas – Royal Caribbean International

| 1999 | Scandinavian/European | XL | 1180 |

Westerdam – Holland America Line

| 2004 | Dutch/British | XL | 800 |

Wind Spirit – Windstar Cruises

| 1988 | British | S | 91 |

Wind Star – Windstar Cruises

| 1986 | British | S | 91 |

Wind Surf – Windstar Cruises
1990/1998   European/British   M   188

Yorktown Clipper – Clipper Cruise Lines
1988/2000   European   S   42

Zaandam – Holland America Line
2000   Dutch/British   L   650

Zenith – Celebrity Cruises
1992   Greek   L   628

Zuiderdam – Holland America Line
2002   Dutch/British   XL   800

Other Options

SAILING SHIPS & YACHTS

Cruising doesn't necessarily mean on a regular cruise ship. Indeed, those with a taste for adventure might like to consider working on a vessel with sails. Unfortunately, however, their relatively small passenger carry means that yachts and sailing ships do not offer an abundance of employment opportunities. Many chartered yachts are hired to experienced sailors as 'bareboats' (with no crew provided) and even larger sailing vessels may use less than a dozen crew members. With the exception of hi-tech sail-cruisers, there are usually no casinos or spa/gymnasium facilities onboard vessels with sails and very few jobs for musicians and entertainers. The opportunities that do exist are particularly good for experienced captains and qualified chefs. But bear in mind that vessels registered in the United States are crewed by American citizens or US work permit holders only.

Excluding the hi-tech sail-cruisers of **Club Mediterranée, Windstar Cruises** and **Compagnie des Isles du Ponant** (listed under *The Cruise Lines*), sailing ships offer a generally slower form of travel and the flavour of a bygone age. The onboard atmosphere tends to be informal on even the most expensive sailing ships and all crew members, irrespective of rank, are likely to have some social contact with the passengers. Seasickness sufferers should note, however, that you are more likely to feel the motion of the ocean on a wind-powered vessel.

The bi-monthly magazine *Traditional Boats & Tall Ships* (Poundbury Publishing Ltd, Prospect House, Peverell Avenue East, Poundbury, Dorchester, Dorset DT1 3WE, England; ☎01305-266360; fax 01305-262760; e-mail tallships@poundbury.co.uk; www.poundbury.co.uk) is a good source of information on sailing ships which you can also check online atwww.tallship.co.uk.

North End Shipyard Schooners
With a couple of traditional sailing ships, this family-run company operates cruises along America's east coast. Of the fleet (*Heritage* and *American Eagle*) *American Eagle* has the claim to fame of being a National Historic Landmark. This is one of several individual sailing ship operators

represented by the **Maine Windjammer Association** (PO Box 1144P, Blue Hill, Maine 04614; ☎ 1-800 807 9463; www.sailmainecoast.com).

Sea Cloud Cruises
Arguably the most luxurious sailing ship currently in operation, *Sea Cloud* was launched in 1931 for the American heiress, Marjorie Merriweather Post, and has since transported numerous celebrities around the seven seas. She now carries 65 passengers – and the same number of crew – on cruises throughout Europe (Mediterranean, North Sea, Blatic) and the Caribbean (West Indies). *Sea Cloud,* her 'sister' *Sea Cloud II,* and the five-star cruise vessels *River Cloud* and *River Cloud II* are under crew management of Hampton Shipping (e-mail jobs@hampton-shipping.com)

SeaDream Yacht Club
Operates the twin, ultra-luxury mega yachts, *SeaDream I* and *SeaDream II*, sailing in the Mediterranean and around the Greek Islands in summer and the Caribbean in winter.

Square Sail Pacific
The star of the television series, The Onedin Line, *Soren Larsen* is a square-rigged brigantine that sails in Pacific waters, including New Zealand, and once every five years undertakes a worldwide voyage. Family-operated and carrying only 22 guests, this classic vessel does take crew but they must have square-rig sailing experience.

Star Clippers
This Florida-based company owns the four-masted *Star Clipper* and *Star Flyer* and the five-masted *Royal Clipper* (the largest square-rigger sailing ship every built). Each of the trio offers employment for at least 70 crew members of mixed nationalities, including watersports instructors. Combining modern comfort with traditional design, these stately vessels cut an impressive figure in Mediterranean, Caribbean and Far Eastern waters.

The Moorings
Offers sailboat, crewed yacht, bareboat, and catamaran sailing boat charters in the Caribbean, Bahamas, Mexico, South Pacific, Mediterranean, North America and Scandinavia.

Windjammer Barefoot Cruises
One of the more likely companies for employment opportunities on sailing ships, Windjammer operates a fleet of historically interesting vessels. These currently include the three-masted *Mandalay*, the barquentine *Flying Cloud,* the schooner *Polynesia* and the 1920s yacht, *Yankee Clipper.*

Yachts and Yacht Crewing Agencies

The largest yacht chartering and management company in the world is **The Moorings** with a fleet of almost 700 vessels, although **Sacks Yacht Charters** also operates sail and motor vessels around the globe. Those seeking work specifically on yachts or sailing vessels might wish to consider enlisting the help of a crewing agency, some of which charge an annual subscription of about £30:

Blue Water (France), La Galerie du Port, 8 Boulevard d'Aguillon, 06600 Antibes, France; ☎4-9334 3413; fax 4-9334 3593; e-mail crew@bluewateryachting.com; www.bluewateryachting.com.

Blue Water (UK), 5 Dryden Street, Covent Garden, London WC2E 9NW, England; ☎020-7829 8446; www.bluewateryachting.com.

Crewseekers Limited, Hawthorn House, Hawthorn Lane, Sarisbury Green, Southampton, Hampshire SO31 7BD, England; ☎/fax 01489-578319; e-mail info@crewseekers.co.uk; www.crewseekers.co.uk.

Crewfinders, 404 & 408 SE 17th Street, Fort Lauderdale, Florida 33316, USA; ☎954-522 2739; fax 954-522 2725; e-mail crew@crewfinders.com; www.crewfinders.com.

Cruising Association, CA House, 1 Northey Street, Limehouse Basin, London E14 8BT, England; ☎020-7537 2828; fax 020-7537 2266; e-mail office@cruising.org.uk; www.cruising.org.uk.

Flying Fish, 25 Union Road, Cowes, Isle of Wight PO31 7TW, England; ☎01983-280641; fax 01983-281821; www.flyingfishonline.com.

Peter Insull Yacht Marketing, Résidences du Port Vauban, 19 Avenue du 11 Novembre, 06600 Antibes, France; ☎4-9334 4455; fax 4-9334 9274; e-mail info@insull.com; www.insull.com.

Reliance Yacht Management, First Floor Suite, 127 Lynchford Road, Farnborough, Hampshire GU14 6ET, England; ☎01252-378239; fax 01252-521736; e-mail info@reliance-yachts.com; www.reliance-yachts.com.

Sea Gem International, 10A Alexandra Road, Bournemouth, Dorset BH6 5JA England; ☎01202-422341; email info@seageminternational.

com; www.seageminternational.com.

World Crews, 52 York Place, Bournemouth BH7 6JN, England; ☎/fax 01202-431520.

Look in trade magazines such as *Yachting World, Yachting Monthly* and *Yachts & Yachting* for related information on yachting schools, clubs and associations, brokers and charter companies. International organisations such as the *American Sailing Association* (13922 Marquesas Way, Marina del Rey, CA 90292, USA; ☎310-822 7171; fax 310-822 4741; e-mail info@american-sailing.com; www.american-sailing.com), *Yachting Australia* (Locked Bag 806, Milsons Point NSW 2061, 16 Atchison Street, St Leonards, NSW 2061, Australia; ☎2-9922 4333; fax 2-9923 2883; e-mail office@yachting.org.au; www.yachting.org.au) or *Irish Sailing Association* (3 Park Road, Dun Laoghaire, Co Dublin, Ireland; ☎1-280 0239; fax 1-280 7558; e-mail reception@sailing.ie; www.sailing.ie) may also provide useful information. In the United Kingdom, contact the *Royal Yachting Association* (RYA House, Ensign Way, Hamble, Southampton, Hampshire SO31 4YA; ☎023-8060 4100; fax 023-8060 4299; e-mail info@rya.org.uk; www.rya.org.uk) or the *Yacht Charter Association* (Deacons Boatyard, Burseldon Bridge, Southampton SO31 8AZ; ☎023-8040 7075; fax 023-8040 7076; e-mail charter@yca.co.uk; www.yca.co.uk).

RIVERBOATS & COASTAL VESSELS

Of course, a cruise doesn't have to be at sea. There are numerous passenger vessels plying rivers across the world. Likewise there are coastal ships that follow interesting itineraries without ever losing sight of land. These cruises are often good news for potential sea-sickness sufferers.

Note, however, that salaries aboard riverboats and coastal vessels are unlikely to be on a par with regular cruise ship earnings. Also, the local workforce may supply the full complement of staff. Many of the tourist vessels that cruise the Nile in Egypt, for example, are operated by international hotel chains (Presidential, Sheraton, Oberoi, Sonnesta, Hilton International), yet employ an entirely Egyptian personnel. Confusingly, riverboats and coastal vessels may also be chartered or marketed by several different travel companies and these are rarely involved in the recruiting process.

The range of available jobs is often so limited that, unless you are a specialist lecturer or a very bad sailor, you might do better to send your details elsewhere. But for those undeterred by the limitations, some of the leading operators of river and coastal cruises are as follows:

American Canadian Caribbean Line (ACCL)
ACCL's three small coastal vessels, *Grande Caribe, Grande Mariner* and *Niagara Prince*, follow unusual North American and Caribbean itineraries. As with all US-registered cruise lines, only American job-seekers should apply.

American West Steamboat Company
This company operates the nostalgic *Queen of the West* paddle wheeler on the Columbia and neighbouring rivers. Sailing out of Portland, Oregon, this US-registered steamer employs approximately 80 all-American crew members. The other sternwheeler, the *Empress of the North*, sails Alaska's Inside Passage.

Blue Lagoon Cruises
This Fiji-based company operates a fleet of boutique small cruise ships (*Lycianda, Mystique Princess, Nanuya Princess* and *Fiji Princess*). Each carries between 42 and 72 passengers on accommodation cruises around the Yasawa Islands and employs an all-Fijian workforce.

Captain Cook Cruises
A well-known Australian operator of small vessels, the Captain Cook fleet includes the 168-passenger *Reef Endeavour*, which cruises the Great Barrier Reef; the tall ship *Spirit of the Pacific* and the cruise ship *Reef Escape* sailing out of Fiji; and the traditional paddle wheeler *Murray Princess*, which pounds the Murray River; as well as nine ships on Sydney Harbour.

Clipper Cruise Line
Not to be confused with sailing ships, this line's coastal cruisers (*Clipper Adventurer, Nantucket Clipper, Yorktown Clipper* and *Clipper Odyssey*) each carry between 100 and 140 passengers. The former three vessels follow varied North American, Mexican and Caribbean routes while the *Clipper Odyssey* explores Australia, New Zealand, Southeast and East Asia. US job-seekers only should apply. *Clipper Adventurer* was a Soviet passenger ship converted for expedition cruising and now sails to the Arctic and Antarctic.

Coral Princess Cruises

This Australian company operates two catamarans (*Coral Princess* and *Coral Princess II*) carrying 54 and 48 passengers respectively on the Kimberley river or Great Barrier Reef. The expedition cruise ship, *Ocean Princess*, carries 76 passengers sailing in the Kimberley region.

Cruise West

This line operates coastal vessels sightseeing and whale watching around Alaska. Except for *Pacific Explorer* and *Sheltered Seas*, the ships are *Spirit of* ... (*...Alaska, Columbia, Discovery, Endeavour, Oceanus* and *Spirit of '98*) with all-American crews. *Spirit of Oceanus* is its first ocean-going vessel.

Peter Deilmann Cruises

The same company that operates the cruise ship *Deutschland* and a sailing ship also operates deluxe riverboats on the Danube, Rhine and other European waterways. The river fleet comprises *Danube Princess, Dresden, Mozart, Princesse de Provence, Cézanne, Heidelberg, Casanova, Katharina,* and *Federic Chopin*. An ability to speak German is important for work with this line.

Delta Queen Steamboat Company

Fans of Tom Sawyer will delight in the prospect of working on a real Mississippi paddle steamer. As a subsidiary of the bankrupt American Classic the company was in danger of disappearing until bought by the Delaware North entertainment group. The **Delta Queen Steamboat Company** currently operates three traditional vessels. *American Queen* and *Mississippi Queen* employ approximately 160 crew members apiece, while *Delta Queen* (a National Historic Landmark) has a crew of 80. Because of their American registry, however, only US citizens need apply.

Glacier Bay Cruise Line

Alaskan adventure cruises are offered by this Seattle-based company aboard its American-crewed catamaran *Executive Explorer* and small coastal cruisers *Wilderness Explorer, Wilderness Discoverer,* and *Wilderness Adventurer*.

Gota Canal Steamship Company

This company's three vintage steamers (*Diana, Juno* and *Wihelm Tham*) currently offer cruises of up to six days on Sweden's Gota Canal between

Stockholm and Gothenburg. Crews are only 12 in size and language skills are a must.

Hurtigruten
Also known as Norwegian Coastal Voyages, this hardy fleet sails year-round along Norway's craggy coastline. It currently includes *Finnmarken, Kong Harald, Lofoten, Midnatsol, Narvik, Nordkapp, Nordlys, Nord-norge, Nordstjernen, Polarlys, Richard With, Trollfjord* and *Vesterålen.* Something of a cross between ferry, cruise ship and cargo ship, these vessels carry up to 1,000 passengers and are a reasonable source of regional employment.

Kristina Cruises
This is a small Finnish line, whose two vessels, the 350-passenger/55-crew, *Kristina Regina* and *Kristina Brahe* plies the coasts of Scandinavia, Barent Sea, west European coast, and the Mediterranean.

St. Lawrence Cruise Lines
This Canadian company employs a small Canadian workforce for seasonal cruising (May-October) on the St. Lawrence and Ottowa rivers aboard the replica steamboat, *Canadian Empress.*

Venice Simplon-Orient-Express (VSOE)
Although its name is synonymous with luxury train travel, VSOE also operates the deluxe *Road to Mandalay* riverboat on Myanmar's Ayeyarwady river.

Victoria Cruises
This American company operates modern riverboats on China's Yangtze river – *Victoria Emperor, Victoria Katarina, Victoria Prince, Victoria Queen, Victoria Rose* and *Victoria Star.* The line's newest and largest ship, the *Victoria Anna,* will be inaugurated in 2006.

Viking River Cruises
One of the world's largest river cruise lines, it has a substantial fleet of vessels journeying along the rivers of Europe, Russia and China. The fleet currently comprises *Viking Burgandy, Viking Century Skye, Viking Century Star, Viking Europe, Viking Kirov, Viking Lavrinenkov, Viking Neptune, Viking Pakhomov, Viking Schumann, Viking Seine, Viking Sky, Viking Spirit, Viking Sun* and *Viking Surkov.* Good opportunities for Eng-

lish- and German-speaking job-seekers.

Yangtze Cruises
A cruise and tour wholesaler of China and the Orient, specialising in Yangtze cruises and tours. The company represents Chinese government-owned cruise liners.

EXPLORER VESSELS & PASSENGER-CARGO SHIPS

From Antarctica to the Amazon, the Galápagos Islands to the North Pole, explorer vessels venture well beyond mainstream shipping lanes in their search for unusual destinations.

Most of them employ small, specialist crews with regional knowledge and relevant expertise. These may include zodiac pilots with experience of polar navigation, for example, or guest lecturers on subjects such as marine biology. With the notable exception of Orient Lines' *Marco Polo* and Hapag Lloyd's *Hanseatic*, entertainment is distinctly limited and the general attire is practical rather than fashionable.

Ships venturing to the Arctic or Antarctic boast an ice-hardened hull and many are ice-breakers chartered from Russian or Ukrainian companies. Most of the vessels exploring the Galápagos Islands are registered in Ecuador and manned by Ecuadorian crews, while those venturing along the upper regions of the Amazon are mostly manned by Peruvians.

As with other 'alternative' styles of cruising, many companies which market explorer vessels do not actually own the ships and are not directly responsible for recruiting personnel. Even explorer companies which do hire crew members have very limited vacancies compared to most regular cruise lines.

Some cargo ships also carry passengers, offering an even different type of travel experience. In such cases, passengers have close contact with the ship's company, have access to normally off-limit areas such as the navigational bridge and eat on a regular basis with the ship's officers. Passenger-cargo ships cannot be compared with regular cruise ships, however, and do not usually require staff such as entertainers, croupiers, hairdressers or shore excursion personnel.

Taking the above factors into account, some of the major names in explorer and passenger-cargo cruising are as follows:

Abercrombie & Kent (A & K)
A & K's *Explorer* carries approximately 100 passengers and 70 crew

members on global explorations that include the Antarctic and the Amazon.

Amazon Tours & Cruises
This Peruvian company employs local crews for its fleet of small river vessels, which explore the less-visited reaches of the Amazon between Iquitos and Leticia. At times the company does take on foreign students on a no-pay basis as lecturers or assistant guides.

Andrew Weir Shipping (St Helena Cruises)
Post 1945, the Royal Mail Ship service to the island of St Helena was provided by Union Castle liners who ceased voyages in 1977. In 1990, the current RMS *St Helena* began sailing regularly between the UK, Ascension Island, St Helena and Cape Town, calling in at Tenerife and Vigo. Nowadays, *St Helena* is based in South Africa and sails the south Atlantic calling in at Namibia, St Helena and Ascension Island and has once again extended her trips to the UK, taking in Tenerife and Vigo. These trips are operated by her managing agents, Andrew Weir Shipping.

Galápagos Cruises
This company's small Ecuadorian-manned and registered vessels offer cruises of discovery around Ecuador's provincial nature haven, the Galápagos Islands. The flagship is the 100-passenger *Galápagos Explorer II*.

Hapag-Lloyd Cruises
For those seeking to combine adventure with luxury, Hapag-Lloyd's *Hanseatic* (marketed by Hanseatic Tours) offer the Arctic and Antarctic among their worldwide itineraries (see Cruise Lines).

Heritage Expeditions
Expedition travel operators specialising in the southern oceans with *Spirit Enderby*, which has a crew of 24, and *Explore*, with a crew of 53.

Lindblad Expeditions
Lindblad owns six ships, *National Geographic Endeavour* (formerly *Endeavour* but renamed as part of the new alliance between Linblad and National Geographic), *Polaris, Sea Bird, Sea Lion* and *Islander*. The company specialises in expedition and educational cruises that include Latin America, Alaska, Antarctica and the South Pacific

Orient Lines
Orient operates one of the very few passenger ships to venture to the Antarctic, the ice-hardened *Marco Polo* (see Cruise Lines).

Quark Expeditions
Quark operates the largest fleet of passenger vessels in the Antarctic. The Adventure Fleet is comprised of *Akademik Shokalskiy, Professor Multanovskiy* and *Professor Milchanov.* The *Lyubov Orlova* is the company's conventional ship. The ice-breaker *Kapitan Khlebnikov* completes the fleet. In the Arctic, in addition to *Kapitan Khlebnikov,* Quark operates expeditions to the North Pole with the nuclear powered *Yamal.*

Spitsbergen Travel
This Norwegian company specialises in voyages above the Arctic Circle aboard its ice-hardened, Norwegian-registered explorer vessels.

THEMED CRUISES

Ships which offer themed cruises may provide specialist employment opportunities, especially for musicians and expert lecturers. P & O, Seabourn and Hapag-Lloyd regularly feature classical music cruises, while Norwegian Cruise Line hosts Country and Western, Blues, Big Band and Jazz. The Delta Queen Steamboat Company (see *Riverboats & Coastal Vessels*) is also noted for its regular Dixie and Big Band Cruises, providing employment for American musicians only. Peter Deilmann Cruises offer classical music cruises on its riverboats.

Independent charterers such as Classical Cruises, Page & Moy or Voyages of Discovery may specialise in themes like archaeology, horticulture, cookery, wine tasting and murder mystery. Orient Lines and Swan Hellenic are also noted for their strong specialist lecture programmes.

Norwegian Cruise Line is the real front-runner when it comes to all kinds of sporting themed cruises, featuring celebrities and expert lecturers in fields as diverse as motor-racing and skiing. NCL regularly hosts Golf Cruises, as do Royal Caribbean International and Clipper Cruise Line (see *Riverboats & Coastal Vessels*).

Musicians, lecturers and others seeking work on a particular theme would do well to keep an eye on special interest newspapers and magazines. These often provide useful information concerning appropriate themed cruises and their operators.

Cruising Itineraries

Most of the major players have ships around the globe, while smaller lines may concentrate on a specific region. You might wish to consider the general itineraries of a company's fleet before applying to them. This way, you can avoid accepting a contract for the Mexican Riviera when you can't stand the heat or a series of Atlantic crossings when you go green on the Mersey Ferry. As a guide, the main cruising areas, together with their respective advantages and disadvantages, are as follows:

Caribbean

Traditionally the preferred destination of beach lovers, rum-drinkers and scuba divers, the West Indies provides the world's most popular year-round cruising region. Romantics should also enjoy those balmy star-filled Caribbean nights. But all that sun and sand can become boring for crew members on long contracts and crime rates in ports such as Montego Bay (Jamaica) and San Juan (Puerto Rico) are high. Hurricanes and long-term tourist exploitation have also left their scars. There are so many vessels now calling at St. Thomas, for example, that the port of Charlotte Amalie sometimes resembles a cruise ship parking lot.

Many Caribbean cruises sail out of Miami or Fort Lauderdale, including a host of three- and four-day 'cheapies', which means good news for party animals, casino and bar staff. Specific opportunities may also exist for steel/calypso bands and port lecturers/shopping advisors. British crew members should also note that British passport/C1-D Visa formalities may be dealt with in the Bahamas.

Most of the major lines have itineraries which include the Caribbean. Try especially Carnival Cruise Lines, Celebrity Cruises, Costa Cruises, Cunard Line, Club Med, Disney Cruise Line, Holland America Line, Norwegian Cruise Line, Princess Cruises, Royal Caribbean International, Seabourn Cruise Line, Windstar Cruises and operators of sailing ships such as Star Clippers and Windjammer Barefoot Cruises.

Caribbean itineraries may include: Antigua, Aruba, Bahamas, Barbados, Cayman Islands, Cuba, Dominican Republic, Fort Lauderdale, Grenada, Guadeloupe, Haiti, Jamaica, Key West, Martinique, Miami, Puerto Rico, St. Kitts, St. Lucia, St. Maarten, St. Thomas, Tortola, Trinidad and Tobago.

Alaska

The standard Alaskan route covers the west coast of North America between Vancouver and Seward (the port for Anchorage) and the cruise season runs between May and September. Wildlife spotters will enjoy this run, the scenery is magnificent and it is certainly good to breathe fresher air, but be prepared for inclement (rather than simply cold) weather. Again, this itinerary can become boring on a long contract, which is one reason why some crew members become ten pin bowling experts during their time here.

Cruising in Alaska is very much dominated by Princess Cruises and Holland America Line (HAL), as they also have large shoreside travel operations here. Carnival Cruise Lines, Celebrity Cruises, Norwegian Cruise Line and Royal Caribbean International are among the other major lines which venture here during the summer months. Explorer specialists, such as Lindblad Expeditions pursue more offbeat itineraries in this region and American job-seekers might wish to contact coastal cruise specialists, such as Clipper Cruise Line and Cruise West.

Alaskan itineraries may include: Glacier Bay, Homer, Juneau, Ketchikan, Seattle, Seward, Sitka, Skagway, Tracey Arm Fjord, Vancouver and Wrangell.

Mediterranean

The Mediterranean provides much more variety than most other regions. From the Greek islands to the French Riviera, the Pyramids to the Colosseum, the Med has everything a seafarer could want: sun, sand, good food, fine wine, ancient history, bars of every description and telephones that work. Be a little wary of contracts leaving from Tilbury or Southampton though. The convenience of home ports (for the British) is really no match for being thrown around the Bay of Biscay (even on a good day). Many cruise ships which follow Eastern Mediterranean itineraries in the summer months reposition to the Caribbean or Western Mediterranean/ Atlantic (with ports in Morocco and the Canary Islands) in the winter.

Numerous companies operate ships for those wishing to head for the Med, including: Classic International Cruises, Club Med, Costa Cruises, Cunard Line, Fred. Olsen Cruise Lines, Louis Cruise Lines, Mediterranean Shipping Cruises, Norwegian Cruise Line, P & O Cruises, Paradise Cruise, Radisson Seven Seas Cruises, Seabourn Cruise Line and Silversea Cruises.

Mediterranean itineraries may include: Agadir, Alexandria, Ashdod (for Jerusalem), Barcelona, Bodrum, Cadiz, Canary Islands, Cannes, Capri, Casablanca, Civitavecchia (for Rome), Corinth Canal, Crete, Cyprus, Dardanelles, Dubrovnik, Genoa, Gibraltar, Greek Islands (inc. Mykonos and Santorini), Haifa, Ibiza, Istanbul, Kusadasi, La Goulette (for Tunis), Lisbon, Livorno (for Florence), Madeira, Malaga, Mallorca, Malta, Menorca, Nice, Piraeus (for Athens), Port Said (for Cairo), Rhodes, Sicily, Sorrento, Tangier, Venice and Villefranche.

Black Sea

Often combined with cruises in the Eastern Mediterranean, the Black Sea offers attractive scenery and the cultural experience of handkerchief-waving folkloric dancers, a matinée at the opera or a bargain 'massage'. Other bargains frequently snapped up by crew members include Soviet memorabilia, cheap watches and tins of fake caviar.

For work opportunities, check out the cruise lines that operate ships in the Mediterranean as some of them also include the Black Sea (Swan Hellenic) in their summer programmes.

Black Sea itineraries may include: Constanta, Istanbul, Odessa, Varna and Yalta.

Northern Europe

The weather's too cold and the guests too old for the 'Kiss-Me-Quick' Romeos of other itineraries. Rather, Northern Europe provides more of a cultural experience with clean Scandinavian cities, fresh Arctic air and yet more folkloric dancers waving handkerchiefs (or could they be the same ones in different boots?). Midnight Sun seekers tend to be richer than regular sun-seekers, so tips can be good. But remember that Scandinavia, in particular, can also be expensive.

With the notable exception of ferry companies and Norway's Hurtigruten, cruising in Northern Europe is generally restricted to the summer months (May-October). Costa Cruise Lines, Crystal Cruises, Cunard Line, Fred. Olsen Cruise Lines, Norwegian Cruise Line, P & O Cruises, Princess Cruises, Radisson Seven Seas Cruises, Saga Holidays, Seabourn Cruise Line, Silversea Cruises and Swan Hellenic Cruises may be of particular interest to those wishing to work in these waters. Also, various German cruise operators, specialists in arctic explorations and regional coastal cruise operators such as Hebridean Island Cruises and

Kristina Cruises.

Northern European itineraries may include: Alesund, Amsterdam, Antwerp, Bergen, Bordeaux, Brest, Channel Islands, Cherbourg, Cobh (for Cork), Copenhagen, Dover, Dublin, Faroe Islands, Flam, Gdansk, Gdynia, Geiranger Fjord, Gravdal, Greenland, Gudvangen, Hamburg, Hellesylt, Helsinki, Honningsvaag, Invergordon, Isle of Mann, Isle of Wight, Kiel Canal, La Coruja, Leigh (for Edinburgh), Molde, North Cape, Oban, Oslo, Reykjavik, Riga, Rouen, Shetland Islands, Southampton, Spitzbergen, St. Malo, St. Petersburg, Stavanger, Stockholm, Stornoway, Tallinn, Tilbury (for London), Tromso, Trondheim, Waterford and Zeebrugge.

Middle East and Indian Ocean

The Red Sea, Arabian Sea and Indian Ocean are most likely to be visited by vessels on world cruises and repositioning cruises (when the ship moves from its regular winter cruising region to its summer cruising region and vice versa). Cruises in this area generally take place between November and April. A notable exception to this rule is African Safari Club's *Royal Star,* which offers year-round cruises in the Indian Ocean out of Mombasa. Other ships cruising this region include those of Cunard Line, Fred. Olsen Cruise Lines, Hapag-Lloyd Cruises, Orient Lines, Princess Cruises, Radisson Seven Seas Cruises, Silversea Cruises, Seabourn Cruise Line and Swan Hellenic Cruises.

Scuba divers should enjoy the Seychelles and Red Sea ports such as Aqaba and Safaga; collectors of handicrafts are likely to buy more African wood-carvings than they can cram in their suitcase; and India has to be on every serious traveller's hit list.

Middle East and Indian Ocean itineraries may include: Aden, Al Hudaydah, Aqaba, Bahrain, Calcutta, Cape Town, Cochin, Comores Islands, Djibouti, Dubai, Durban, Madagascar, Madras, Maldives, Mauritius, Mombasa, Mormugao, Mumbai (formerly Bombay), Muscat, New Mangalore, Port Suez, Safaga, Seychelles, Sharm el Sheik, Sri Lanka and Zanzibar.

Southeast Asia and the Far East

Opportunities to discover the mysteries of the East occur on World Cruises and lengthy voyages, many of which pass through oriental waters. Find yourself on a Slow Boat to China and you might also pick up bargains in Bali, silks in Singapore and whatever-you-will in Thailand. The cruising season varies, but most ships sail here between October and March.

The current batch of Orient-based cruise lines are mainly one-ship operations, too numerous to list and catering primarily to the Asian passenger market. Some of these vessels are nothing more than seamy 'gambling and prostitution' operations. But successful mainstream oriental lines such as Singapore-based Star Cruise are developing rapidly and many shipping executives believe that, as the Caribbean reaches saturation point, the Far East could become cruising's future playground.

Alongside Star Cruises, companies to try include Cunard Line, Peter Deilmann Cruises, Hapag-Lloyd Cruises, Orient Lines, Princess Cruises, Radisson Seven Seas Cruises, Royal Caribbean International, Seabourn Cruise Line, Silversea Cruises and Swan Hellenic Cruises. Japanese-speakers should also try Mitsui OSK Passenger Line.

Southeast Asian and Far Eastern itineraries may include: Bali, Da Nang, Guangzhou, Hai Phong (for Hanoi), Hainan, Ho Chi Minh City, Hong Kong, Inchon (for Seoul), Java (inc. Jakarta and Semarang), Kagoshima, Kobe, Komodo, Laem Chabang (for Bangkok), Langkawi, Lombok, Manila, Mindanao Island, Nagasaki, Nha Trang, Osaka, Penang, Phuket, Port Klang (for Kuala Lumpur), Pusan, Shanghai, Singapore, Sulawesi, Spice Islands, Sumatra, TCai – pei, Tianjin (for Beijing), Visayan Islands, Xingang (for Beijing), Yangon and Yokohama (for Tokyo).

Australasia and the South Pacific

Sail in the wake of Captains Cook and Bligh to find sparkling seas, picture postcard beaches and the real Bali Ha'i. Discover fire walkers in Fiji and fire water in Tahiti (watch that *kava*!), be a beach bum on Waikiki, dive the largest reef in the world and trade those boring luncheon vouchers for a 'barbie' in Bora Bora. Well, somebody's got to do it.

If you'd like that somebody to be you, try Cunard Line, Orient Lines, P & O Australia, and Princess Cruises; smaller upmarket companies such as Radisson Seven Seas Cruises and Seabourn Cruise Line; German companies such as Peter Deilmann Cruises and Hapag-Lloyd Cruises; the major Japanese lines; and regional coastal specialists such as Australia's Captain Cook Cruises and Fiji's Blue Lagoon Cruises. The main cruising season for this region is between April and November.

Australasian and South Pacific itineraries may include: Adelaide, American Samoa, Auckland, Bay of Islands, Bora Bora, Brisbane, Cairns, Christchurch, Cook Islands, Darwin, Devonport, Easter Island, Fiji (including Viti Levu), Fremantle, Great Barrier Reef, Hawaiian Islands (including Kaui, Maui and Oahu), Hobart, Mariana Islands (including Guam), Marlborough Sounds, Marquesas Islands (including Hiva Oa), Melbourne, Milford Sound, New Caledonia Islands (including Loyalty Islands and Isle of Pines), Port Moresby, Raiatea, Solomon Islands, Sydney, Tahiti, Tonga, Vanuatu, Wellington and Western Samoa.

North American East Coast

North American cruising may be dominated by Florida and Alaska, but the East Coast from South Carolina to Canada's Gulf of St. Lawrence also provides seasonal cruising (usually May through to October). 'New England in the Fall' itineraries are offered by various leading lines and coastal Maine is a haven for windjammers and sailing vessels of all descriptions. Further east, the Atlantic island group of Bermuda provides a popular destination. But be warned of Bermuda's hidden danger – not the Triangle but a crash course (literally) in moped riding. Tragically, too many crew members survive one but not the other.

Celebrity Cruises, Crystal Cruises, Cunard Line, Fred. Olsen Cruise Lines, Norwegian Cruise Line, P & O Cruises, Princess Cruises, Royal Caribbean International, Seabourn Cruise Line, Silversea Cruises, Thomson Cruises and various sailing ship operators (see *Sailing Ships & Yachts*) all bring vessels to these waters.

North American East Coast itineraries may include: Bermuda, Boothbay Harbour, Boston, Cape Cod, Charleston, Halifax, Montreal, Nantucket, New York City, Newport, Portland, Prince Edward Island, Quebec City, Rockland, Savannah, St. John's, St. Lawrence Seaway and Williamsburg.

Central and South America

From the natural beauty of Costa Rica and the Chilean Fjords to the rare species of the Amazon and Galapagos Islands, this is a region for nature buffs. And if nightlife is more your scene than wildlife, this is also the route for you. Acapulco, Buenos Aires, Rio de Janeiro are exciting, sensual cities, which should satisfy even the keenest night owl. As for bargain hunters, you can buy all your souvenirs here and still have enough to feed the throng of vagrants who will be following you around. Finding a working phone to call the folks back home could be a problem, as can calling for help, should you inadvertently stray into an undesirable neighbourhood – and it has to be said, some of these ports can be dangerous.

True, the best view of Rio is seen when arriving by sea, but that's not the reason why people choose to stay onboard.

While cruises along the Mexican Riviera take place year-round (often integrated into Caribbean itineraries), navigation of coastal South America is generally restricted to the months between September and April.

The cruise lines to try include Carnival Cruise Lines, Fred. Olsen Cruise Lines, Mediterranean Shipping Cruises, Compagnie des Iles du Ponant, Crystal Cruises, Cunard Line, Holland America Line, Norwegian Cruise Line, Orient Line, Princess Cruises, Royal Caribbean International, Thomson Cruises, P & O Cruises, Seabourn Cruise Line, Silversea Cruises, Radisson Seven Seas Cruises; major German operators, such as Hapag-Lloyd Cruises; and operators of explorer vessels (see *Explorer Vessels & Passenger-Cargo Ships*).

Central & South American itineraries may include: Acapulco, Amazon, Belem, Belize City, Buenos Aires, Cabo San Lucas, Cartagena, Cozumel, Falkland Islands, Fortaleza, Galapagos Islands, Galveston, Guayaquil, La Guaira (for Caracas), Lima, Los Angeles, Manaus, Manzanillo, Mazatlan, Montevideo, New Orleans, Panama Canal, Playa del Carmen, Puerto Caldera (for San José), Puerto Limon, Puerto Montt, Puerto Vallarta, Punta Arenas, Punte del Este, Recife, Rio de Janeiro, Salvador da Bahia, San Diego, Santarem, Santiago, Santos, Ushuaia, Valparaiso and Zihuatanejo.

Transatlantic Crossings

It is surprising how few transatlantic crossings there are any more. Apart from ships navigating the South Atlantic as part of a broader itinerary (from Europe to the Caribbean via Madeira and the Canary Islands, for example), only Cunard's *QM2* offers a regular route across the Atlantic. The fact that her design and speed is suited to this passage does not detract from the monotony of six grey days at sea and frequently heavy swells. And forget the idea of time off in New York or Southampton. No sooner do you reach your destination than you turn straight round and do the whole thing over again. On the bright side, sailing past Liberty Island is the most exciting way to enter Manhattan. And you will save money, since there are no ports of call in which to spend it. Carnival Cruise Lines has crossings from Ft Lauderdale to St Maarten, Funchal, Malaga, Livorno and Rome. Also departures from Rome to Barcelona, Palma de Mallorca, Malaga, Funchal, St Maarten and Ft Lauderdale.

Transatlantic itineraries may include: Cherbourg, Cobh (for Cork), New York City and Southampton.

Around the World

Circumnavigating the world, on the other hand, is a much brighter prospect, and it may be worth suffering the *QE2* 'ferry service' to stake your claim on the world cruise. Alongside the 'Queen', several other ships follow annual round-the-world itineraries, including the *Oriana* (P & O Cruises), *Saga Rose* (Saga Holidays), *Maxim Gorki* (Phoenix Reisen), *Astor* (Transocean Cruise Lines), and *Black Watch* (Fred. Olsen Cruises).

Most world cruises start in January and last approximately three months, which sounds an exciting prospect. But there is a down side: lots of hard-working sea days without a break; you will be lucky to get off in even a third of the ports; and the frequently low (even half empty) passenger carry is not conducive to high earnings for those in the service sector. Although many passengers will complete the whole voyage, others may join the ship simply for a section of a world cruise (Sydney to Singapore, for example), which provides some sort of turnover.

There is a popular theory at sea: the more expensive the cruise, the older the clientele. Judging from the large number of walking frames parked outside guest accommodation on round-the-world cruises, it may be true. But there are no prizes for witty staff members who, when asked

Some crew members may offer more personal services'

the average age of the passengers, promptly answer 'deceased'.

Taking into account the fact that global itineraries can become predictable, some crew members actually turn down repeat offers ('Ho, hum, not another World Cruise') in favour of shorter passages on other ships. But for the first-timer, to sail around the world in 80 (or, more commonly, 90) days is an experience that no would-be traveller should miss.

Round-the-world itineraries may include: Acapulco, Aden, Auckland, Bali, Cape Town, Darwin, Fiji, Hawaii, Hong Kong, Lisbon, Los Angeles, Manila, Mombasa, Mumbai, New York, Panama Canal, Rio de Janeiro, Singapore, Suez Canal, Sydney, Wellington, Yokohama and many other ports.

Nowhere

Last but not least, we come to the 'Party Cruise' which is, in essence, the cruise to nowhere. Of course, there may be a destination, maybe even two, but the destination is not the focus. These itineraries are invariably short (usually three or four days) and are primarily aimed at that huge untapped market of people who have never before set foot on a cruise ship and are happy to spend their money. Such cruises are cheap and cheerful, in fact very cheerful, with a high rate of alcohol consumption. The passengers tend to also be younger and noisier than the seasoned cruiser. Of course, some crew members may offer more personal services than others to ensure that their guests have a good time, while the DJ may complain at actually having to work. For stewards, barmen, croupiers and anyone else depending on tips or commission, it's one hell of a cruise. For everyone else, it's a cruise from hell.

If this sounds like your scene, try companies such as SeaEscape, which offer competitively-priced 'mini-cruises'.

See *Which Line?* and *Addresses of Cruise Lines & Other Companies* for further details.

Addresses of Cruise Lines & Other Companies

Please note that the following list of addresses and (especially) telephone numbers is subject to change. Details should always be verified before posting applications, expensive publicity packages, and so on. Never send originals of references or photographs and other material that you do not intend the receiver to keep. Even stamped addressed envelopes and offers of return postage will not always get them back.

If telephoning, be advised that the code for the US from Great Britain is 001; the code for the UK from the United States is 001 44. For all other countries, dial 00 plus the country code (given in brackets before the number). Websites, where available, are also given.

Abercrombie & Kent Ltd
St George's House, Ambrose Street, Chletenham, Gloucestshire GL50 3LG, England
☎0845-0700 610
Fax: 0845-0700 607
www.abercrombiekent.co.uk

African Safari Club
Imperial House, 21-25 North Street, Bromley, Kent BR1 1SD, England
☎0845-345 0014
Fax: 020-8466 0020
e-mail info@africansafariclub.com
www.africansafariclub.com

Aida Cruises
Am Strande 3 d, 18055 Rostock, Germany
☎381-444 0
Fax: 381-444 8888
www.aida.de

Amazon Tours & Cruises,
275 Fontainebleau Boulevard, Suite 173, Miami, Florida 33172, USA

☎305-227 2266
Fax: 305-227 1880
e-mail info@amazontours.net
www.amazontours.net

Amazon Tours & Cruises
Requena 336, Iquitos, Peru
☎94-6523 1611
Fax: 94-6523 1265
www.amazontours.net

American Canadian Caribbean Line Inc
461 Water Street, Warren, RI 02885, USA
☎401-247 0955
Fax: 401-247 2350
e-mail info@accl-smallships.com
www.accl-smallships.com

American West Steamboat Company
2101 4th Avenue, Suite 1150, Seattle, Washington 98121, USA
☎206-292 9606
Fax: 206-340 0975
e-mail info@awsc.us
www.columbiarivercruise.com

Andrew Weir Shipping Limited
Dexter House, 2 Royal Mint Court, London EC3N 4XX, England
☎020-7575 6480
Fax: 020-7575 6200
www.aws.co.uk

Blue Lagoon Cruises Fiji
183 Vitogo Parade, PO Box 130, Lautoka, Fiji Islands
☎666 1622
Fax: 666 4098
www.bluelagooncruises.com

Captain Cook Cruises
6 Jetty, Circular Quay, Sydney, NSW 2000, Australia
☎2-9206 1122

Fax: 2-9251 4725
www.captaincook.com.au

Carnival Cruise Lines
3655 NW 87th Avenue, Miami, Florida 33178, USA
☎305-599 2600
Fax: 305-406 4700
e-mail shipcruisestaff@carnival.com
www.carnival.com

Celebrity Cruises
1050 Caribbean Way, Miami, Florida 33132, USA
☎305-539 6000
Fax: 305-536 6577
www.celebrity-cruises.com

Classical Cruises
132 East 70th Street, New York, NY 10021, USA
☎212-517 7555
Fax: 212-517 0077
www.classicalcruises.com

Classic International Cruises
274 Main Road, Sutton-at-Hone, Dartford, Kent DA4 9HJ, England
☎0845-603 1180
Fax: 01322-860751
www.classicintcruises.co.uk

Clipper Cruise Line
11969 Westline Industrial Drive, St Louis, Missouri 63146, USA
☎1-800-325 0010
Fax: 314-655 6670
e-mail clipper@clippercruise.com
www.clippercruise.com

Club Med Cruises
11 Rue de Cambrai, 75957 Paris, Cedex 19, France
☎1-5335 3553
Fax: 1-5335 3612
www.clubmed.com.

Club Med (North America)
75 Valencia Avenue, 12th Floor, Coral Gables, Florida 33134, USA
☎305-925 9106
Fax: 305-925 9052
www.clubmed.com

Compagnie des Iles du Ponant
60 Boulevard Marechal Juin, 44100 Nantes, France
☎2-4058 1495
Fax: 2-4058 2702
www.ponant.com

Coral Princess Cruises
PO Box 2093, Cairns, Queensland 4870, Australia
☎7-4040 9999
Fax: 7-4035 5995
www.coralprincess.com.au

Costa Crociere
Via Octobre XII, 2, 16121, Genoa, Italy
☎010-548 31
Fax: 010-548 3290
e-mail info@costa.it
www.costa.it

Costa Cruise Lines
World Trade Center Building, 80 SW 8th Street, Miami, Florida 33130,
USA
☎305-358 7325
Fax: 305-375 0676
www.costacruises.com

Cruise West
2301 5th Avenue, Suite 401, Seattle, Washington 98121, USA
☎1-888-851 8133
Fax: 206-441 4757
www.smallship.com

Crystal Cruises Inc
2049 Century Park East, Suite 1400, Los Angeles, California 90067,

USA
☎310-785 9300
Fax: 310-785 0011
www.crystalcruises.com

Cunard Line (UK)
Fleet Personnel Department, Mountbatten House, Grosvenor Square, Southampton SO15 2BF, England
☎0845-071 0300
Fax: 023 8063 4500
www.cunard.co.uk

Cunard (USA & Canada)
Suite 400, 6100 Blue Lagoon Drive, Miami, Florida 33126, USA
☎305-463 3000
Fax: 305-463 3010
www.cunard.com

Cunard (Asia/Pacific)
Level 1, 189 Kent Street, Sydney, NSW 2000, Australia
☎2-9250 6666
Fax: 2-9250 6699
www.cunard.com

Peter Deilmann Cruises
1800 Diagonal Road, Suite 170, Alexandria, Virginia 22314, USA
☎1-800-348 8287
Fax: 1-703-549 7924
www.deilmann-cruises.com

Delphin Seereisen GmbH
Neusalzerstr. 22E, D-63069, Offenbach, Germany
☎69-9840 3811
Fax: 69-9840 3840
e-mail delphin@delphin-kreuzfahrt.de
www.delphin-kreuzfahrt.de

Delta Queen Steamboat Co
Robin Street Wharf, 1380 Port of New Orleans Place, New Orleans, Louisiana 70130, USA

☎504-586 0631
Fax: 504-585 0630
www.deltaqueen.com

Discovery World Cruises
1800 SE 10th Avenue, Suite 205, Fort Lauderdale, Florida 33316, USA
☎866-623 2689
Fax: 954-761 7878
e-mail info@mvdiscovery.com
www.discoveryworldcruises.com

Disney Cruise Line
Suite 400, 210 Celebration Place, Celebration, Florida 34747, USA
☎407-566 3500
Fax: 407-566 3751
www.disney.go.com

easyCruise
The Rotunda, 42/43 Glouvester Crescent, London NW1 7DL, England
☎0906-292 9000
www.easycruise.com

Equity Cruises
77/79 Great Eastern Street, London EC2A 3HU, England
☎020-7729 1929
Fax: 020-7739 7512

First Choice
First Choice House, London Road, Crawley, West Sussex RH10 2GX, England
☎01293-588405
Fax: 01293-588510
www.firstchoice.co.uk

Fred. Olsen Cruise Lines,
Fred. Olsen House, White House Road, Ipswich IP1 5LL, Suffolk, England
☎01473-292200
Fax: 01473-292201
www.fredolsencruises.co.uk

Galápagos Inc
Suite 112, 7800 Red Road, Miami, Florida 33143, USA
☎305-665 0841
Fax: 305-661 1457
e-mail info@galapagos.net
www.galapagoscruises.net

Glacier Bay Cruiseline
2101 4th Avenue, Suite 2200, Seattle, Washington 98121, USA
☎206-623 7110
Fax: 206-623 7809
www.glacierbaycruiseline.com

Göta Canal Steamship Company Ltd
Rederi AB Göta Kanal, Pusterviksgatan 13, 41301 Gothenburg, Sweden
☎31-806315
Fax: 31-158311
www.gotacanal.se

Hapag-Lloyd Cruises
Ballindamm 25, D-20095, Hamburg, Germany
☎40-3001 4606
Fax: 40-3001 4613
www.hlkf.de

Hebridean Island Cruises Ltd
Griffin House, Broughton Hall, Skipton BD23 3AN, North Yorkshire, England
☎01756-704704
Fax: 01756-704794
www.hebridean.co.uk

Heritage Expeditions (NZ) Ltd
53B Montreal Street, Christchurch, New Zealand
☎3-365 3500
Fax: 3365 1300
e-mail info@heritage-expeditions.co.nz
www.heritage-expeditions.com

Holland America Line
300 Elliott Avenue West, Seattle, Washington 98119, USA
☎206-281 3535
Fax: 206-281 7110
Job Line: 206-286 3496
www.hollandamerica.com

Hurtigruten
Troms Fylkes, Dampskipsselskap ASA, Pb 6144, Tromsø, Norway
☎7764 8200
Fax: 7764 8240
www.hurtigruten.com

Imperial Majesty Cruise Line
2950 Gateway Drive, Pompano Beach, Florida 33069, USA
☎954-956 9505
Fax: 954-971 6678
e-mail employment@imperialmajesty.com
www.imperialmajesty.com

Island Cruises
Diamond House, Peel Cross Road, Salford, Manchester M5 2AN, England
☎0870-850 3927
e-mail enquiries@islandcruises.com
www.islandcruises.com

Japan Cruise Line
Umeda Haushin No. 1 Building 15-F, 2-5-25, Umeda, Kita-ku Osaka 530-0001, Japan
☎66-347 7521
Fax: 66-341 8980
www.venus-cruise.co.jp

Kristina Cruises Ltd
Kirkkokatu 16, 48100 Kotka, Finland
☎5-21144
Fax: 5-2114500
www.kristinacruises.com

Lindblad Expeditions Inc
96 Morton Street, 9th Floor, New York, NY 10014, USA
☎212-765 7740
Fax: 212-265 3770
www.expeditions.com

Louis Cruise Lines
150A Franklin Roosevelt and Omonias Avenue, PO Box 55612, 3045
Limassol, Cyprus
☎2-557 0000
Fax: 2-557 3320
e-mail crewing@louiscruises.com
www.louiscruises.com

Maine Windjammer Association
PO Box 1144P, Blue Hill, Maine 04614, USA
☎207-374 2993
Fax: 207-374 2952
e-mail info@sailmainecoast.com
www.sailmainecoast.com

Mayflower Ocean Lines
10097 Clearly Boulevard, Suite 323, Plantation, Florida 33324, USA
☎954-452 8461
Fax: 954-749 8234
www.mayfloweroceanlines.com

Mediterranean Shipping Cruises
Via A. Depretis 31, 80133 Naples, Italy
☎081-794 2111
Fax: 081-794 2707
e-mail cruiseinfo@msccrociere.it
www.msccruises.com

Mitsui O.S.K. Passenger Line Ltd
3-6 Kioicho, Chiyoda-Ku, Tokyo 102-8552, Japan
☎3-5211 5280
Fax: 3-5211 5307
www.mopas.co.jp

The Moorings
19345 US Highway 19 N, Clearwater, Florida 33764, USA
☎888-952 8420
www.moorings.com

North End Shipyard Schooners
PO Box 482, Rockland, Maine 04841, USA
☎1-800-648 4544
e-mail schooner@midcoast.com
www.midcoast.com/~schooner/

Norwegian Coastal Voyage
3 Shortlands, London W6 8NE, England
☎020-8846 2666
Fax: 020-8846 2678
www.norwegiancoastalvoyage.com

Norwegian Cruise Line
7665 Corporate Center Drive, Miami, Florida 33126, USA
☎305-436 0866
Fax: 305-436 4138
www.ncl.com

Ocean Village
Richmond House, Terminus Terrace, Southampton SO14 8PN, England
☎0845-358 5000
Fax 023-8052 3720
www.oceanvillageholidays.co.uk

Oceania Cruises
8300 NW 33rd Street, Suite 308, Miami, Florida 33122, USA
☎305-514 2300
Fax: 305-514 2222
www.oceaniacruises.com

Orient Lines (UK)
1 Derry Street, Kensington, London W8 5NN, England
☎020-7591 8000
www.orientlines.com

Orient Lines (USA)
7665 Corporate Center Drive, Miami, Florida 33126, USA
☎305-436 4000
e-mail info@orientlines.com
www.orientlines.com

P&O Cruises
Richmond House, Terminus Terrace, Southampton SO14 3PN, England
☎023-8065 5058
Fax: 023-8065 7030
www.pocruises.com

Page & Moy Cruises
136-140 London Road, Leicester LE2 1EN, England
☎0870-010 6430
Fax: 0870-010 6449
www.cruisecollection.com

Paradise Cruise
1540 South King Street, Honolulu, Hawaii 96826, USA
☎800-334 6191
Fax: 1-808-983 7780
e-mail info@paradisecruises.com
www.paradisecruises.com

Phoenix Reisen
Pfälzerstr. 14, D-53111 Bonn, Germany
☎228-72628-0
Fax: 228-72628-999
www.phoenixreisen.com

Princess Cruises
24844 Avenue Rockefeller, Santa Clarita, California 91355, USA
☎661-753 0000
Fax: 661-259 3108
e-mail careersatsea@princesscruises.com
www.princesscruises.com

Quark Expeditions
1019 Boston Post Road, Darien, Connecticut, USA

☎203-656 0499
e-mail enquiry@quarkexpeditions.com
www.quarkexpeditions.com

Radisson Seven Seas Cruises
600 Corporate Drive, Suite 410, Fort Lauderdale, Florida 33334, USA
☎800-285 1835
Fax: 402-501 5599
www.rssc.com

ResidenSea
5200 Blue Lagoon Drive, Suite 790, Miami, Florida 33126, USA
☎305-264 9090
Fax: 305-264 5090
www.residensea.com

Royal Caribbean International
1050 Caribbean Way, Miami, Florida 33132, USA
☎305-379 2601
Fax: 305-539 6168
e-mail infouk@rccl.com
www.royalcaribbean.com

Sacks Yacht Charters
1600 SE 17th Street, Suite 418, Fort Lauderdale, Florida 33316, USA
☎954-764 7742
Fax: 954-523 3769
e-mail info@sacksyachts.com
www.sacksyachts.com

Saga Holidays
The Saga Building, Middelburg Square, Folkestone, Kent CT20 1AZ,
England
☎01303-711111
Fax: 01303-7711010
www.saga.co.uk

Sea Cloud Cruises
Ballindamm 17, D-20095 Hamburg, Germany
☎40-309592-0

Fax: 40-309592-22
e-mail jobs@hampton-shipping.com
www.seacloud.com

Seabourn Cruise Line
6100 Blue Lagoon Drive, Miami, Florida 33126, USA
☎1-800-929 9391
Fax: 305-463 3010
www.seabourn.com

SeaDream Yacht Club
2601 South Bayshore Drive, Penthouse 1B, Coconut Grove, Florida 33133, USA
☎800-707 4911
Fax: 305-631 6110
e-mail info@seadreamyachtclub.com
www.seadreamyachtclub.com

SeaEscape Cruises,
3045 N Federal Highway, Landmark Building 7, Fort Lauderdale, Florida 33306, USA
☎954-453 2200
Fax: 954-453 6555
www.seaescape.com

Silversea Cruises
110 East Broward Boulevard, Fort Lauderdale, Florida 33301, USA
☎945-522 2299
Fax: 954-522 4499
www.silversea.com

Squaresail Pacific Ltd
PO Box 310, Kumeu, Auckland 1250, New Zealand
☎9-411 8755
Fax: 9-411 8484
e-mail escape @sorenlarsen.co.nz
www.sorenlarsen.co.nz

St Lawrence Cruise Lines
☎613-549 8091

Fax: 613-549 8410
www.stlawrencecruiselines.com

Star Clippers
7200 NW 19th Street, Suite 206, Miami, Florida 33126, USA
☎305-442 0550
Fax: 305-442 1611
e-mail info@starclippers.com
www.starclippers.com

Star Cruises
Star Cruises Terminal, PO Box 288, Pulau Indah, Pelabuhan Barat, 42009
Pelabuhan Klang, Selangor Darul Ehsan, Malaysia
☎3-3101 1313
Fax: 3-3101 1406
www.starcruises.com

Spitsbergen Travel
Box 548, 9171 Longyearbyen, Norway
☎7902 6100
Fax: 7902 6101
www.spitsbergentravel.com

Swan Hellenic
Richmond House, Terminus Terrace, Southampton SO14 3PN, England
☎02380-683606
Fax: 02380-657030
www.swanhellenic.com

Thomson Cruises
Greater London House, Hampstead Road, London NW1 7SD, England
☎0870-165 0079
Fax: 020-7387 8451
www.thomson-holidays.com

Transocean Cruise Lines
Stavendamm 22, D-28195 Bremen, Germany
☎421-3336-0
Fax: 421-3336-100
e-mail mail@transocean.de

www.transocean.de

Venice Simplon-Orient-Express
Sea Container's House, 20 Upper Ground, London SE1 9PF, England
☎0845-077 2222
Fax: 020-7805 5908
www.orient-express.com

Victoria Cruises
57-08 39th Street, Woodside, NY 11377, USA
☎212-818 1680
Fax: 212-818 9889
e-mail contact@victoriacruises.com
www.victoriacruises.com

Viking River Cruises
Schaferweg 18, CH-4057, Basel, Switzerland
☎0800-845 464
Fax: 61-638 6040
www.vikingrivercruises.com

Voyages Jules Verne
21 Dorset Square, London NW1 6QG, England
☎020-7616 1000
www.vjv.co.uk

Voyages of Discovery
Lynnem House, 1 Victoria Way, Burgess Hill, West Sussex RH15 9NF,
England
☎0144-462150
Fax: 0144-462160
e-mail info@voyagesofdiscovery.com
www.voyagesofdiscovery.com

Windjammer Barefoot Cruises
1759 Bay Road, Miami Beach, Florida 33139, USA
☎305-672 6453
Fax: 305-674 1219
e-mail info@windjammer.com
www.windjammer.com

Windstar Cruises
300 Elliot Avenue West, Seattle, Washington 98119, USA
☎206-281 3535
Fax: 206-286 3229
e-mail info@windstarcruises.com
www.windstarcruises.com

Yangtze Cruises
566 7th Avenue, Suite 506, New York, NY 10018, USA
☎212-382 3725
Fax: 212-382 3701
e-mail info@yangtzecruises.com
www.yangtzecruises.com

OTHER USEFUL ADDRESSES

British & International Sailors' Society
Orchard Place, Southampton, Hampshire SO14 3AT, England
☎023-8033 7333
Fax: 023-8033 8333
e-mail admin@biss.org.uk
www.biss.org.uk

CLIA (Cruise Lines International Association)
80 Broad Street, Suite 1800, New York, NY 10004, USA
☎212-921 0066
Fax: 212-921 0549
e-mail clia@cruising.org
www.cruising.org

The Marine Society and Sea Cadets
202 Lambeth Road, London SE1 7JW, England
☎020-7261 9535
Fax: 020-7401 2537
e-mail enq@marine-society.org.uk
www.marine-society.org.uk

The Mission to Seafarers
St Michael Paternoster Royal, College Hill, London EC4R 2RL, England

☎020-7248 5202
Fax: 020-7248 4761
www.missiontoseafarers.org

NUMAST (National Union of Marine, Aviation and Shipping Transport Officers)
Oceanair House, 750-760 High Road, Leytonstone, London E11 3BB, England
☎020-8989 6677
Fax: 020-8530 1015
e-mail enquiries@numast.org
www.numast.org

National Union of Rail, Maritime and Transport Workers (RMT)
Unity House, 39 Chalton Street, London NW1 1JD, England
☎020-7387 4771
Fax: 020-7387 4123
e-mail info@rmt.org.uk
www.rmt.org.uk

PSARA (Passenger Shipping Association Retail Agents Scheme)
Walmar House, 4th Floor, 288-292 Regent Street, London W1B 3AL, England
☎020-7436 2449
Fax: 020-7636 9206
e-mail admin@psa-psara.org
www.psa-psara.org

Seafarers' Benefits Advice Line
80 King William Walk, Greenwich, London SE10 9HH, England
☎0845-741 3318
Fax: 020-8269 0794
e-mail sbal@btinternet.com
www.seabal.co.uk

Appendix 1

LANDLUBBER'S GLOSSARY OF NAUTICAL TERMS

Abeam	At or from the side of the ship
Aboveboard	Areas of the ship above the waterline
Accommodation ladder	External folding ladder, used to climb aboard the ship from a pilot boat, etc.
Aft	Near, towards or in the rear section of the ship
Alleyway	Corridor or passageway
Aloft	Above the ship's superstructure, such as at or near the masthead
Alongside	When the ship is beside the pier (or another vessel)
(A)midships	In or towards the middle of the ship
At anchor	When the ship is anchored offshore (as opposed to docking alongside)
Anchor ball	Black ball that is hoisted on the bow, to signify that the ship is at anchor
Astern	Behind the ship, beyond the stern
Avast	Stop
Backwash	Disturbed water, caused by propeller action when ship is reversing
Ballast	Extra weight in the hold
Bar	Sandbar, often caused by shoreline currents
Batten down	To secure open hatches or equipment likely to fall, while the ship is under way
Beam	Width of the ship at its widest point
Bearing	Compass direction from the ship to another object or location
Belowboard	Areas of the ship below the waterline
Berth	Docking space for the ship; also a bed inside the ship
Bilge	Spaces at the very bottom of the ship's infra structure
Binnacle	Ship's compass

Bow	Front or most forward part of the ship
Bowthruster	Device to propel ship away from the quayside
Bridge	Centre of command and navigation (always at the front of the ship)
Bulkhead	Inner partitioning wall
Bulwark	Ship's outer wall
(To) Bunker	To take on fuel
Bunkers	Fuel storage area
Capstan	Large spindle for attaching or winding in ropes (hawsers) and cables
Cast off	Release ropes prior to departure
Chart	Navigational map
Cleat	Wedge-shaped device for making fast ropes (hawsers) or cables
Coaming	Raised lip on doorsills and hatches to prevent water from entering
Colours	Ship's emblem or flag of nationality
(The) Chief	The Chief Engineer
Comment cards	Forms filled in by passengers, as a means of rating the cruise
Companionway	Interior stairway
Course	Ship's direction (in degrees)
Cross alley	Alley crossing another (often used for bringing on stores, etc.)
D.S.	Abbreviation for Diesel Ship
Davit	Device for raising or lowering storage crates or lifeboats
Deadlight	Ventilated porthole cover
Debark	Abbreviation of disembark
Deck(head)	Floor
(To) Disembark	To leave the ship/go ashore
Dock	The act of bringing the ship alongside the dock, i.e. quay, berth or pier
Draft	Distance from the ship's waterline to the bottom of its keel
Embark	To enter or come on board the ship
Even keel	The ship in a true vertical position as opposed to listing to the side
F & B	Abbreviation of Food & Beverage
Fantail	The rear overhang of the ship

Fathom	Distance of depth (1 fathom = 6 feet)
Fender	Anything that cushions (protects) the ship's hull against the dock or other craft
Flagstaff	Flagpole on the stern of the ship
Fly/Cruise	Package deal consisting of flights to and from the ship as well as the cruise itself (also known as Air/Sea)
Fo'c's'le	Abbreviation of forecastle (section under the bow)
Fore	The front (bow) of the ship
Forward	Towards the front (bow) of the ship
Free port	Port or place exempt from customs duty
Funnel	Ship's chimney
Galley	Ship's kitchen
Gangway	Construction, ladder or ramp giving access to and from the ship
*G.R.T. (grt)**	Gross Registered Tonnage*
Hatch	Cover leading to a hold
Hawse pipe	Large pipe in the bow holding the anchor chain or hawser (not to be confused with a hose pipe)
Hawser	Huge rope used for securing or towing the ship
Helm	Ship's centre of steering
Hold	Interior storage area towards the bottom of the ship
House flag	Flag denoting the cruise line to which the ship belongs
Hull	Framework (shell) of the ship
I.B.	Abbreviation for Ice-breaker
I.M.O.	Abbreviation for International Maritime Organisation, governing body for safety and other standards at sea
Inboard	Towards the centre of the ship (inboard cabins therefore have no portholes)
Jacob's ladder	Rope ladder (often with wooden rungs)
Keel	Longitudinal extension of the ship's underside, important for balance
Knot	Unit of speed (1 nautical mile per hour)
Landlubber	Anyone who is unfamiliar with life on the ocean wave
League	Measure of distance (1 league = approximately

	3.5 nautical miles)
Leeward	Side of the ship that is sheltered from the wind
Line	Any rope that is smaller than a hawser
(To) List	To lean to one side (of drunken sailors as well as ships)
Log (book)	Ship's record of navigation, etc.
M.S.	Abbreviation for Motor Ship
M.T.S.	Abbreviation for Motor Turbine Ship
M.V.	Abbreviation for Motor Vessel
Maiden voyage	Ship's first official cruise
Manifest	List of passengers, crew or cargo
(To) Muster	(To) Assemble passengers and/or crew
Muster Station	Emergency assembly point
Nautical mile	Approximately 1.15 of a statute mile (6,080ft/ 1,870m)
(The) Old Man	(The) Captain (but never call him that to his face)
Open Sitting	Access (for passengers) to dine at any unoccupied table at any time during the restaurant opening hours (as opposed to an assigned table and dining time)
Outboard	Towards, at or beyond the ship's sides (therefore, outboard cabins usually have portholes)
Pax	Abbreviation for passengers
Pig (Pig & Whistle)	Crew Bar
Pilot	Independent navigational advisor at times of entering/leaving port, etc.
(To) Pitch	To rise and fall (of ship, especially in rough seas)
Plimsoll line	One of several marks painted on the ship's hull above the waterline to prevent overloading
Port	Left side of the ship
Port charges	Passenger charges and taxes which must be paid to government authorities in ports; these are normally included in the price of the cruise
Porthole	Circular ship's window
P.O.S.H.	Acronym for 'Port Out, Starboard Home', i.e. the more expensive cabin allocation on the England-India route
Prow	Bow of the ship

Quarterdeck	Rear section of the upper deck
Quay	Dock, pier or berth
Rating	Non-officer position/rank
(The) Ratings	Overall grades determined by the scores given by passengers on their comment cards at the end of the cruise
Repositioning Cruise	Interim itinerary taking the ship from one season's route to another
Rudder	Fin-like steering device below the waterline
Running lights	Three lights (green on the starboard, red on the portside and white at the top of the mast) that must be lit if the ship is sailing at night
S.S.	Abbreviation for Steam Ship
S.T.R.	Abbreviation for Steamer
Screw	Ship's propeller
Scuppers	Deck drainage system
Shake-down Cruise	Ship's unofficial first cruise, to sort out problems (at least in theory) before the official Maiden Voyage
Shell door	Outer opening above water level, enabling access for stores, pilots, passenger gangways, etc.
Sitting	Allocated passenger dining time i.e. first (earlier) or second (later) sitting
(The) Skipper	(The) Captain
Sounding	Measurement of water depth
Stabilizer	Gyroscopic retractable fin on either side of the ship to minimise rolling motion
Stack	Ship's funnel or 'chimney'
(The) Staff	Staff Captain
(The) Staff Chief	Staff Chief Engineer
Starboard	Right side of the ship
Stern	Back (or aft) of the ship
Stow	To load with cargo or provisions
T.B.A.	Abbreviation for To Be Assigned (cabins, etc.)
T.S.	Abbreviation for Twin Screw
T.S.S.	Abbreviation for Turbine Steamship
Tender	Small boat (often lifeboat) used to transport people to and from shore when the ship is at anchor

Transfers	Transport between the ship and airports, hotels, etc.
U.S.P.H.	Abbreviation for United States Public Health (inspection)
Under way	When the ship is about to depart
Wake	Trail of disturbed water behind a moving ship
Watch	Period (usually of 4 hours) spent on duty, not just watching
(To) Weigh anchor	To raise the anchor
Wheelhouse	Centre of navigation (the Bridge)
Windward	Side of the ship towards the wind
Working alley	Main passage in the crew area
Yaw	Deviation from the ship's course, generally caused by rough seas

*A passenger ship's tonnage is calculated not by its actual weight, but by the total of permanently enclosed spaces, excluding the bridge, radio room and other specified areas. 1 GRT=100 cubic feet of enclosed space, and is the basis by which port and other dues are calculated.

Appendix 2

FAMILY TREE OF JOBS

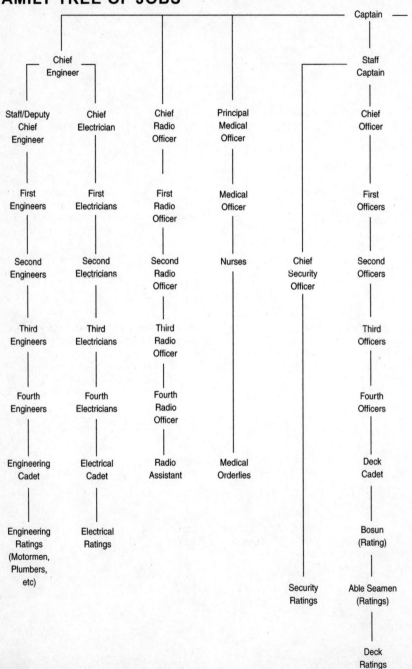

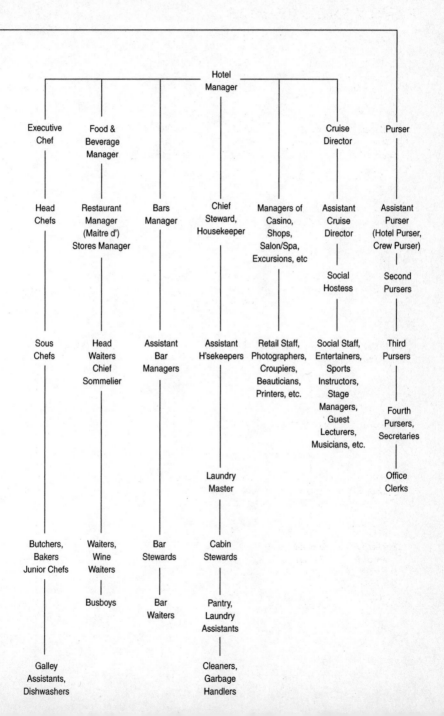

Appendix 3

FURTHER READING

Many of the major travel guide publishers include cruise guides in their range of books, most of which are updated every year. These include Fielding's, Fodor's, Frommers, Berlitz, Globetrotter, A Brit's Guide, Thomas Cook and Macmillan's Unofficial guides.

Globetrotter Cruise Guide, published by New Holland Publishers (UK) Ltd (Garfield House, 86-88 Edgware Road, London W2 2EA, England; ☎020-7724 7773; fax 020-7724 6184; www.newhollandpublishers.com). Part of the extensive Globetrotter Travel Guide range, the *Globetrotter Cruise Guide* is available from bookshops worldwide.

In addition to cruise guides, the following publications may help you to become better acquainted with the world of cruising:

Cruise Industry News Quarterly is an international magazine covering all areas of the cruise industry. Copies are available direct from their American office (441 Lexington Avenue, Suite 1209, New York, NY 10017, USA; ☎212-986 1025; fax 212-986 1033; www.cruiseindustrynews.com) for an annual subscription of $30 for four issues a year.

Cruise Travel is 'America's No. 1 Cruise Vacation Magazine,' a bimonthly publication containing articles and information about the cruising industry. Published in the USA by World Publishing Company (990 Grove Street, Evanston, Illionois 60201, USA; ☎847-491 6440; fax 847-491 6462; www.cruisetravelmag.com).

Jobs Afloat is published by a British employment agency and gives an update on current job availability on cruise ships and yachts. Contact Travelmate (52 York Place, Bournemouth BH7 6JN, England; ☎01202-431520) for details.

Lloyds Register of Ships and *Lloyds Register of Shipowning Groups* are both published annually by Lloyds Register of Shipping (3rd Floor, Lombard House, 3 Princess Way, Redhill RH1 1UP, England; ☎01737-379000; fax 01737-379001; e-mail info@lrfairplay.com; www.lrfairplay.com). Recent editions of this comprehensive global listing of ships and shipowners can be found in most good reference libraries.

The Motor Ship contains names and addresses of shipowners, consultants, shipbuilders/repairers, engine builders. Published annually by

Cumulus Business Media (Anne Boleyn House, 9-13 Ewell Road, Cheam, Surrey SM3 8BZ, England; ☎020-8722 6039; www.motorship.co.uk). Copies may be found in public libraries.

Porthole is a bi-monthly cruise magazine, published in the United States by Panoff Publishing (4517 NW 31st Avenue, Fort Lauderdale, Florida 33319, USA; ☎954-377 7777; fax 954-746 5244; www.porthole. com).

Rolling Pin International is a European hotel and catering trade magazine which sometimes advertises cruise ship job vacancies, particularly in the catering and housekeeping sectors. For subscription rates and other information, contact Johann Haiden Strasse 29, A-8020 Graz, Austria; ☎316-584946; fax 316-584946-19; e-mail office@rollingpin.at; www.rollingpin.at.

Sea Breezes is a long-established (since 1919) monthly magazine 'of Ships and the Sea', often containing features pertinent to the cruising industry. For subscription rates contact Mannin Media Group (Media House, Cronkbourne, Douglas, Isle of Man IM4 4SB, England; ☎01624-696565; fax 01624-625623; www.manninmedia.co.im).

Shipping – Today & Yesterday is a monthly magazine, covering all areas of shipping including cruising. Subscription rates are available from the publishers, HPC Publishing (Drury Lane, St Leonards-on-Sea, East Sussex TN38 9BJ, England; ☎01424-720477; fax 01424-443693; e-mail admin@shippingtoday.com; www.shippingtoday.com)

The Telegraph (not to be confused with the daily) is the monthly newspaper of NUMAST mentioned above. It is not available through newsagents but is distributed to companies and colleges specialising in the maritime industry. Personal copies can be sent to your home address for an annual subscription of £27 (UK and Europe) and £54 (elsewhere). ☎020-8989 6677 for more details.

Travel by Cargo Ship by Hugo Verlomme lists the many operators of passenger-cargo vessels. It was last updated in 1995 and is now out of print but may be available in libraries and through www.amazon. com. Another similar book, *Cargo Ship Cruising: A Guide to the Joys of Sailing the World in Passenger-Carrying Cargo Ships* (published 1997) by Robert B. and Barbara W. Kane is also available through www.amazon.com.

Travel Trade Gazette is a publication about the travel industry in general including cruising. It also publishes the annual *Travel Trade Gazette Directory* which includes addresses of cruise lines and operators and can be found in most public libraries in the UK. For more details contact CMP Information Services (Sovereign House, Sovereign Way, Tonbridge, Kent TN9 1RW, England; ☎01732-377591; fax 01732-367301; www.cmpdata.co.uk).

What Cruise is a bi-monthly cruise magazine, published in the UK by Cruise Travel Publications Ltd (Hitech House, Roebuck Road, Chessington, Surrey KT9 1LH, England; ☎020-8287 5537; www.whatcruise.co.uk; Subscriptions: DMZee Marketing; ☎01234-216016; fax 01234-261251.

There are also various *How to Get Work at Sea*-type publications, available only by mail order, seen in the advertisement columns of newspapers. Some of these will give worthwhile information; most will be overpriced, and a few will be downright rip-offs. *Caveat emptor.*

Vacation Work Publications

Vacation Work Publications, 9 Park End Street, Oxford OX1 1HJ
Tel 01865-241978 Fax 01865-790885

Visit us online for more information on our unrivalled range of titles for
work, travel and gap years, readers' feedback and regular updates:

www.vacationwork.co.uk

Books are available in the USA from
The Globe Pequot Press, Guilford, Connecticut
www.globepequot.com